The Philosoph
Volume 2

Cathal Haughian

Before
The
Collapse

Final Edition

Many thanks to Enetia Robson, PhD. (University College of London)
Editor
Many thanks to my private secretary 陈菲霓 'Chen Feini'

Dedicated to The Readership of the Financial Times

We have had a fierce debate about the Global Economic Depression and this book is that debate presented to you. This is an unusual book for one reason. It was written by a group of capitalists, executives, government officers and economists who didn't realize that's what they were doing at the time. We were debating specific articles in the Financial Times with no attempt to develop a larger theme. It's like Reality TV, but much more real...because none of us knew that there was a camera in the room.

The 'camera in the room' was a fellow reader called Cathal Haughian. He has been an FT reader for many years, he tends to take a low profile, preferring to think and to synthesize ideas rather than formulate or promote an ideology. He and I have never met face to face, but I think it is safe to say that he is an interesting character.

I asked Cathal why he put this book together. Here is some of what he said. I paraphrase:

'The FT publishes articles that tell you what the UK establishment wants people to think. So they were of limited utility. I've been following the debate between FT readers for years ... actually I was analysing everything, and saw how the establishment line influenced the readership and how the readers were influencing one another. Everyone was trying to identify the problem and solve it. I was just using everyone's experience and knowledge to draw the design of the present system in my imagination.

Before the third money printing program (QE) by the US Federal Reserve I was considering the possibility that I may have to write the book with my own hand. After QE3, the quality of the debate drastically improved. The readership all realized that the ship was rudderless and the ruling group were afraid. One cannot deny what's obvious: if they know what they are doing then why are 48 million Americans on food aid?

There are three Systems that shape the Human Life World: Capitalism, Imperialism and the Natural System. The crisis can be triggered by all three and all three seek solutions. Religion is part of the Imperial system though it can drive or hinder Capitalism. Capitalism has three levels. The real economy interlocks with the Natural System. The monetary system, founded upon the Fiat Dollar, interlocks with the Imperial System. The financial system mediates between the real and monetary systems and its nature is different in different places. All three systems are under extreme stress.

Unless a remedy is proposed soon the system will tear itself apart. The book is very much a collective effort, though on an unconscious level. You shared the same will but your minds were separate. It was a nice challenge for me, it was difficult but I searched for what I needed — the knowledge and experience of the FT readership — the bankers, CEOs, economists, political and dynastic elite.

The book is **not** meant to be read sequentially, pick the topic which matches your curiosity and read it in the here and now.'

You will find all shades of opinion on these pages. Some veer to the right, some to the left, some want less government, some want more. However...I suspect that the one thing we would all agree upon is this:

You should make up your own mind.

Cathal has put this book together to help you do that.

MarkGB, 27th June 2015

Table of Contents

Table of Contents

Between the covers of this book is a synthesis of thought pertaining to the economy since the plague of Depression returned in 2008. The Great Recession, as of 2015, remains in place as the elite cower behind their printing presses. There have been many brave attempts to explain our plight, by many intelligent men, and yet our pain is without cease. I have monitored the evolution of their ideas since 2008; they became more concrete, systematized and coherent through time.

All these thinkers shared a common problem. Isolated within their own work environments they were forced to analyse what they saw as the malaise of the capitalist system through their own experiences and expertise. Of necessity they could not help but reduce the complexity of the system to single causes of the economic stagnation they were witnessing. As individuals they felt driven to enquire, for the sake of the countless unemployed and homeless, why capitalism has become such an impoverished provider.

There are scores of forces at work. Herein is a synthesis of their substance; a collage of our best minds working feverishly for years. Even though they failed as individuals the totality of their thought constitutes a success. The Mind must form organically. They read the first editions and began to appreciate their knowledge and experiences at the system level. Even Hegel, equipped with such a powerful imagination, fell victim to his vanity: The individual mind fills in ignorance of the World by projection of unconscious preconceptions and assumptions. So this book will not tell you what to think. It's a synthesis designed to let you write your thesis.

This is practical philosophy. I have neither time nor sympathy for obscure words and those that hide their ignorance behind them. All terms are clearly defined. I am confident that my meagre contribution shall be least worthwhile to contemplate. Read it once to create the categories and concepts required for a practical understanding of the global economic system; and twice to organise your mind and make personal preparation.

The capitalist system employs tens of thousands of professional economists who have also failed. These include central bankers, pundits writing for newspapers and so on. It is important to note why they failed: it's because they don't have a clue about supply. It would take at least 5 years in a management role to fully understand supply in a given industry. For example, to understand 'supply side logistics' you would need several years of experience as a manager for Amazon or an equivalent company. To understand the supply of car parts you would need several years of work as a corporate officer in an automotive company.

Our professional economists spent ten years walking around a university campus. Combined, they have never designed, built, manufactured, marketed or sold a single object or product in their entire lifetimes. Supply remains an abstraction for them. Ultimately, bookish learning is inherently limited: it can introduce the mind to new concepts and categories, but these will remain abstractions in the imagination, to be talked about at best but deformed until made real and crystallized by experience. For one to enjoy true confidence and authority one's education must be tempered by experience. Only a fool would begin to appreciate an oil painting by reading a book about it. Alas, that is the summation of the efforts of the economics profession. Their foetal minds, as unexposed to reality as those of unborn infants, required the conformity and certainty offered by ideology.

Furthermore, the Nobel Prize in economics has never been awarded to a Chinese economist. Economic planners in China have taken hundreds of millions of peasants out of poverty in recent history. Given the results of this national economy something would seem amiss. It's probably got something to do with 'confidence'. The keystone upon which Neo-Liberal Theory rests is 'confidence'. To inculcate 'confidence' within the citizenry and other economic agents, authority figures are required to endorse the status quo. The citizens' 'confidence' in their intellectual system is so fragile that dissent cannot be risked.

So thinkers in Beijing are excluded from the Pantheon of Failure which houses the Nobel Prize in Economic Sciences. The topics and notions addressed herein range from War; Ecology; Geo-Politics; Supply; Demand; Printing Money (QE); Psychology; Money; Profit; Religion; Culture and so on. My debt to the contributors is immense, their motive being a practical concern for the welfare and well being of our fellow man. Most insist on using pseudonyms for political, contractual and commercial reasons. I'm not aware of any contributor under the age of 60 and through private correspondence I've discovered many are in excess of 80. Amazing! I have always wondered how they could write about the 1930s as if it were just last week.

They run your power companies, infrastructure projects, pension funds and each one has for several decades invested in and managed the real, financial or monetary system. Their mind is not filled with abstractions and theories but shaped and crystallised by experience. The system is called capitalism and they are the capitalists: they know how the system works, why it works and when it doesn't. Obviously the 1st edition was awful, so I set-up a Darwinian process whereby Capitalists could submit entries — contributions that were deeper and clearer kicked out the less fit. This edition is pretty good.

It is painfully obvious that the majority of mankind hold onto certainties and strongly held beliefs pertaining to the economy. Many people have opinions which are shaped by biases that they will seek to confirm within these pages. Perhaps it would be best for readers to take in and reflect upon the evidence presented here of the fundamental nature of the global economic system and its significance for living a good life in an unbiased manner before forming any judgement. One can overcome the ego by adopting a mental state of suspended judgement.

In 2007 I understood the system well enough to anticipate and profit from the Great Financial Crisis. This book is the product of seven more years of daily study. I did not adopt a viewpoint, write anything, complain, criticise or lose faith. Contemplation is the highest and most constant form of pleasure. And this has been an enjoyable and difficult task, a real challenge.

I hadn't kept a digital catalogue of everyone's ideas. So instead, I had to dredge my memory for the entry that would represent the brush-stroke I needed. This was mentally challenging, some of the entries were written over five years ago. For me, every entry is a brush-stroke and I'm painting a picture that reveals the underlying nature of capitalism and capitalistic society. Finally, a stable set of *ideas* are described that a capitalistic nation can rest upon.

I have deliberately avoided the use of statistics as these are normally employed to shore up 'confidence' by and in the authorities and thus no longer relate to value creation. Since 'confidence' is a key determinant, I have permitted some contributions which, although they are strongly subjective, manage to highlight this 'intangible good.' These are easily identified and also serve my primary goal: to elevate the inner life of Man as central to an understanding of the economy.

In actuality, *confidence* is not the keystone of the capitalist system. The foundation of the system is civilisation. The keystone of civilisation is *belief*: namely the *belief* that the goal of the state and civil society is the well-being of the citizenry. If this *belief* is shared by all citizens there can be friendship in spite of caste, class and origin. In its absence there is crime, civil strife, factions, wars of aggression and revolution.

Cathal Haughian

The starting point has to be to see the World, not just Europe or US, as a whole. For only by acknowledging that the rise of China and WTO-style globalization have changed everything, save mainstream macroeconomic theory, can we begin to grasp just how profound and unique is the present juncture.

Unemployment and under-employment are problems almost everywhere. China's disciplined, industrious, and super-exploited workers can manufacture just about everything from shoes, to computers and locomotives, more cheaply than workers in Europe, the US or Latin America. Chinese expertise is rendering millions redundant while also spreading deflationary pressures like a virus.

As the Middle Kingdom captures an ever larger share of the global economy's research and development projects, there will be fewer products with which even the skilled, industrious German workforce can remain competitive. China's share of the value-added dollar will also increase, and unmanageable global imbalances will finally bring the ill-conceived WTO experiment to a wrenching halt.

There's a second major factor roiling the jobs market in emerging markets. This is the US's industrial agricultural juggernaut and its enormous volume of cheap exports. We flood poor nations in the Caribbean, Central America, and elsewhere with cheap corn, rice, soy, chickens, pork and many other comestibles, then act shocked when the unemployed agricultural workers in those countries flock to our increasingly violent and unstable cities, where they fuel the ranks of the "reserve army of the unemployed," or join the underground gangs which smuggle illicit drugs and many of our illegal immigrants.

Meanwhile the American people subsidize the accompanying loss of topsoil, depletion of aquifers, and rampant pollution of our waterways with agricultural chemicals and animal waste from the factory farms. It's a terrible, unsustainable bargain for everyone except captains and shareholders of Agricultural Corporations. In the interim, asking the German people repeatedly to fork over the cash so Mr. Draghi can buy sovereign bonds to finance deficits in southern Europe, seemingly forever, may strike Martin Wolf and Paul Krugman as a sensible idea, but its benefits would be minimal and short-lived, while failing to address the structural imbalances in the global economy. Without far more comprehensive change, Europe may be left to stagger toward unimaginable catastrophe.

Don Williams – U.S. Viewpoint

1) Americans have tolerated this elitist Dance of the Seven Veils for several decades now, only to see our real median income fall 17% and our federal debt soar to $18 Trillion—about $152,000 for a taxpayer earning between $70,000 and $120,000 per year. What economist, I wonder, gave Bill Clinton the idea that Americans would get rich selling GM cars to China if we opened up our doors to Chinese exports?
http://www.manufacturingnews.com/news/10/0615/WTO.html
Or that Mexican billionaires would be opening up job fairs in America if we just approved NAFTA?

2) Globalization will be unstable absent a global government and I see none in existence that would serve the middle class worker. We don't even have a national government that serves its citizens in America.

3) Real trade would occur naturally if each nation focused on excelling at what it does best. But we don't have that — we have Wall Street exporting US capital and technology to our rivals on a massive scale in search of the cheapest labour while expecting impoverished American workers to sacrifice their lives in defence of this self-serving plantation.

4) Why not simply ask how Washington could best serve the American People—and what arrangements with the rest of the world would be needed to bring that about? What benefit does that $1 Trillion per year military budget provide to the average American, for example? Or lending tax dollars to Wall Street at 0.5% so that Wall Street can either hand the money back to us at loan shark rates or make massive profits handing the money back to the Treasury at 3 % interest, sit on the money as reserves for massive gambling debts or lend it to foreign competitors so that they can invest it into cutting the throats of US workers?

5) We are abusing the dollar's status to sanction Russia not because that benefits the American People but because Exxon and Chevron want to make hefty profits on their Caspian Sea investments and pushing Russia

aside as supplier of fossil fuels to the EU would promote that goal.

6) Of course, once the US oligarchs conquer Russia and China then we will all be slaves. You only have to look at how the American People were treated after we --at great sacrifice-- won the Cold War to see what that means: Falling real median income while the Rich increase their share of income from 8% to 25% and rising. Democracy in which elections are held because it doesn't matter which of the two candidates we choose – both have been co-opted by the Rich well before they were allowed to run.

7) The corruption of Congress and of our leaders has made America brittle in ways not seen from outside. If Al Qaeda had any brain cells, they would recruit in our massive prisons. It is worth remembering that two US spy rings handed Stalin the detailed design of the plutonium implosion bomb and the members of those spy rings had lived through the misery of the Great Depression.

Metal Industrialist

I grew up in a rust belt manufacturing city and I saw its decline. I saw the cost of that decline in the local economy and individual struggle (and death). The notion that we can have a decent society without decent jobs is a crock. Those who supported outsourcing and off-shoring as well as the death of unions have dealt tens of millions a body blow from which they will not recover. Our country is vastly weakened as a result. If this is the result of the new globalized utopia, bring back nationalism - the quicker the better.

Venture Capitalist

In 1992 Ross Perot stated that the giant sucking sound was American Jobs going overseas. In his opposition to NAFTA, Perot hit the nail squarely in the centre. In almost every city in the United States, old abandoned factories are being converted into apartments. This is all well and good but jobs have flown out the window to China, India, Vietnam, Mexico and a thousand other places. The very rich control everything, including the press and broadcast media. Unless a poor kid is a whiz in mathematics and can do engineering there is a job waiting for him or her flipping hamburgers.

Many young people are employed in the killing fields of the Middle East if they do not wish to work in a mall. Why is this inequality even in any doubt as it has been obvious for more than 20 years? When share prices collapse the rich will be bailed out because they are supposedly 'too big to fail'. Capitalism for the poor and socialism for the upper crust is the order of the day. Not everyone can do mathematics, but everyone has to eat.

Gareth Davies

Why are we surprised? The greed of Wall Street killed America when they genuflected before the great Sino experiment in slavery as a tool for political control.

Enetia Robson, PhD

In 313 C.E. Constantine the Great declared toleration for Christianity, which later became the official state religion of the Empire, undermining the authority of the emperors whom their people saw as gods. In 330 C.E. he split the empire into two parts: the western Roman and the eastern half in Constantinople, named after himself. This city flourished while the west declined. After the western part of the Roman Empire fell, Byzantium continued to exist for hundreds of years.

A decrease in agricultural production led to higher food prices in the west, which had a large trade deficit with the eastern empire, from which the west purchased luxury goods. Without much to trade in exchange, the Roman government adulterated the coinage by cutting the silver content, leading to inflation. Piracy and attacks from Germanic tribes disrupted the flow of trade, especially in the west.

Adding to these woes, political amateurs controlled Rome. Army generals dominated the emperorship. Many were corrupt. The military became increasingly mercenary with no real loyalty to Rome. As money grew tight, the government hired cheaper Germanic soldiers to fight in Roman armies. Rome was being defended by Germanic soldiers fighting Germanic tribesmen, so collapse was no surprise. In 476 C.E. Romulus, the last of the Roman western emperors, was overthrown by the Germanic leader Odoacer, who became the first Barbarian to rule in Rome. The 1000 years of Pax Romana was over. Perhaps people today might learn lessons from the fall of this ancient union of Europeans.

***

I once worked for King Abdullah and the Bin Laden family, in the desert outside Mecca. We'd pay Bedouin adults to attend an educational facility. Our target was young adults though many students were unaware of their age due to the local culture of not marking and celebrating individual birthdays. During the insurgency, which began after 9/11, the Kingdom changed somewhat. Mosques were closed at night so that earnest youth could not live in them. By and large, it was converts to Islam that tended to be zealots for Saudis were content to express their religiosity in everyday custom and norm. Diplomacy and courtesy came naturally to them, for these are attributes of tribal society.

The place was flooded with high quality hashish that penetrated every town and tribe. The youth were pacified, but the purest form of their ancient culture may never return. For the Koran forbids intoxication and traditional Saudi culture expressed knowledge stored in the Koran exceedingly well.

They can be generous and warm people to foreign friends though they reside in the largest prison on the planet. Western security corporations support the local police with full spectrum surveillance. It is common for Westerners to think that Saudi women are treated unfairly. After living in 50 countries, I can confirm that the spiritual and mental grade of men and women are generally equal in homogeneous communities. How can it be otherwise? Saudi men treat their wives as their king treats them and the wife treats her servants in the manner that she is treated by her husband. Man and wife are usually cut from the same cloth.

The clergy are paid to please the king and should be seen as an organ of the State. The degree of social control and punishment is extreme. As a people, they've made some changes in attitude in order to comprehend the West. They've adopted the concepts of consumption and entertainment wholeheartedly. I was there at the tail end of the insurgency, embedded within the native population. I used to watch Mankind encircle the Kaaba. Submission: how does it feel?

We could discuss the organic basis for submission, by asking, for instance, how our ancestors survived by submitting to their captors after warfare, during the first cruel chapters of Mankind's historical journey.

But that would only encourage false confidence. For the sake of example, before and during the beginning of the recent war in Libya, I spent 200 days in the Sahara desert. I didn't see many women or children. You cannot imagine what it is like to live in an Islamic society and it is best that you don't try to do so. Without similar lived experience you would not be able to understand and even worse, your mind would create and depend on concepts and categories that are malformed. Such things are a poor guide to living.

However, you can gain valuable insight and understanding of Islamic societies if I explain their economy, habitat and forms of governance and warfare. For the terms used shall correspond to your lived experience. It's important to understand the Middle East and North Africa because these regions are an important source of net energy gain (oil) for the globalised economy.

Religion can be seen as proto-government. Religious systems can be seen to have resulted from the trials and errors of our ancestors who required a stable hierarchy of *power*. The successful prototypes such as Judaism, Christianity and Islam are only considered successful on the grounds that their adherents survived. Men and women have different motivations to adhere: the men are promised complete control of their women's reproductive systems while women are promised property. This arrangement in Islamic culture is called marriage.

Islamic societies are unstable since one man can purchase four wives: this arrangement ensures males do not cooperate well in the capitalist mode of production. Upon reflection, it's more accurate to say that men deliberately hinder each other's wealth accumulation. A substantial gain in relative wealth for one man leaves another Muslim man deprived of a spouse, since he will use his excess of wealth to have a second family. So polygamy is a legal right though few ever get to afford it.

Unfortunately, the Koran strongly urges the believer not to trust anyone, including family: Koran [64,14] - 'O ye who *believe*! Truly, among your wives and your children are enemies to yourselves: so beware of them!' This also hinders wealth creation and encourages inbreeding: if a man marries outside the tribe then the family loses a great deal of wealth. He must hand over property. His womenfolk don't trust the other tribe to reciprocate. Thus marriages may be arranged on an intra-clan or intra-tribal basis. There was a common theme that the poorer the family the closer the marriages became. For instance, in Pakistan a young man from a poor family may marry his mother's sister as they wish not to lose what little capital they have.

Alas, this leaves social life insular which hinders company formation and international expansion: Koran [3,118] – 'O you who *believe*! Do not take for intimate friends from among others than your own people, they do not fall short of inflicting loss upon you; they love what distresses you; vehement hatred has already appeared from out of their mouths, and what their breasts conceal is greater still.' Moreover, trust is an essential ingredient for a capitalistic economy. Where social trust is absent ultra strong government is required to authenticate and enforce contracts. To a far lesser degree, similar phenomena curtail economic expansion in Southern Italy, where the family is clannish and insular.

Other economic weaknesses result from believing that human life and reality in general is deterministic or fatalistic: Koran [2, 6-7] – 'As to those who reject *Faith*, it is the same to them whether thou warn them or do not warn them; they will not believe. Allah hath set a seal on their hearts and on their hearing, and on their eyes is a veil; great is the penalty they (incur).' To what degree Islam is deterministic is the subject of academic argument in spite of the claim by Islamic scholars that the Koran is to be considered perfect. According to the above extract, everything is determined by the will of God, even your inner life phenomena. The Koran never makes clear why those who reject faith are punished as they never had the agency to reject faith in the first place.

From an economic viewpoint such debate is irrelevant for the common response to queries concerning the future is 'God willing' or 'if God wills'. If you ask a merchant if a widget will be available next week he will reply 'If God wills'. If all present actions cannot influence the future, then what's the point in going to work? Long term planning is stillborn and fruitless. Because of which, with respect to day-to-day living, the Koran has produced a culture whereby it is socially acceptable to bear an attitude that it makes no difference what I do in the present, because the future is unaffected.

In addition, you will note that Muslims don't appear to be outraged by slaughters and massacres carried out by members of their moral community. They can, in old age, even behead their own daughter without weeping. Within Islamic communities, there is little to no social peer pressure to express empathy. God is willing that the afflicted suffer. The person who is suffering has obviously wronged God, they assume automatically without thinking about it.

In 2002, Saudi Arabia's religious police stopped schoolgirls from leaving a blazing building because they were not wearing correct Islamic dress. One witness said he saw three policemen "beating young girls to prevent them from leaving the school because they were not wearing the abaya". 15 schoolgirls died. Neurology is informative: neurons that don't fire together don't wire together. You either use an ability or you lose it. Similarly there are special combat soldiers, who are exposed to social peer pressure to condition the brain to bypass the empathy zone. In contrast, the Christian is commanded to love his neighbour, which results in complex economies capable of providing high grade medical care, therapy, nutrition, education and shelter.

On the other hand, praying five times per day has an excellent disciplining effect, even though it breaks up the day. And Mohammed's contempt for usury is commendable. Similarly, Tibet and India provided an example of a philosophy of life, Buddhism, which was adapted to provide a proto-government.

All governments raise taxes and religions continue to do so. It is in their interest that the taxable base grows through population growth. Of course, like all governments, religions are capable of good and evil: for they have no conscience. Only the individual man has a conscience that can be his guide in life.

The advent of Reason eclipsed faith in heavenly bodies, and so the modern secular state was fashioned after a likeness to the proto-government which preceded it. The secular designers used their religious hierarchy of power as a template. Western nation states were inspired by Rome. Islamic peoples have sympathy for dictatorship as Mohammed ruled by diktat. Today, we see religious peasants in Turkey celebrating the return of dictatorship.

The transition from religious to secular government is hard to pull off because the people may lose *faith*. Essentially, any group of people coalesces on the basis of *faith*. You take away the *faith* and the edifice crumbles. This *faith* is essentially the belief that there is a benefit to being in the group that outweighs the cost. Also, there is an instinctual element to it: humans are social animals. As people get wiser with age, they make the calculation rather than relying on instincts to inform their behaviour.

So even at the micro-foundational level, a family break up shows what happens. The child grows up and leaves the house and then parents get a divorce. But the same principle applies to larger groupings, such as nations. Elaborate myths and symbols are erected that indulge our instinctual tendency towards belonging but our intelligence demands that we make a calculation. The intelligence community knows this. For example, the C.I.A. in the U.S.A. as well her Majesty's secret services knew that the KGB was using operatives in Hollywood to interject subversive messages into the content of popular media. When the congress found out, there were hearings and blacklists.

So now we know that one way to destroy a rival power is to destroy the nation. This is done with propaganda designed to rip apart the calculation that the benefits of being in a nation is worth the costs (following the rules, paying taxes, etc.) But at the same time that your intelligence apparatus is busy Balkanizing the rest of the world, it must also bolster the *belief* in the host nation that the people belong together. Clearly, Mossad would encourage the *belief* among Israelis and Jews the world over that they need a homeland. But at the same time, they want their neighbouring nations to disintegrate. This is because they fear that these neighbours are adversaries so it makes sense to weaken them by subverting their raison d'être.

Of course, the ruling group of Great Britain has accumulated vast knowledge and institutional means to curtail the ambition and hubris of her Majesty's secret services and neutralise blowback. The security apparatus of younger nation states often falls prey to opportunism and myopic policies. Pakistan's unholy decision, decades ago, to play host for factories of jihadis has destroyed faith in the nation. For children are now massacred, which is one of the few acts of violence admonished in the Koran. By 2011, one in five Pakistanis reported they would flee if they had the means to do so. A more nuanced analysis is necessary to appreciate how civil society in Israel has become malignant.

Israeli society lacked the institutional means to constrain expansionist impulses which has resulted in a conflict without any prospect of ultimate resolution. The seizure of land and capture of 4-5 million hostile foreigners requires military governors, secret police, propaganda and a perpetual siege. Democracy and civil liberty, when draped in 'empire' produces an unstable set of ideas and conditions.

As such, it's presently difficult, to transition from one form of governance to another because foreign powers will take advantage of the uncertainty. This is why China cannot afford to entertain the idea of democracy because rival powers will subvert the transition to cause chaos, e.g. as was done in Russia in 1992, whereby the U.S. reneged on her promise to fund Russia's transition to a capitalistic economy. That betrayal caused Russia's economy to disintegrate and severely weakened her military power. Her natural resources were bought for a pittance and plundered.

Modern history is replete with such power struggles though there is no better player than the most sophisticated Nation State in world history. For more than 100 years, Great Britain has colluded with radical Islam, highlighting its long-standing preference for Islamist regimes over secular nationalist, communist, or democratic groups. Today is just another node in that long history.

The British government promised Arab Islamists led by Hussein a new Caliphate based in Mecca and Medina in 1914, in return for help against the Ottomans. Fortunes were spent aiding the Muslim Brotherhood in Egypt to combat the threat of secular nationalism there. Millions were spent educating and arming the 'Taliban' (which literally means 'students') in Madrassas in Pakistan, to ensure a steady supply of zealots who were sent into Afghanistan to fight the USSR.

The UK encouraged Islamist clerics to base themselves in London (including Bin Laden, whose office was in Wembley) in the 1980s, while Thatcher praised the execution of democrat leaders such as Bhutto in Pakistan. The UK sent Bin Laden's jihadis into South Yemen, then a communist republic, and provided training centres and weapons to them there. This being the sole reason why Yemen is now a factory for jihadis, something still used to UK advantage.

The UK has waged a successful campaign against Arab secularism which has brought down Ghaddafi, Saddam, and they've had their eyes fixed on Assad, the last of them for quite some time. Meanwhile, the UK fauns over conservative Islamists in Saudi Arabia, Qatar and Kuwait. Why? Because religious governments are not constrained by a political constitution that is reasonable to the majority of the people, rulers of proto-governments may be happy to serve foreign interests rather than the well-being of their own people.

Is ISIS a case of blowback? It was not even 2 years ago that the UK was assisting the incubus that became ISIS with training and aid, another node in UK policy of supporting Islamist insurgencies against secular groups in the Middle East. Syria went from 10,000 dead to nearly 200,000 dead, three million displaced, Iraq collapsed, and ISIS emerged. Isis is rather more than blowback, it was clearly more opportunism and divide-and-conquer politics.

Like Secretary of State for India, Wood, wrote to Lord Elgin in 1862: "we have maintained our power in India by playing one part against the other and we must continue to do so. Do all you can, therefore, to prevent all from having a common feeling." Divide et impera, the stratagem of ancient times, was also applied by Britain and France to divide Middle Eastern tribes and sects after World War One. Today, the hordes of refugees and terrorists herded to mainland Europe are countermeasures by adversarial powers that understand how this game is played. They are designed to undermine *faith* in the European nation.

The concept of nation and national identity may be constructed by shared race, language, religious belief, values and historical experiences. Groups with different and strongly held belief systems concerning existential issues do not readily cohere. Western Europe has managed to deliver relatively coherent societies mostly due to indifference (tolerance). When groups enter the country holding belief systems that are at odds with the prevailing rationalist indifference, that coherence will start to break apart. We are already seeing this, particularly in Scandinavia. Religious governments, such as Saudi Arabia, send monies and radicalised clerics to extend their sphere of military and political power with the added advantage of undermining *faith* in potential enemy nation states.

Why has the UK's strategy been so successful? The weakness in the

Middle East and North Africa is precisely the fact that these states (Iraq, Syria, Lebanon, Libya, (Trans) Jordan) are artificial. They do not reflect national identities because such identities have never existed. Before WW1 the Middle East was part of the Turkish Empire for hundreds of years. Before the Turks they were part of the Arab empire.

Before the Arabs these territories were held by the Byzantines and the Persians. Before that it was the Romans, who took them over from the Greeks who had conquered them from the Persians. And that already takes us back about 2,500 years. And if we go back to the Assyrians and Babylonians i.e. over 3,000 years, we should remember that those were also empires in their own right.

During these imperial millennia people moved around all these lands, settling and re-settling all over the Fertile Crescent. There are therefore no national peoples or national identities. After WW2 the dictators who controlled these artificial states sought to legitimise them by propagating an Arab and pan-Arab identity. This attempt failed badly and now we are witnessing an attempt to create a pan-Islamic identity. This is also doomed to failure, wrecked on the shoals of sectarianism, economic and ecological collapse. Thus, the Middle East is falling back on the traditional sources of identity and protection—tribe, clan and religious sect.

With respect to Yemen, the underlying problems are economic and social. For decades they have been rapidly increasing population size despite the lack of natural resources. They are running out of water and it is only a matter of time before the place becomes another Somalia. Like much of the Middle East it has now fallen prey to the conflict between Iran and Saudi. Iran has now taken Lebanon (through Hezbollah), Iraq, Syria (the Assad bits) and now Yemen. The Sunnis are losing and are resorting to ever more extreme Islamist jihadist groups like ISIS and Al-Nusra to fight the Iranians. The endgame will start when the Shia in Saudi Arabia's Eastern Province rises up with Iranian support.

The cold, hard truth is that the Saudi's have never been battle-tested. They have relied upon the US to support a myth of a nation counter-balancing Iran. They will learn in war, money means nothing if your forces will not fight and die. The Saudis have massed tanks on the Yemeni border and leased soldiers from Pakistan though mercenaries are not noted for their willingness to die in combat.

In our quest for understanding, let's analyse Egypt and we'll see a similar story. Demographics are the time bomb ticking away under Egypt. It's a small strip of habitable land along a river in a vast desert and hence it has one of the highest effective population densities on the planet without the sort of export economy that makes it sustainable. It needs to import half of its food, is turning into a net importer of energy and has few exports to trade in return. Income from tourism is nowhere near the peak of $12.5b in 2010, it roughly halved. Egypt's balance of trade is negative and has worsened since 2010.

Egypt has 40% youth unemployment. It shares borders with some of the most unstable regions worldwide. Oil prices are down, which is beneficial to prices at the pump, but detrimental to the incomes of Egypt's sponsors on the Arabian Peninsula without whom Egypt would probably not be able to balance its budget. Government debt is 87% debt to GDP, up from 74% in 2011 and continuing to grow. It's a very bleak picture. It is politically correct to admonish the generals to be less bloody. The Muslim brotherhood is not a terrorist organization but a grass roots collection of local conservatives who think that limiting women's rights and getting everyone to their prayers five times a day is the way forward.

With reference to Islamic terrorism, we must begin by understanding how the mind forms. How the individual interprets his existence and the World influences decision making processes in the unconscious. Life, for the Muslim, is full of meaning: Koran [2, 155] – 'We shall certainly test you by afflicting you with fear, hunger, loss of properties and lives and fruits.' It is a trial: Koran [47, 31] 'And We will surely test you until We make evident those who strive among you [for the cause of Allah] and the patient, and We will test your affairs.' Therefore, the Muslim seeks the means of acquittal. It is received wisdom that there are two sure ways for judgement of acquittal: the conversion of a disbeliever or the waging of holy war.

Thus, terrorism is the most significant challenge to the advanced countries of the world today. Within the advanced economies and societies it must be effectively countered through surveillance, counter intelligence focused on counter terrorism, and effective police methods. Look for a globalized integrated international security state embracing all of the advanced and some of the advancing countries. Membership in this security state will be the defining characteristic of tomorrow's G20.

(Virtually the entire Muslim world will be outside this security structure primarily due to increased violent instability in the region driven by adverse climate change.)

Adverse climate change is going to drive increased instability across Africa, the Middle East, and South Asia. Lack of water and deteriorating agriculture are going to be transcendent challenges to this region. This means that adverse climate change is going to be a big driver of future terrorism. Climate is going to be seen as a crippling deficiency across Africa, the Middle East, and South Asia—a problem to be at best managed, not solved—with the arsenal of 50 thermonuclear warheads central to the fate of singular failed state Pakistan. The security state will evolve to anticipate and counter potentially super massive human migrations.

The U.S. sits in the North American quadrant of the world with Canada, Mexico, Central America, and the Caribbean. It has about 10 percent of the world's population in 25 percent of its space. It is in a very geographically advantageous space. Undoubtedly the American public is going to be more mindful of improving the domestic neighbourhood and avoiding dissipating endless trillions in the remainder of the world chasing non-existent solutions to very intractable problems. As a world leader, one would expect the US to invest in cooperation and progress where possible and avoid and contain the intractable.

Today in the West, religion functions as passive redundancy in the case of secular systems failure. Religious organs can coordinate shelter, provisions, medical aid and offer hope if or when the nation state is defeated in war or declares bankruptcy. In recent years, Grecian and Irish citizens have been fortified by religious institutions while their nation states have been severely weakened. From the perspective of economic governance, Christianity is demonstrably the best religion. In the most advanced capitalist nation state, the Catholic Church offers an excellent network of shelter, education and medical services to the laity of the United States. As a capitalist economy weakens or becomes unstable religious institutions need to become active and resources need to be directed to them, while keeping in mind how they operate and behave when not balanced by Secular Law.

You should now understand why Mohammad sowed mistrust and paranoia of other religious/proto governments. He was fortifying *faith* in his nation, that it was a better and safer bet than other prospects. Modern media have undermined *faith* in backward and corrupt nations which pressures their ruling group to risk extreme options, such as war or empowered religious authority, which forces the human group to congregate. Why are Islamic societies and communities violent? First, you need to appreciate what civilisation is. A civilisation arises from, is shaped by and rests upon a stable set of ideas. Human groups inherit ideas that spring forth from philosophical discourse and contemplation.

Philosophers can be categorized by their mode of thinking; it can be analytical (e.g. Wittgenstein), critical (e.g. Nietzsche), system level (e.g. Plato) or practical (e.g. Confucius). Once they are recognised as a matchless authority by a critical mass of the populace, society is ordered in deference to, and in harmony with, their intellectual output. Thus, deference is a key civilisational trait. Their ideas become expressed as social peer pressure, custom or law. For the sake of example, you may note how corporal punishment was phased out in the West after Locke judged it to be unwise. If their output threatens to destabilise the existing set of ideas that supports the status quo they are imprisoned, executed or their commentaries are banned, e.g. in 1210 the Council of Paris banned the study of Aristotle's output.

Islamic communities were unable to create a stable set of ideas that complex economies and powerful Nation States could rest upon and be stabilised by. Thus, Islamic civilisation in and of itself has never existed. The Arab world was created in much the same way as Latin America was. Five hundred years ago Spaniards and Portuguese invaded America and destroyed the indigenous empires and civilizations. They then imposed their languages (Spanish and Portuguese) and their religion (Catholic Christianity). They also exported settlers. Some of these set up European settlements and sometimes exterminated the locals e.g. in Argentina and Uruguay. Others took local women which led to the creation of a mestizo population e.g. in Chile. In yet other parts (Paraguay, Peru) the settlers were few in number and the population remains primarily indigenous.

The Arab world was created a few hundred years earlier when tribesmen from Arabia, united and fortified by their new religion, invaded Byzantine and Persian territories. They too, imposed their religion and their language on their newly conquered peoples. They too settled and took local women. The difference was that the conquered people were more sophisticated and civilised than the Arabs were. There was no 'Arab' culture. Most Arabs couldn't read or write. Hence, the Koran (the Recital) is so called. It was a reverse takeover with the primitive Arabs taking over and preserving (for a while) the civilization of the peoples they had conquered. Iran is far more stable than Saudi Arabia for the Shia sect incorporated ideas from these ancient civilisations.

The Koran proposed polygamy, a fatalistic attitude and mistrust of family which are an unstable set of ideas.

Violence governs reality where thought does not.

Contributors: Paul A. Myers (USA), Felix Drost (Europe), Coarse Theorem, Physiocrat (Scandinavia), Helloway (UK)

***

Have you ever wondered whatever happened to any duty of care towards the worker, which these appropriators have morally owed to us, since we acquiesced to relinquish our individual power of initiative to them? Is it not revealing that they prefer advice such as 'pull yourself up by the bootstraps' rather than action that may cost them?

And then there would seem to be a variation in the legal system's effectiveness in dealing with individual culpability on the part of worker malfeasance and group culpability on the part of elite malfeasance. More often than not, crimes always seem to be the responsibility of an individual's personally sanctioned deviance rather than a consensus-sanctioned imposition on the individual. The crisis in 2008 illuminates this truth: the individual was robbed by the ruling group to 'bail out' the ruling group who were culpable of malfeasance.

Though this is not a crime for the difference between subsistence production and collaborative production being that the worker does not own his output, the capitalist or the State does.

So now you know why the CEO of Wells Fargo shall remain a free man. Though if the motivations and rewards of Capitalism don't map and reinforce our morals then the system alienates us from our values.

No wonder we're in a bad place.

Talk to any small business owner, and they know we've been in a Depression since 2006. For ten years the government has talked about green shoots but here's what reality has sounded like: QE1, QE2, Operation Twist, food stamps, zero or negative interest rates, a dropping labour participation rate, off-shored jobs, cash for clunkers, soaring health care and education cost, increasing property taxes, kids graduating with debt but no jobs and unable to start a family.

But the economy doesn't scare me the most. What scares me most is what is obviously taking over. Our institutions, our laws and our principles are being set aside so the truth can't come out: We're in a Depression and it's getting worse. A big difference between the Depression we're in now—and the 'Great Depression' of the 1930's —was that there was a sense of solidarity back then. Everyone knew and admitted that they were in a Depression, so there was this national sense of *we're all in this together.*

The Depression we're in now is denied by every branch of the establishment—the government, the judiciary and mainstream media. Everyone feels alone and isolated, there is no sense of support. For those too proud to beg for public assistance, it is every man for himself. I've known several who have pulled the plug, and this current Depression was at the root of their problems. One was a veteran, could only find part time work at a home depot, so also worked part time at the animal shelter. Then he had a medical situation and some major car repairs. He never asked for help and no one saw it coming, but he remained his own man to the end, and that was important to him, although it left a wake of sadness that lingers still.

That right there is the unmitigated evil of all this. Not that people have problems but the evil nature of a system that steals from us all—via inflation and bail-ins—then denies individuals the legal right and ability to be a basic human being and support themselves. And when we forget about our veterans don't act surprised when they forget about us. As it stands, one-in-five Americans experience mental illness in a given year.

Drug treatments are pushed and profitable, but in the words of one British clinician "they simply do not work without psycho-emotional support that helps the patient work through the underlying problems that give rise to their symptoms.

Despite the efforts of science mental illness is on the increase, and it is important to understand that science has a limited scope in its ability to remedy the crippling misery of psycho-emotional suffering. What really works is the dynamic of human relationships in which empathy and compassion administer the ointment of loving kindness, in which sufferers feel deeply understood in contact with a well trained therapist.

The government, pharmaceutical companies and the health establishment have all tried to find quick, cheap fixes but they don't work. Money has to be invested in treatment programs that support talk therapies, alongside the efforts made in neuroscience to understand the organic basis of mental illness.

The problem is that scientific methods cannot regulate human inter-relational dynamics, and so the establishment cannot control the therapeutic processes that do the real work of treatment. That makes the institutions uncomfortable and reluctant to fund the supportive care that the mentally ill deserve; and so society limps along with millions of its members unable to function."

You could argue that we're all the slaves of defunct economists— these are the 'experts' who more than any other (and certainly more than mental health experts) our leaders listen to. And what have these influential economists taught us in recent years? That individualism is more efficient than collective action, that personal insecurity will make markets work better—often called flexibility—and that competition not collaboration or cooperation will drive human progress. They are theories that increasingly look economically unsound and have, to my mind, destroyed the fellow-feeling that our well-being depends upon.

That veteran died because he wasn't able to change. It wasn't his fault— our society had only offered him a very limited framework of opportunities to work with. He was vulnerable to changes wrought by automation and globalisation. He and countless others who feel economically insecure obsess about changes to the climate, the economy, jobs and relationships while the Capitalist class—that makes almost all corporate decisions—ensure they and those closest to them are insulated from risk.

Darwin taught us that it's not intelligence or strength that determines survival, but adaptability to change and certainly decision makers and the wealthy have more room for manoeuvre.

And we're not an especially adaptable species—just note how long it takes to educate one worker—decades now. We know, deep down, that our individual survival is completely dependent on the whole system surviving. So every day we're tempted by 'click-bait' to read 'news' in search for and sensitive to change—even in distant and faraway places. Why? Because our very survival depends on Globalisation.

Globalization is evolving into a fully interconnected and inter-dependent human system which is not man-made but a necessary evolutionary state. We evolved from and still exist within the vast natural system around us which is basically a single, interconnected and inter-dependent ecosystem. Humanity as a species have to adapt to this system and the adaptation can only happen through "equivalence of form", by us becoming global and integral too.

The only but very significant difference is that while every other organism in nature follows integration and achieves dynamic equilibrium instinctively; human beings are inherently individual, unique and self-centred. We are still tribal and so limited to only looking after and serving our closest circles.

We can be this way and happy. But such an attitude won't stop the growth of homeless encampments along the LA River, lines of people lining up for free food at churches, people begging for food in front of grocery stores, homeless families camped out in their cars, sick, homeless, little old ladies pushing shopping carts with all their belongings. It's rough out there.

This paradox between our inherent nature and the integral conditions around us caused the global economic crisis and if we are unable to solve this paradox by adapting to our evolutionary conditions we may not qualify to evolve any further.

Our only hope is the human mind. The positive point is that what is unique in human beings is the human mind — capable of critical, objective self-assessment, initiating necessary self-change. We have reached the stage where we have to start using this unique human quality.

We have been stubbornly pushing a completely unnatural, virtual lifestyle and economic system, whereby we brainwash people to desire things they do not really need, to pay for that with means they do not have, and as a result we have this illusion of "constant quantitative growth", built on excessive, constantly growing "aggregate demand"—driven by debt which can neither be sustained nor repaid.

We still exist within a natural system whether or not we want to admit it, and that natural system works on completely different laws. The natural laws are about balance and homeostasis, life based on natural necessities and available resources, and instead of the exclusive, exploitative competition we pursue; in nature the elements mutually complement one another.

We need to reconsider how we look at trade and economy, and the relationship between producer and consumer. Especially today, as we have evolved into a globally interconnected and interdependent system.

Initially, when trade and economy was still based on natural foundations, there was a simple and natural relationship between the producer and consumer: one had a service the other needed and the other bought the service or product for an agreed price. They had a mutual relationship between them which was important for both of them to maintain. Especially since one fellow's expenditure was the other's income, and vice versa. Such a system allowed for a beautiful harmony whereby the individual could only desire the product of his own labour.

With the advent of Capitalism this relationship was broken: the producer started focusing on profit, making it the absolute priority.

The costumer became a necessary evil, to be exploited as much as possible in order to generate the maximum available profit. Nobody talks about "service", serving anybody anymore.

With modern marketing it mutated even further: artificial, never even dreamed about, most of the time harmful products—pleasures are promoted but the side-effects keep mounting up (obesity and addiction come to mind). Consumers are brainwashed to keep buying even when they are without need, in a "Matrix"-like environment where every product is designed to become obsolete when the warranty expires.

A person that would have been happy with a bicycle is frustrated with his Mazda because he desires a Porsche, the person who would have been happy with a small house is unhappy with his 4 room apartment as he desires the mansion of the celebrity, etc. Moreover they have to keep consuming beyond their available means, thus individuals and nations alike are buried by intolerable debt.

We need to return to natural necessity and available means based trade and economy, building human connections and serving each other. It is not an ethical or ideological choice, this artificial, excessive bubble, the illusion of constant growth is falling apart, it is unsustainable in a closed and finite, integral natural system. Our choice is whether we change proactively, understanding the conditions we have to adapt to, or we will change by suffering as a result of crisis and other volatile events.

When homestead owners agreed to abandon independent production in favour of Capitalism, they did not envisage the 'tooth and claw' mentality that grips America today. It is destructive and unnecessary. Society only requires a level of competition that results in and rewards cooperation: In your nearby town there must be plenty of restaurants—the competition between them forces the management and employees of each restaurant to cooperate—so they can all keep their income. Watch an episode to Hells Kitchen and notice that restaurants going out of business are stricken by disputes. The staff and management don't cooperate and get along.

Throughout this Depression Wells Fargo executives have been rewarded to get it morally wrong. Why would they act in a morally right way? They are Too Big To Fail. Why would executives and staff—who are not afraid of going out of business—care about the consumer?

An ex-employee warned me, in 2003, that the home mortgage industry was heading for collapse. He worked at Wells Fargo Mortgage in Minneapolis. He was the guy people called when they were late on their mortgage payment and wanted to get their account back to good standing. He was under constant pressure to get these people to open credit accounts of one sort and another—even though the whole reason he was talking to them was that they were delinquent on their existing Wells Fargo Mortgage.

And then there is "Drawering." Drawering happened to people who had a history of sending in their mortgage payment very near or just past the due date, and who had a fair amount of equity in their homes. Sometimes their check would show up a day before the due date. It would be put in the drawer until the day after the due date, when it was processed. They'd deduct the late fee from the mortgage payment, so that month's payment showed as being for less than the full amount.

Doing that a few times could put a borrower a full payment behind before they knew it, particularly if they weren't monitoring their account. The fees would mount up, the borrower could be put into delinquency, and possibly even foreclosure. Wells Fargo employees got rewarded for raking in all the fees, and for eventually reconciling the account in the bank's favour. And in the case of foreclosure, the bank seized the under-lying asset.

So there won't be any change. Nothing's changed since 2003. Why would there be change? They are not individually culpable of group malfeasance. A bad reputation won't put them out of business. Why would anyone change without pain?

And pay no mind to public outrage, the corporations are several moves ahead of any progressive agenda. You can't stop buying from them because they have eliminated the competition, mostly through government intervention on their behalf to obtain monopolies, subsidies, tax breaks, and to place onerous regulation and expensive "bars to entry" in the form of licensing and regulation on their competitors. In the case of agriculture, they have actually made it illegal for would-be competitors to sell many types of farm produce.

It can be pretty tough to compete with the big corporations in these circumstances. The truth about many corporate products is, nobody wants their shoddy products, much of which is manufactured without regard even to public safety, let alone utility. The consumer would infinitely prefer to buy a quality product, were it available at a competitive price. But a competitive price is not possible when the big corporations enjoy so many government-conferred advantages.

These defensive measures by corporations are a system result— Capitalism produces for profit and competition forces the rate of profit to fall. So there is no evil motive or agent at work.

Corporate officers can only act within the framework of opportunities presented to them by Capitalism. We can't remove the government-conferred advantages enjoyed by the corporate world because the politicians have been bought (by campaign contributions) and the rate of return on Capital would go to zero.

If that happens, capital can't accumulate and the system would seize up. So be careful what you wish for. There has been progress since 2008, we now know exactly what's gone wrong and we know how to deal with the mountain ranges of ageing debt. But a concrete model of how to deal with the internal contradictions in Capitalism—most importantly the diametric opposition between profit and wages—remains incomplete. Do we build profit into the system framework or add buying power for the mass consumer (who happens to also be the global labour force?)

Don't think such questions are radical or even theoretical: subsidies are a form of profit already added to the system framework. Perhaps you've also noted the proliferation of books and pundits prophesying imminent doom and gloom. These pundits are mistaken and their message mistimed. Sure, the system is in crisis but we know it can be prolonged up until we, the Dominant Class, are impacted by the collapse of the working classes, and the impact that collapse has on our Profit.

Capitalism is malleable and can work perfectly well with different economies for different classes. In the USA there's the USofA economy thats wealth and income is inflating (thanks to money printing, off-shoring, imported labour etc.) The USofB economy appears to be slowly imploding (rising costs of education, health care etc. against stagnant or declining take home pay.) The USofC has collapsed with tens of millions on food stamps. And the rest without much wealth and discretionary spending.

The result is a demoralised public that's becoming confrontational e.g. Black Lives Matter. The family unit is in tatters, especially in poor places. Many are uncaring and incapable of rational, constructive discourse. They'd rather protest or go to court to resolve personal disputes.

Some are even willing to bear the extraordinary capital cost of going it alone in some sort of pessimistic society e.g. gold-bugs and heavily armed preppers. Unfortunately for them, their very survival is completely dependent on the whole system surviving. If we forget about the whole system they'll be extinguished. And if you forget about society then society will forget about you.

So there's still time, but not much. The central question is whether we can change our economic arrangements without extraordinary pain? So far we've done everything to avoid pain—with Central Banks buying government bonds and even moving into equities—they've bought us time but the ultimate result is very fragile.

Our artificial bubble is breaking at multiple levels: the human resources are already exhausted, hallmarked by social inequality, unemployment, intolerable debt burden, depression, substance abuse, separatism, wars, and riots, not to mention our destruction of the natural environment.

There are no financial, economic or political solutions for this system failure, only an educational one. We need to re-tune ourselves so we adapt to the natural system we exist within.

Make this your moral goal.

Jiddu Krishnamurt

'It is no measure of health to be well adjusted to a profoundly sick society.'

Enetia Robson, PhD

In many areas of the UK there is no provision for mental health problems for those under 19. About 6,000 adults and 200 children with mental health issues were detained in police cells in 2014 because of a shortage of space in NHS hospitals. 236 children were detained in a police cell under Section 136 of the Mental Health Act 1983, which rules that the mentally ill can be held in a hospital or police station for up to 72 hours.

A noisy, brightly lit police custody suite, with drunken hooligans and gangsters passing through, is not appropriate for someone in the midst of a breakdown. 22% fewer people were held in cells under the Mental Health Act in 2013/14 than in the previous 12 months. But the Police Federation of England and Wales said ministers must "do more" to ensure mental health patients were treated by the NHS "instead of leaving it to police officers". Suicides within two days of release from police cells have increased.

Bed shortage means that acute patients can be sent to cities far away from their own area. There is only one outstanding mental health hospital in London and surrounds—Mile End. It does not have same sex wards, so sick young women can find themselves in danger of attracting sexual attentions. Mile End is the hospital to which the seasoned mentally ill hope to be sent, however, because patients there are treated better than in other hospitals.

Effective diagnosis is difficult. Police might take a person acting bizarrely in public to an A&E dept and that dept be so short staffed and have so little expertise in mental health problems that patients are allowed to leave and wander the streets.

CBT is a fairly good treatment for people with moderate to mild symptoms but it does not tackle long term depression. Only competent counselling helps serious disturbance but the best counselling is expensive. Psychiatrists have the power to section ill people for up to six months at a time and they diagnose and prescribe for conditions such as Bi Polar and so called Schizophrenia. The drugs used to help calm patients are very difficult to live with, usually having a long list of known side effects. Nor do they do very much in the way of curing anything. They control the patients and make them tractable enough to be kept together in locked acute wards, where the patients gradually recover on their own for all the actual psychotherapy the average acutely disturbed person receives.

Their drugs are called 'anti-psychotics' because they reduce the visible symptoms. The main ones belong to a group of 'atypical tranquilisers' called the mono amine-oxidases. They are dopamine antagonists. Examples include Olanzepine, Quetiapine and Risperidone. Unfortunately these drugs are highly toxic and have side effects including liver failure, obesity, making some women lactate, uncontrollable shaking of the limbs, slow movement and even an inability to see, among other effects. Often the ill are given these drugs on the blanket assumption that the patient has schizophrenia when that is not the case. These drugs are as close to the type of poisons used in medieval treatments as it is possible to be in modern times. Psychotherapy such as that practised by Freud and Jung and several other schools can be helpful but these are not generally available on the NHS.

Cathal Haughian

Well trained and effective therapists are expensive because they are in short supply. Therapists can be categorized by their motivation to study psychology. First, there are those with psychological problems who seek to self diagnose. Next, there are those who have been let down or injured by people close to them, so they seek the means to control others. Finally, there are those moved by their kind and caring nature. The State should take steps to ensure the final group is the majority as it is safe to assume they will be most efficient. For efficiency reduces cost, though this is not sufficient:

Mentally ill people are vulnerable and often without the means and wherewithal to have private health insurance. Therefore, in the United States there is a mismatch between top therapists and those in greatest need of counselling. A profit driven marketplace for psycho-emotional therapy may not be suitable for society.

With respect to education and prevention, I must say that the family unit is far more influential and important to young people than any teacher could be. Teachers can operate as a third parent, or second parent if the family breaks down, but a youth needs a stable environment for healthy emotional and instinctual development. Excellent diet, physical exercise and regimented sleep patterns are essential while the brain is developing. The teacher mediates between the needs of the child, family and organs of the State. The education of children becomes increasingly difficult as the rate of family breakdown increases. Some countries drop examination standards so as to shore-up self esteem in the youth.

Young people require a stable foundation and that is the family. Outsourcing and off-shoring, supported by famous Western economists, disfigured the family unit in the United States.

Successful education systems are a form of behavioural conditioning. Memorisation is a form of mental effort; effort is rewarded with praise and social status within the student peer group; a recursive process is implemented until any given pattern of behaviour is ingrained. Students with psychological needs for approval from authority figures excel. Diligence, deference and obedience are key civilisational attributes which are required by society. The educational system identifies such students for the organs of the State, just as has happened over centuries in China.

Analytical, logical, systematic thinking skills would undermine this process. Thus, the study of mathematics is reduced to the rote memorisation of formulae and process. Ultimately, the student cannot be allowed to develop a mind that can build a rational framework to interpret society: as this would lead to a cost-benefit analysis of said society.

If the costs are greater than the benefits, then the mind will begin to function separately from society; giving birth to a *thinking will*. Just consider high achievers in the U.S. education system, which accumulate vast debt while being ignorant of what debt is. Remaining unable to articulate why their society lost the Vietnam War; ignorant of its cost and consequence; for if they weren't unable, they may finish their education in a public library. Or upon graduation from university lose *faith* and emigrate to an opposing nation state.

In order to interpret depression correctly the teacher would need to discuss the phenomenology of the mind and society. Sadly, very few societies have the *confidence* to permit that discussion and so citizens are left bereft of the means to interpret and express their inner life within a rational framework. Thus, emotions and related phenomena get trapped in the unconscious. The field of hypnotherapy considers 'trapped anger' to be a major cause of depression.

The citizens of Switzerland are encouraged by the State to develop a *thinking will*; for it must govern itself and society; through the process of *direct democracy*.

* Many thanks to ZG Hermann and Thomas Greaves

The three tenets of Western dominance:

Free markets — what are these — the ones where central banks set the price of money, assets and everything else, if indirectly? The free markets where the most levered and insolvent ride high again, subsidised by the poor, prudent and the young?

Democracy — what is the relevance when all economic wealth distribution and relative prosperity is now determined by a couple of people in central banks—like the Soviets? What is democracy when the core function is usurped by unelected technocrats who also happen to have failed on a disastrous scale? The money changers run America and the World.

American *power* — cannot beat shoeless Neanderthals in mountains and have done nothing but wreak anarchy everywhere they go? For what?

Our ideology is based on the premise that free markets, American *power* and democracy actually exist – that belief is utterly bizarre.

Mysterion

This is neither a loss of *faith* nor a failure of *confidence*—it is a retreat from hubris. And that is a positive development.

After WWII intellectual life on either side of the iron curtain developed as if on two sides of a mirror. Bitter political opposition encouraged each side to assume a form that was the exact inverse of their enemy's in every sphere: culturally, economically and politically. Just as the Eastern Bloc states had their weighty tomes of Marxist doctrine the West needed a matching solid theoretical basis for its claims to superiority. Mainstream economics, especially the strand known as neoclassical economics, was that theory. It functioned as a political tool – as anti-Marxism. Just as the USSR had its Institute of Marxism-Leninism the USA had the economics departments of MIT and the University of Chicago.

Marxist Economics told a story of a capitalist world which would inevitably collapse in revolution. Iron laws of history would cause the profitability of commerce to fall over time. Capitalists would be compelled to extract more and more labour from the working classes to maintain their profits until eventually the proletariat would be forced to rebel and overthrow the economic order. Just like a spinning top each capitalist economy would increase in instability until it eventually toppled over into Communism, a stable state. Whereas Marxists asserted that capitalism was subject to inevitable catastrophic failure, US economists were drawn to assert the opposite: free market economies were fundamentally self stabilising. They claimed that irresistible forces inevitably pushed an economy back into equilibrium when faced with any kind of "external shock".

Opposition to Marxist States left us with a set of false beliefs about the inherent stability of a capitalist economy. These eventually played out as hubris in the build up to the Great Financial Crisis. Banks built mathematical models that used equilibrium thinking and then came to rely on them. Neoclassical thinkers (neo-liberals) fought for the de-regulation of the banking industry in the belief that the closer the real world came to their models the better for all of us. The central bankers looked on happily at what they called 'The Great Moderation'. Not only was equilibrium thinking validated, the intermittent swings away from the centre point got ever smaller. Or they did until the whole construction tore itself apart from the inside without any kind of 'external shock' at all. If as a result we are finally beginning to put long finished conflicts behind us, so much the better for us all.

Janus

The West began its decline in 1914. It is only because its starting position in 1914 (ruling the entire world) was so dominant that the decline still hasn't reached a bottom. The decline began in 1914 because of the great civil war AKA WW I which destroyed a generation of young men (and many of the young ruling class man at that).

Then the civilizational war between the West and Christian Orthodoxy 25 years later put a nearly fatal nail in the West, leaving only that poor facsimile of the West, the USA, standing tall to lead what remained of the West. With a culture only millimetres deep and a population bred from much of the worst stock of Europe, it didn't take long before the patina of the glue of Western culture in the USA fell apart; all it took was a demographic bulge of poorly educated adolescents (AKA baby-boomers). Then the USA puked its nasty brew of culture back onto mother Europe.

The basic problem with the West is that it has become unhinged from its traditional culture. It no longer values honour, pride of craftsmanship, authority, responsibility, family, duty, and other long term civilizational attributes. The result is a fertility rate below replacement rate which causes the population to decline significantly every generation. Combine the shrinking workforce with huge increases in the length of retirement (non-productive lives), made for a crisis situation. Instead of dealing with the crisis with an eye on the civilization, the boomers took the easy way out and imported people from other civilizations to make up the worker deficiency. For the most part, these imported bodies have not made the contributions expected of them, and far worse they have made the idea of rescuing traditional Western culture even less likely.

The West lost about 5,000 soldiers in Iraq War II. A civilization which complains about losing 5,000 out of a population of over 700 million is a civilization of wimps. The West is soft, and it is soft because it lost its traditional culture and it lost its identity.

John Bloom

Trickle-down economics doesn't work. In fact, the opposite is true: wealth accumulates into a small number of hands and, in free market conditions, the vast majority become wage-slaves. The suppression of revolt by the wage-slaves can be a bloody business so we have instead a society aimed at "demoralising" the masses, not in the sense of making them miserable but rather diverting their attention with amoral pursuits — hollow mass entertainment, the churn of "celebrity", overeating, glitzy electronic trinkets, alcohol, drugs and sex, sex, sex. "The West has become unhinged from its traditional culture. It no longer values honour, pride of craftsmanship, authority, responsibility, family, duty, and other long term civilizational attributes" Janus writes, and I agree with him except that I would add that this is no accident. It is because if honour, pride, responsibility and duty took hold the glitzy culture of trinkets would crash and that of course would lead to major societal changes.

*The creditor class is concentrated. The debtor class is dispersed and thus disorganised; namely households with a mortgage, young workers with student loans and students accumulating debt. The trickle up effect is in the form of interest charges; over time the rate of return on loaning money is compounded so that gross wealth inequality is the result.

Stuttgart 88

In my opinion the real message from the West's victory in the Cold War is that mixed economies work better than centrally planned ones. Instead the West's victory has opened the door for market fundamentalists to take charge of the intellectual agenda. Whilst it is obvious that it's a good thing that half the world (or whatever fraction it was) was set free from totalitarianism, in a way it hasn't been unambiguously positive for the West. Just as the West was taking a big shift to the Right by deregulating and liberalising many markets, including labour markets, the world was being flooded by cheap labour. The collapse of communism removed a valuable counterbalance. Business owners no longer had to respect the fact that workers might vote for a shift to the far left because such a shift was rendered intellectually redundant. Without this threat to keep business owners on their toes, workers' slice of the pie has continued to decline.

Albert Ross

What we are seeing is just what Lord Macaulay foresaw in 1857, when he wrote: "A democracy cannot survive as a permanent form of government. It can last only until its citizens discover that they can vote themselves largesse from the public treasury. From that moment on, the majority (who vote) will vote for the candidates promising the greatest benefits from the public purse, with the result that a democracy will always collapse from loose fiscal policies, always followed by a dictatorship."

Jeannick

It is a common idea that all civilizations grow, flourish and decay. Free markets are usually wrong, either too high or too low, but right on average. Democracy is always undermined by its governance class, who rig it for their benefit. The US laughed its head off at the Soviets crumbling under their military burden. In 1993, a Pentagon internal report estimated a light infantry soldier, trained, equipped, ready, to cost 193.000 $ apiece. During a recent budget hearing, in answer to a question the under-secretary of defence stated that to the best of his knowledge a soldier in Afghanistan cost 850.000 $. The Roman Empire fell while still a dominant military power; they just ran out of money.

The decline in US *power* started in the 70s with Nixon. The gold standard kept the USA in an enviable position with the fact that their WW2 loans were being paid in solid currency. Whilst the Americans have not been afraid to show their military might the world over, this is no longer as lucrative as it used to be, as cheaper arms manufacturers have eaten into their market share.

Is it that easy?

The West has been reduced to banana republic money printing to survive its current form – why on earth should this yield intellectual *confidence*?

Snow

It's not loss of *confidence* in free markets, democracy and American *power*. It's that the 3 ideas don't work. The (financial) markets don't work due to massive fraud engineered by the financial industry who "democracy" (regulators and lawmakers) allowed and still perpetuate (money printing on steroids to cover up failed policies). Democracy failed to represent the electorate and instead represents special interests — no difference to many systems "undemocratic" countries use — so what's the motivation for these countries (by those who really decide) to change, really?

Democracy failed because it isn't democratic. The 3rd leg of the stool, U.S. *power*, is merely a reflection of global corporate *power* ("markets" and "democracy" all rolled into one) and how "country" *power* as a concept is waning. In 1990, 80% of the world's 25 largest companies were American and now it's 30%. "U.S. *power*" is not as relevant as "global corporate *power*" (all the largest U.S. companies except Wal-Mart make most of their revenues outside of the U.S.).

Perguntador

I'd say oligopolies are, by definition, a failure of free markets. Many markets tend to become oligopolies or cartels in the long run. The drive to concentration and/or price-fixing is a defensive measure — wrong, of course, as competition should be a cornerstone of a market economy — but quite common and widespread. Why is it that every reasonably developed country finds it necessary to create, at a point of its development, a public body in charge of defending competition and busting the "trusts"? The USA started in the 1920s by dismantling the Rockefeller oil empire. The truth is, the essentially competitive nature of entrepreneurs is just a myth. It can be true as long as they are the challengers, the new kids on the block. But not any more when they become the establishment, the target of the new challengers. Markets need to be well-regulated to remain competitive. But that, of course, is anathema to market fundamentalism.

General Economist

The reason we are losing confidence is that (especially in UK and US, and apart from Germany) we are running at a loss. In the UK, the loss is something like £75 billion pounds per year (the current account deficit). The reason we are running at a loss is the failure to distinguish between productive and unproductive investment, the failure to have a banking system that favours wealth extraction over wealth creation, the failure to tax away location and resource rent. And we need private profit because?

The simple answer is that private profit encourages individuals and companies to do things in ways that satisfies individual requirements more exactly, and in a way that uses less scarce resources. While under the current system, private profit has both good and bad parts. On one hand it encourages activities and labour saving, which should enable some relief from the universal toil; on the other hand it is pillaging those things which should be commonly preserved, and setting up private toll booths on things that used to be free (or could be rationed using public taxation).

Don

Malaise by any other name smells just as sweet. I don't think the average citizen living in the EU or US worries for one second about the animating values of Western civilization. Earning a living, being secure against crime, and enjoying personal liberty are occupation enough. Western civilization may be the worst sort, but for the alternatives.

Don Williams – US Viewpoint

And yet, from the far side of the world, 19 men committed suicide on Sept 11, 2001 in order to strike at that exalted civilization. And the billionaire-owned news media rushed to conceal from the voters of our great democracy why that attack had occurred.

And our leaders then proceeded to discard civil liberties that were centuries old in order to respond — with no one in our news media asking why we were fighting and why the attack had occurred. And Washington has since run up $12 Trillion in debt within 13 years — a debt that would effectively bankrupt most of America's 120 million households if we had to pay it off today.

Read the words of Christian priest Salvian from 440 AD — and ask why the common Roman citizens no longer fought to defend their government from the German invasion:

'In what respects can our customs be preferred to those of the Goths and Vandals, or even compared with them? And first, to speak of affection and mutual charity (which, our Lord teaches, is the chief virtue, saying, "By this shall all men know that ye are my disciples, if ye have love one to another "), almost all barbarians, at least those who are of one race and kin, love each other, while the Romans persecute each other. For what citizen does not envy his fellow citizen? What citizen shows to his neighbor full charity?

[The Romans oppress each other with exactions] nay, not each other : it would be quite tolerable, if each suffered what he inflicted. It is worse than that ; for the many are oppressed by the few, who regard public exactions as their own peculiar right, who carry on private traffic under tile guise of collecting the taxes. And this is done not only by nobles, but by men of lowest rank; not by judges only, but by judges' subordinates. For where is the city even the town or village which has not as many tyrants as it has curials? . . . What place is there, therefore, as I have said, where the substance of widows and orphans, nay even of the saints, is not devoured by the chief citizens? . . .

None but the great is secure from the devastations of these plundering brigands, except those who arw themselves robbers.

[Nay, the state has fallen upon such evil days that a man cannot be safe unless he is wicked] Even those in a position to protest against the iniquity which they see about them dare not speak lest they make matters worse than before. So the poor are despoiled, the widows sigh, the orphans are oppressed, until many of them, born of families not obscure, and liberally educated, flee to our enemies that they may no longer suffer the oppression of public persecution. They doubtless seek Roman humanity among the barbarians, because they cannot bear barbarian inhumanity among the Romans. And although they differ from the people to Whom they flee in manner and in language; although they are unlike as regards the fetid odor of the barbarians' bodies and garments, yet they would rather endure a foreign civilization among the barbarians than cruel injustice among the Romans.

So they migrate to the Goths, or to the Bagaudes, or to some other tribe of the barbarians who are ruling everywhere, and do not regret their exile. For they would rather live free under an appearance of slavery than live as captives tinder an appearance of liberty. The name of Roman citi'en, once so highly esteemed and so dearly bought, is now a thing that men repudiate and flee from. . . . It is urged that if we Romans are wicked and corrupt, that the barbarians commit the same sins, and are not so miserable as we. There is, however, this difference, that the barbarians commit the same crimes as we, yet we more grievously. . . .

All the barbarians, as we have already said, are pagans or heretics. The Saxon race is cruel, the Franks are faithless, the Gepidae are inhuman, the Huns are unchaste, in short, there is vice in the life of all the barbarian peoples. But are their offenses as serious as ours? Is the unchastity of the Hun so criminal as ours? Is the faithlessness of the Frank so blameworthy as ours? Is the intemperance of the Alemanni so base as the intemperance of the Christians? Does the greed of the Alani so merit condemnation as the greed of the Christians? If Hun or the Gepid cheat, what is there to wonder at, since he does not know that cheating is a crime? If a Frank perjures himself, does he do anything strange, he who regards perjury as a way of speaking, not as a crime?'

James Harvey Robinson, ed., Readings in European History: Vol. I: (Boston:: Ginn and co., 1904), pg. 28-30

When wealth becomes deeply concentrated, a republic becomes deeply corrupt and the politicians stab the common citizens in the back in order to serve the wealthy few. This means the many will no longer fight to protect a system if they see that system as worse than a foreign invader.

Our intellectuals haven't lost self-*confidence*. It is merely that much of what they say has been exposed as utter claptrap. But they just need to make up new narratives to promote their wealthy masters' agenda and dine out on that. Argue, for example, that Russia with a $2.5 Trillion GDP is mounting a war of conquest against a NATO with $34 Trillion GDP.

A ship with dry rot may float — until a storm arrives.

*The U.S. Ambassador April Glaspie informed Saddam Hussein that the US did not take a position on Arab-Arab disputes. Saddam understood that to mean that the United States would not react to his invasion of Kuwait. Saddam invaded. US officials informed the Saudi king that an invasion was imminent. The shakedown worked well. The Saudis believe he paid US$280bn (in 1990 values) for protection which was every penny attainable. *Belief* was broken so a faction within KSA dissented, resulting in attacks against US targets and an internal insurgency.

With respect to the words of Christian priest Salvian, we can see that *belief was broken* first, and then *faith was lost*. *Faith and belief* are a stable set of ideas. Only *Confidence* and *Direct Democracy* are stable, as other forms of democracy demand *trust* in the unknown agenda of nameless factions within the elite. Thus, such other forms wither as *confidence* evaporates.

Confidence and *Fiat Currency* are related ideas that are unstable. We can see the signs today, with respect to the US dollar, that they may require *totalitarian government* if there is no relationship to gold. In addition, powerful offensive capabilities are required to destroy any opposing nation that seeks to undermine *Confidence* in the *Fiat Currency*. Recently Mr. Turner, a British economist, has proposed 'to use overt permanent money finance of fiscal deficits in appropriately moderate amounts to avoid deflation and stimulate the economy.' Or, in plain English, just print *fiat currency* to fund the deficit of the UK.

Unhappily for Mr. Turner, major and adversarial world powers have recovered from WW2. They cannot be militarily defeated and search to destroy *confidence*. *Confidence* in U.S. military *power* and *fiat currency* has been shaken by manifold events since Sept 11, 2001.

Globalised Capitalism is not about managing scarcity. How could it be? The Germans care not for deprivation in Spain for Mankind did not evolve beyond the tribe. Capitalism is about *power, faith, belief, trust, gold* and *confidence* in the *fiat*.

Higher education is just a convenient vector. The key is to farm the young by pulling forward demand through debt. Pull forward the credit to be spent now, push back the debt to be paid now into another electoral cycle. Trouble is the UK has been doing this for many years now so new administrations inherit the last cowboy's debt-bombshell and have to double down.

Housing is exactly the same. Providing the credit has become problematic in itself — requiring the law and the market for money to be corrupted so as to provide a subsidy to the banks in the USA: Young adults, with little or no guidance or financial maturity are socially coerced into college with implied promises of success. They're given loans to buy degrees that cannot possibly earn enough to cover their indebtedness. They have no flexibility to refinance their loan as you would with your home when interest rates drop. They're held hostage to usurious rates! Even in bankruptcy they cannot shed these chains.

The above compels students to go to university as employers begin demanding degrees for ever more menial tasks: Red queen syndrome. Individuals can opt-out knowing they don't need a degree for a basic office job, however because the rest opt-in (and the credit allows for this) when they leave school and apply for that office job they won't get an interview because employers demand a degree. It's pure and simple inflation. They printed too many degrees and now they are worthless. The continued underwriting of this via credit entrenches the problem.

John Robertson (Pseudonym)

It is easier to see what is going on if we put things in a historical perspective. Is Capitalism the first social system since the dawn of civilisation to 'trickle down'?

Since it is based on self-interest this seems highly unlikely.

It would be drawn up in the self-interest of those that came up with the system, i.e. those at the top. The 20th Century saw progressive taxation and high inheritance taxes to do away with old money elites and so looking at the playing field now can be rather deceptive. Today's ideal is unregulated, trickle down Capitalism.

We had unregulated, trickle down Capitalism in the UK in the 19th Century. We know what it looks like:

1) Those at the top were very wealthy
2) Those lower down lived in grinding poverty, paid just enough to keep them alive to work with as little time off as possible
3) Slavery
4) Child Labour

Immense wealth at the top with neither stream nor trickle in sight, just like today. The beginnings of regulation to deal with the wealthy UK businessman seeking to maximise profit was the abolition of slavery and child labour. The businessman was compensated for the loss of his property though it's telling that the slaves were not. At the end of the 19th Century, with a century or two of Capitalism under our belt, it was very obvious that a Leisure Class existed at the top of society.

The Theory of the Leisure Class: An Economic Study of Institutions:

"That the contemporary lords of the manor, the businessmen who own the means of production, have employed themselves in the economically unproductive practices of conspicuous consumption and conspicuous leisure, which are useless activities that contribute neither to the economy nor to the material production of the useful goods and services required for the functioning of society; while it is the middle class and the working class who are usefully employed in the industrialised, productive occupations that support the whole of society." Thorstein Veblen

This was before the levelling of inequality by progressive taxation and high inheritance taxes in the 20th Century. It can clearly be seen that Capitalism, like every other social system since the dawn of civilisation, is designed to support a Leisure Class at the top through the effort of a working and middle class.

After the mass movements of the 20th Century demanded progressive taxation or equalization measures the Leisure Class has learnt to stay well hidden. Though in the UK, associates of the Royal Family are well covered in the press and show the Leisure Class is still here with us today.

It was obvious in Adam Smith's day:

"The Labour and time of the poor is in civilised countries sacrificed to the maintaining of the rich in ease and luxury. The Landlord is maintained in idleness and luxury by the labour of his tenants. The moneyed man is supported by his extractions from the industrious merchant and the needy who are obliged to support him in ease by a return for the use of his money. But every savage has the full fruits of his own labours; there are no landlords, no usurers and no tax gatherers." – 1776

With more modern Capitalism it's better hidden.

The Rothschild brothers of London writing to associates in New York, 1863:

"The few who understand the system will either be so interested in its profits or be so dependent upon its favours that there will be no opposition from that class, while on the other hand, the great body of people, mentally incapable of comprehending the tremendous advantage that capital derives from the system, will bear its burdens without complaint, and perhaps without even suspecting that the system is inimical to their interests."

Dr. Hu - USA   *******   **Oct, 2014**

And so, after the race to the bottom reaches bottom, then what? Can anyone wonder why, after twenty-plus years of corporations rushing to low-wage, low-regulation venues in search of greater profits, we've succeeded all too well in lowering wages, benefits—and consumer demand —in the developed world. Some call it 'convergence'. But the consequences are pernicious and destabilizing.

The global labour pool, expanded by the addition of 2 billion low cost workers, exerts strong deflationary pressures everywhere. Benefits we in the West once not only took for granted, but expected to "progress"— vacation time, health care, safe working conditions, a clean environment —have eroded under withering global competition. And yet the WTO model marches on. Vietnam attracts Samsung factories, and never gives a thought to selling the products in their own domestic market—assuming more affluent consumers in the US, Europe, Japan, South Korea, etc. will do the buying. 'Export-driven development' limps on, in spite of weakening demand from indebted Middle Class consumers.

China climbed briskly up the value-added ladder for toys, shoes, and textiles in the '90s to high speed locomotives, wind turbines, and solar panels today. They so "over-built" that "over-capacity" which rendered millions of developed world workers redundant. And they kept on building to the point that they're now jettisoning many of their own workers into that burgeoning reserve army of the unemployed. Cheap money from the Fed's and others' copious punch bowls, in a relentless search for greater returns, found its way into ever riskier investments, adding to the supply glut. And now the world shudders at the faintest hint of locking away the punch and embarking on the long, joyless process of "getting sober."

In our ardour to avoid recession and inevitable wave of 'creative destruction' needed to begin rebalancing this badly distorted global economy we've set ourselves up for a tsunami-sized disaster.

Tim Young – UK Viewpoint

The establishment's analysis of global imbalances is that they expect there to be an expansionary solution, and I just don't think that, in a world of finite natural resources, in which efficiency increases slowly and largely exogenously by technical progress, an expansionary solution exists. If say, Germany, decided to consume its export earnings as they wish, and spent them on, say scotch, it might be easy for the distilleries to find labour, but they would also need more barley, more heat for the mash, more copper for the stills etc. This would drive up the prices of other goods, and less of them would be consumed, and economic output could be expected to fall back again.

And this situation is getting worse, day by day, as the productivity of China etc. increases, and they can competitively secure a greater proportion of global output. At the moment, the situation is being resolved because China etc. are content to consume a smaller proportion of their growing wealth, and, in our ignorance fostered by cynical politicians and naïve commentators, we are prepared to borrow it to maintain our consumption. As I say, the ordinary people do not even understand that this is what they are doing — they expect that the natural order is for their consumption to remain the same or even grow. And, unless some miracle turns up like fusion power that dramatically increases global output, we are heading for catastrophe when the emerging countries decide to start drawing on their savings with us, and either we consume a lot less or we repudiate their savings.

If we cannot adjust our economy to producing enough output which increases in value as China gets richer, like Germany has with its machine tools and cars, the obvious solution is that we recognise our declining competitiveness, and cut our consumption in line with our falling share of global output now. Given that two obvious extremes in our present economies are (1) public deficits and (2) inequality, I would tackle the problem by increasing wealth taxes. While this would not deal with the international imbalances directly, the resulting reduction in spending and pay down of foreign holdings of gilts would reduce our current account deficit. Of course, such change might have to be introduced gradually, and even more public expenditure might be required to facilitate adjustment, but the important thing is to recognise the solution and get started on it.

Since of course such a contractive solution is likely to be extremely unpopular, it is going to be difficult to sell to the public, and so I would appeal to influential commentators to consider them seriously, and set aside their Keynesian ideas which do not apply to a world which Keynes did not envisage.

Duvin Rouge – French Viewpoint

'An attempt to deny reality' rather than a 'managed depression'. The latter assumes some level of understanding and control. Both are lacking. Firstly, a crisis of overproduction cannot be understood by economics based upon a marginal conception of value.

Secondly, governments and central banks are unable to control the process of de-leverage because they cannot control the creation of money, especially credit money since the era of fiat money. What should be worrying the capitalist ruling class is: is this more than a crisis of overproduction? Is what lies behind the excessive creation of credit money a crisis of long-term profitability? In other words, despite the rise of China and the plundering of the Soviet bloc which had increased the rate of exploitation, have profits been artificially supported by credit/debt, so that the real rate of profit is so low that the whole system is in danger of collapse?

Mysterion

Here's a better question — Suppose we had been told 20 years ago that by late 2014, policy would have dictated rates of c.0.5% should be in effect for more than five years in Europe, and in Japan for two decades, that by general agreement they had not actually relieved the 'depression' in those zones in any way, and that economists who had advocated the policy were now resorting to empty auxiliary hypotheses about a mysterious state of 'Secular Stagnation' as their only explanation of why the policy hadn't worked. What would we have concluded about the efficacy of the policy?

B

We avoid the heart of the crisis. Capitalism relies on growth, growth in population matters a whole lot more than the growth in productivity. The chronic drop in birth rate in the developed world means less demand for houses, cars, furniture; as a result companies hire less and invest less. No amount of money printing is going to change this!!!

Hope Springs

It is the relative price (and value) of labour. With the irreversible opening of markets, which continues hugely to benefit the less developed world, we in the West are, in aggregate, living above our means. There is an inexorable downward pressure on labour costs which is strongest in least skilled occupations and those most easily substituted by off-shoring, but which is also not completely absent in the highest skilled occupations. The forces affecting the price/value of labour may be contributing to a lack of profitable investment opportunities. If this is true, the implications are pretty profound. Ultimately, it means that real asset prices that are driven by labour costs, among other things — especially property — could look very different in the future.

Olaf von Rein – UK

No more than 1.4% of all new loans go towards business (where one might charitably presume that they will contribute towards growth of our asset base). The rest, more or less, goes towards inflating the price of existing assets (cf. house price inflation). In the work-out from the credit crisis, we all had a choice: Run a large balance sheet (work-out via inflation) or run a small balance (work-out via defaults). The world tries to hang on to a large balance sheet (the US and UK with a little more panache than the EZ and Japan). But the size of the balance sheet does not really correlate with income. Income is going be the same, give or take. Low yields are then simply the flip side of the balance sheet choice we made. The elephant in the room ignored by Summers, Krugman, Yellan, Bernanke — is why the balance sheets of some countries (e.g. the UK) are so much longer (per capita) than those of other countries (e.g. Germany) in the first place? And the answer is universal asset backed pensions!! These savings have NO WHERE to go other than mostly towards existing assets. The low yields on an inflated asset base are simply the way that a universal asset back pension system succumbs to demographic pressures.

Is it that easy?

"Managed depression" - Glorious prosperity and hedonism for some; abject misery for most.

MarkGB   ***   **Sep,2014**

All empires throughout history have employed a number of 'strategies' to create or defend hegemony. These include:

1. They wrap up their territorial/economic ambitions in the fabric of a more noble objective

2. They seek to impose their values and/or religious beliefs on other cultures

3. They demonize their rivals, inventing a narrative that is laughable from the perspective of a few hundred years, or even decades, but seems perfectly acceptable to the majority of people at the time

4. They sacrifice 'human rights' at the drop of a hat when it suits them

5. They take their countries to war at times which are very convenient from the perspective of a government wishing to distract their population from economic or domestic concerns

6. They carry out false flag incidents, and lie about military intelligence in order to demonize their rivals and justify war

7. They persecute and attempt to undermine journalists, honest politicians and/or members of the public who attempt to expose their hidden agendas; and in many cases such people subsequently seem to find themselves involved in unfortunate accidents or mysterious suicides

8. They lie to their people about their activities at 1 to 7, leaving historians to spill the beans for them at a later date.

9. They manage to convince their populations that history stopped with them…that there is no number nine…this is the most insidious lie of all. Just a few years ago, Mr. Bush and Mr. Blair presented fabricated evidence to the US Congress and the UK Parliament, in order to justify the invasion of Iraq – number 6. Many of us were fooled, we thought 'no they wouldn't lie to us'. They did. Number nine was alive and well and living at number ten.

If we want to understand geopolitics, now or in the past, we have to learn that the really big lesson of history is that governments lie to their people, paint themselves as whiter than white, and their opponents as very dark indeed. This has gone on throughout history, and it is going on now. There is absolutely no doubt in my mind that right now—the US is 'at it', Russia is 'at it', Ukraine is 'at it', China is 'at it', and they are all 'at it'.

We always see, and are encouraged to look at, our opponents 'games'. We are always encouraged to ignore our own games. That is what is going on here.

Anyone who doubts this should read the recently declassified 'Northwoods Document' produced by the Joint Chiefs of Staff in March 1962, outlying a plan for false flag incidents and press manipulation to create support for a US invasion of Cuba. The plan included hijackings and other covert operations, which were designed to create a public groundswell of support. It was thrown out by President Kennedy. Anyone who thinks that this kind of thing doesn't go on now is naive.

Anyone who thinks the Neocons are just a group of non-compromising supporters of Western values should read the original version of the Wolfowitz doctrine, which was leaked and then hastily re-written when people saw it for what it was.

Personally I condemn empire and hegemony whether it's the Russians, the Americans, the Brits or the French, and if the Telly Tubbies ever decide to do it I shall condemn it in them too.

Further, anyone who thinks you can demoralize an opponent like Mr. Putin by accusing him of stuff that you do yourself is either incredibly arrogant or incredibly foolish.

I don't buy your analysis and I don't buy your certainty. I leave the last word with Mr. Chomsky:

"There is a principle of ideology that we must never look at our own crimes, we should, on the other hand, exalt in the crimes of others and in our own nobility in opposing them"

Noam Chomsky, Professor of Linguistics, MIT – Four Horsemen

Ealing

Yanukovich had been courted for years by the EU and it looked as though the deal was finally approaching fruition. Yanukovich was, of course, the legitimate President elected by a democratic vote which had been described by international observers as "a model of democracy". The EU worked assiduously to bring him on side and they were almost at the point of handing him the pen to sign. Had he done so, he would have been feted in the West as a great and visionary leader.

But at the last minute, Putin made several points which caused Yanukovich to walk away, principally the fact that Ukraine had received heavily subsidised oil and gas for decades, relied hugely on Russian trade, had a huge expat population in Russia on whose remittances Ukraine relied on, and Ukraine was far behind in its debt payments to Russia for energy already delivered. This debt (which Ukraine couldn't possibly pay) would be called in should Ukraine join the EU.

This was undoubtedly a "threat" from one perspective, or a "dose of reality" if you prefer, but the point Putin was making was that the promises from the EU, should Yanukovich succumb to those appeals, were more ephemeral that the advantages close alliance with Russia secured. Yanukovich thought hard. His decision to stick with Russia sealed his fate and that of his country. He had to go. All the qualities which made him a potentially worthy partner for the EU now evaporated and he became (what he almost certainly always was) a venal grasping politician. The Maidan coup overthrew a legitimately elected President who, as soon as he made the "wrong" decision, had to be exposed as someone completely evil because otherwise there would be no possible justification to dispose of him. He was fine to deal with when being enticed by the EU, but became a monster that had to go when he decided to stop talking.

The narrative that Yanukovich was removed because he was a criminal would have been completely reversed if he had decided to sign up with the EU. Had that happened and had he been removed by the pro-Russian side, he would now be considered a martyr. He was so close, but in the end was convinced that the EU promises of support were less reliable that Moscow's delivery of gas in a cold winter.

Yanukovich was not removed simply because he was venal. He was removed because he made the "wrong" decision in the West's analysis, and he, and his entire country, will pay for that "mistake" for years to come.

Morally, and financially of course, so will the EU.

Sarasota Bill

Russia has been invaded too often throughout history for it not to affect its world view. Where the West sees free countries choosing to associate with NATO and the EU, Russia sees past enemies moving closer to her borders. After Hitler and Napoleon killed millions and millions of Russians they are not willing to accept protestations of benign intent. (Not to mention the millions murdered by Stalin) The treaty with Hitler taught them that lesson. We in the West must learn to look at situations through the eyes of those we engage with.

iTrade

The media are essentially naive or overly idealistic, or put another way, not really acknowledging just how long it takes to develop a stable set of ideas, and counter ideas, over what it takes to create a true democratic political environment and political system that can be stable yet challenging, representative but decisive. Can we really say in the West that we have achieved this? US democracy is ever more compromised (special interests and lame ducks); UK has been slowly tearing itself apart, but not proportional representatively, unlike European versions which have evolved political classes into an exalted Indian Caste system of affirmative action. To criticise the current Russian government, or previous versions, for not having embraced the true spirit of our Western Political Democracies is just pure folderol, betraying a lack of clear historical appreciation, likely dulled by the self satisfaction that is inherent even as our own rot begins to crumble.

Maljoffre

Russia is effectively encircled by US and NATO (the largest and most powerful military alliance in the world that reaches right up to Russia's borders) bases. The US and NATO have stationed nuclear-capable missiles near that border forcing Russia to reply in kind. Any country that is militarily threatened will, in its defence, use the most powerful weapons it has in its arsenal. The US military dominates the sea lanes off the coast of China and sends spy planes over China's airspace while it has defence agreements with Japan and vows to support that nation in any dispute with China.

Russia is right to feel threatened. The US anti ballistic system in Eastern Europe is according to the US government there to protect Europe from Iran. Iran, that stopped its nuclear program a decade ago according to both non US, and even US intelligence. Combine that with the change of US military doctrine that allows for first strikes with nuclear weapons and it is more than clear that the US is threatening the very existence of Russia. Beyond that, the US supported (if not fomented) rioters in Kiev who overthrew the elected government that was replaced with a rabidly anti-Russian one in Ukraine, where president Poroshenko, just yesterday said the Ukraine, Russia's neighbouring state, is ready for "total war" with Russia.

In response, Russia and China, both nuclear-armed states with a multi-million man army, are forming a military alliance to counter US aggr-ession.

Ealing

The media's virulent anti-Russian invective is followed carefully as if it has been mandated. Nevertheless, when describing the conditions in Lugansk, which only avoided a humanitarian catastrophe when the Russians sent a desperately needed convoy back in the summer, in the teeth of opposition from Kiev, it should be reasonable for the FT to state that the town is not really "caught in the middle" of the conflict. It has been pummelled non stop by artillery fire.

This was artillery fire from the Kiev forces. Everyone in Lugansk knows that, which is why a large number of the people of Lugansk fled to the perceived safety of Russia. The Lugansk rebels were obviously not shelling their own people, however difficult this might be for some of the more rabidly anti-Russian faction to accept.

There is a journalistic black hole in the story of Ukraine, where possibly the largest forced migration in Europe since the World War 2 has been happening in total silence. It would be wonderful if the FT would interview some of the one million people who have fled east Ukraine in terror of their lives, and ask them how they felt about the Government in Kiev, and why they felt they had to abandon everything they had and flee, and why they chose Russia for sanctuary.

The answers, of course, are absolutely obvious, and run totally counter to the West's chosen narrative, as a consequence of which not a single western journalist has even tried to ask the questions. When the answers are bound to destroy the fiction that all Ukrainians support Kiev, that Kiev is a good and fair Government, and that Russians are all evil to the core, nobody can be found to report this. The refugees do not agree at all with the line the West insists upon, and so a million desperate people are completely ignored.

How can it be that one million people can be displaced in Europe and nobody is prepared to talk to them? Every western media source has had one or more reporters speaking regularly with Syrian refugees, why can't we find a single journalist to speak to these Europeans? The answer, of course, is because the refugees from Lugansk will give the unvarnished and unwelcome truth, so a thundering silence must be all that's heard from them.

*Reader, please note that this entry highlights the increasingly difficult task of inculcating and maintaining *faith and belief* in the nation. All power blocks are using increasingly overt means: Euro News, Russia Today, etc. A heavy hand of content filtering and presentation skewing is ineffective, particularly when enemy states are sending counter messages to the intellect. Invitations to the instinctual and emotional mind are best while the brain is in a trance state via subtle suggestions.

A common strategy to permanently weaken another nation is to poach their best and brightest youth. Not all immigrants are the same: smart young men with no dependants are economically and militarily better. Ambitious and productive individuals pursue opportunity rather than a place in the status quo. They can be tempted to emigrate to opposing nations. Just contemplate how German scientists benefited the US war economy.

***

The present showdown between West, Russia and China is the culmination of a long running saga that began with World War One. Prior to which, Capitalism was governed by the gold standard system which was international, very solid, with clear rules and had brought great prosperity: for banking Capital was scarce and so allocated carefully. World War One required debt-capitalism of the FIAT kind, a bankrupt Britain began to pass the Imperial baton to the US, which had profited by financing the war and selling munitions.

The Weimar Republic, suffering a continuation of hostilities via economic means, tried to inflate away its debts in 1919-1923 with disastrous results—hyperinflation. Then, the reintroduction of the gold standard into a world poisoned by war, reparation and debt was fated to fail and ended with a deflationary bust in the early 1930's and WW2.

The US government gained a lot of credibility after WW2 by outlawing offensive war and funding many construction projects that helped transfer private debt to the public book. The US government's debt exploded during the war, but it also shifted the power game away from creditors to a big debtor that had a lot of political capital. The US used her power to define the new rules of the monetary system at Bretton Woods in 1944 and to keep physical hold of gold owned by other nations.

The US jacked up tax rates on the wealthy and had a period of elevated inflation in the late 40s and into the 1950s — all of which wiped out creditors, but also ushered in a unique middle class era in the West. The US also reformed extraction centric institutions in Europe and Japan to make sure an extractive-creditor class did not hobble growth, which was easy to do because the war had wiped them out (same as in Korea).

Capital destruction in WW2 reversed the Marxist rule that the rate of profit always falls. Take any given market — say jeans. At first, all the companies make these jeans using a great deal of human labour so all the jeans are priced around the average of total social labour time required for production (some companies will charge more, some companies less).

One company then introduces a machine (costed at $n) that makes jeans using a lot less labour time. Each of these robot assisted workers is paid the same hourly rate but the production process is now far more productive. This company, ignoring the capital outlay in the machinery, will now have a much higher profit rate than the others. This will attract capital, as capital is always on the lookout for higher rates of profit. The result will be a generalisation of this new mode of production. The robot or machine will be adopted by all the other companies, as it is a more efficient way of producing jeans.

As a consequence the price of the jeans will fall, as there is an increased margin within which each market actor can undercut his fellows. One company will lower prices so as to increase market share. This new price-point will become generalised as competing companies cut their prices to defend their market share. A further n$ was invested but per unit profit margin is put under constant downward pressure, so the rate of return in productive assets tends to fall over time in a competitive marketplace.

Interest rates have been falling for decades in the West because interest rates must always be below the rate of return on productive investments. If interest rates are higher than the risk adjusted rate of return then the capitalist might as well keep his money in a savings account. If there is real deflation his purchasing power increases for free and if there is inflation he will park his money (plus debt) in an unproductive asset that's price inflating, E.G. Housing. Sound familiar? Sure, there has been plenty of profit generated since 2008 but it has not been recovered from productive investments in a competitive free market place. All that profit came from bubbles in asset classes and financial schemes abetted by money printing and zero interest rates.

Thus, we know that the underlying rate of return is near zero in the West. The rate of return falls naturally, due to capital accumulation and market competition. The system is called capitalism because capital accumulates: high income economies are those with the greatest accumulation of capital per worker. The robot assisted worker enjoys a higher income as he is highly productive, partly because the robotics made some of the workers **redundant** and there are fewer workers to share the profit. All the high income economies have had near zero interest rates for seven years. Interest rates in Europe are even negative. How has the system remained stable for so long?

All economic growth depends on energy gain. It takes energy (drilling the oil well) to gain energy. Unlike our everyday experience whereby energy acquisition and energy expenditure can be balanced, capitalism requires an absolute net energy gain. That gain, by way of energy exchange, takes the form of tools and machines that permit an increase in productivity per work hour. Thus GDP increases, living standards improve and the debts can be repaid. Thus, oil is a strategic capitalistic resource.

US net energy gain production peaked in 1974, to be replaced by production from Saudi Arabia, which made the USA a net importer of oil for the first time. US dependence on foreign oil rose from 26% to 47% between 1985 and 1989 to hit a peak of 60% in 2006. And, tellingly, real wages peaked in 1974, levelled-off and then began to fall for most US workers. Wages have never recovered. (The decline is more severe if you don't believe government reported inflation figures that don't count the cost of housing.)

What was the economic and political result of this decline? During the 20 years 1965-85, there were 4 recessions, 2 energy crises and wage and price controls. These were unprecedented in peacetime and The Gulf of Tonkin event led to the Vietnam War which finally required Nixon to move away from the Gold-Exchange Standard in 1971, opening the next degenerate chapter of FIAT finance up until 2008. Cutting this link to gold was cutting the external anchor impeding war and deficit spending. The promise of gold for dollars was revoked.

GDP in the US increased after 1974 but a portion of end use buying power was transferred to Saudi Arabia. They were supplying the net energy gain that was powering the US GDP increase. The working class in the US began to experience a slow real decline in living standards, as 'their share' of the economic pie was squeezed by the ever increasing transfer of buying power to Saudi Arabia.

The US banking and government elite responded by creating and cutting back legal and behavioural rules of a fiat based monetary system. The Chinese appreciated the long term opportunity that this presented and agreed to play ball. The USA over-produced credit money and China over-produced manufactured goods which cushioned the real decline in the buying power of America's working class. Power relations between China and the US began to change: The Communist Party transferred value to the American consumer whilst Wall Street transferred most of the US industrial base to China. They didn't ship the military industrial complex.

Large scale leverage meant that US consumers and businesses had the means to purchase increasingly with debt so the class war was deferred. This is how over production occurs: more is produced that is paid for not with money that represents actual realized labour time, but from future wealth, to be realised from future labour time. The Chinese labour force was producing more than it consumed.

The system has never differed from the limits laid down by the Laws of Thermodynamics. The Real economy system can never over-produce per se. The limit of production is absolute net energy gain. What is produced can be consumed. How did the Chinese produce such a super massive excess and for so long? Economic slavery can achieve radical improvements in living standards for those that benefit from ownership. Slaves don't depreciate as they are rented and are not repaired for they replicate for free. Hundreds of millions of Chinese peasants limited their way of life and controlled their consumption in order to benefit their children. And their exploited life raised the rate of profit!

They began their long march to modern prosperity making toys, shoes, and textiles cheaper than poor women could in South Carolina or Honduras. Such factories are cheap to build and deferential, obedient and industrious peasant staff were a perfect match for work that was not dissimilar to tossing fruit into a basket. Their legacy is the initial capital formation of modern China and one of the greatest accomplishments in human history. The Chinese didn't use net energy gain from oil to power their super massive and sustained increase in production. They used economic slavery powered by caloric energy, exchanged from solar energy. The Chinese labour force picked the World's low hanging fruit that didn't need many tools or machines. Slaves don't need tools for they are the tool.

Without a gold standard and capital ratios our form of over-production has grown enormously. The dotcom bubble was reflated through a housing bubble, which has been pumped up again by sovereign debt, printing press (QE) and central bank insolvency. The US working and middle classes have over-consumed relative to their share of the global economic pie for decades. The correction to prices (the destruction of credit money and accumulated capital) is still yet to happen. This is what has been happening since 1971 because of the growth of financialisation or monetisation.

The application of all these economic methods was justified by the political ideology of neo-Liberalism. Neo-Liberalism entails no or few capital controls, the destruction of trade unions, plundering state and public assets, importing peasants as domesticated help, and entrusting society's value added production to The Communist Party of The People's Republic of China.

The Chinese have many motives but their first motivation is power. Power is more important than money. If you're rich and weak you get robbed. Russia provides illustrating stories of such: Gorbachev had received a promise from George HW Bush that the US would pay Russia approximately $400 billion over 10 years as a "peace dividend" and as a tool to be utilized in the conversion of their state run to a market based economic system. The Russians believe the head of the CIA at the time, George Tenet, essentially killed the deal based on the idea that "letting the country fall apart will destroy Russia as a future military threat". The country fell apart in 1992. Its natural assets were plundered which raised the rate of profit in the 90's until President Putin put a stop to the robbery.

In the last analysis, the current framework of Capitalism results in labour redundancy, a falling rate of profit and ingrained trading imbalances caused by excess capacity funded by the FIAT. Under our current monopoly state capitalism a number of temporary preventive measures have evolved, including the expansion of university, military, and prison systems to warehouse new generations of labour.

Our problem is how to retain the "expected return rate" for us, the Dominant Class. Ultimately, there are only two large-scale solutions, which are intertwined. One is expansion of state debt to keep "the markets" moving and transfer wealth from future generations of labour to the present Dominant Class. The other is war, the consumer of last resort. Wars can burn up excess capacity, shift global markets, generate monopoly rents, and return future labour to a state of helplessness and reduced expectations. The Spanish flu killed 50-100 million people in

1918. As if this was not enough, it also took two World Wars across the 20th century and some 96 million dead to reduce unemployment and stabilize the "labour problem." Is this a rational and humane solution? Well, that would depend on which class you're in.

Capitalism requires World War because Capitalism requires profit and cannot afford the unemployed. The point is Capitalism could afford social democracy after the rate of profit was restored thanks to the depression of the 1930's and the physical destruction of capital during WW2. Capitalism only produces for profit and social democracy was funded by taxing profits after WW2.

Post WW2 growth in labour productivity, due to automation, itself due to oil and gas replacing coal, meant workers could be better off. As the economic pie was growing, workers could receive the same %, and still receive a bigger slice. Wages as a % of US GDP actually increased in the period, 1945-1970. There was an increase in government spending which was being redirected in the form of redistributed incomes.

Inequality will only worsen, because to make profits now we have to continually cut the cost of inputs, i.e. wages and benefits. Have we not already reached the point where large numbers of the working class can neither feed themselves nor afford a roof over their heads? 13% of the UK working age population is out of work and receiving out of work benefits. A huge fraction is receiving in work benefits because low skill work now pays so little. We must act before the masses agitate and congregate for power — Communism, Theocracy, etc.

The underlying nature of Capitalism is cyclical. Here is how the political aspect of the cycle ends:

➤ 1920s/2000s – High inequality, high banker pay, low regulation, low taxes for the wealthy, robber barons (CEOs), reckless bankers, globalisation phase
➤ 1929/2008 – Wall Street crash
➤ 1930s/2010s – Global recession, currency wars, trade wars, rising unemployment, nationalism and extremism
➤ What comes next? - World War.

If Capitalism could speak, she would ask her older brother, Imperialism, this: "Can you solve the problem?" We are not reliving the 1930's, the economy is now an integrated whole that encompasses the entire World. Capital has accumulated since 1945, so under- and unemployment is a plague everywhere. How big is the problem? Official data tells us nothing, but the 47 million Americans on food aid are suggestive. That's 1 in 7 Americans and total World population is 7 billion.

The scale of the solution is dangerous. Our probing for weakness in the South China Sea, Ukraine and Syria has awakened them to their danger. The Chinese and Russian leaders have reacted by integrating their payment systems and real economies, trading energy for manufactured goods for advanced weapon systems. As they are central players in the Shanghai Group we can assume their aim is the monetary system which is the bedrock of our Imperial Power. What's worse, they can avoid overt enemy action and simply choose to undermine "confidence" in the FIAT.

Though given the calibre of their nuclear arsenal, how can they be fought let alone defeated? Appetite preceded Reason, so Lust is hard to Reason with. But beware brother. Your Lust for Power began this saga, perhaps it's time to Reason.

Appendix:
Reason has been said to be the slave of the passions, so yes we do need to be careful about choosing a theory that fits our preconceptions. This applies not just to individuals but to society as a whole. At society level we call this ideology. Political economy was the ideological reaction to classical economics that appeared to show that all profit came from labour (even before Marx). This is why the subtitle of Das Kapital is 'A Critique of Political Economy'. It was a criticism of the argument that each factor of production gets its 'just' reward.

In his attack on this 'surface level' economics, he draws heavily from classical economists like Ricardo, but his labour theory of value is completely different as it includes the market. In simple terms Marx effectively said if commodities of different uses can be exchanged and so measured by a single quantitative measure, money (price/value), then there must be one factor that is common to all commodities. What else is there but labour time?

Not the concrete labour time of individual commodities, but the socially necessary labour time of society. Hence prices of individual commodities will only by luck equal their labour values, but in the aggregate, over the course of the business cycle, aggregate prices should equal aggregate values. This gives us an objective measure of value, however difficult it may be in practice to actually measure. We don't have to resort to subjectivism and ultimately to 'animal spirits' to explain crises.

All this requires a clear understanding of the difference between value and wealth. Increases in labour productivity, or climate changes resulting in increased yield, etc, can mean we can have more use-values (more material things) for the same amount of labour time. We are wealthier, we are better off, but in terms of (labour) value we are no better off. This, arguably, is the story of post-war developed countries.

Since the $ decoupled from gold US imperialism has taken full advantage of the ability to pay its debts by just printing money. The Chinese have been happy to accept these IOU's and in effect have been producing for US citizens (and others in the West) without getting the full value of their labour; a form of slavery. By pegging the RMB to the USD, China has ransacked American production. In order to maintain this advantageous peg, China had to hide their excess profits by loaning them back to the US. If China tried to cash out they would realize 20 years worth of deferred inflation all at once, that is why they may not get all of "their" value back. They would be paying a 20 year tab for borrowing a huge part of US economy.

So, their fear of importing inflation is being dispersed by super-massive infrastructure projects that will build a Eurasian land mass economy. It seems the game is to spend the money outside China; Chinese companies and labour will be favoured. This will export inflation. If the Chinese were to suddenly dump or try and convert these IOU's into assets of real value (as they already have been doing to a small degree,) this would reveal an insolvent FED, tank the Dollar and fuel hyperinflation. That will spell the end of the $ based monetary system and throw US imperialism into crisis. The tensions with China will almost certainly lead to war.

Contributors: Duvin Rouge, TAC, Quietly Spoken, John Robertson, Nelson Alexander

German Viewpoint - German Mittelstand Company, CEO

Capitalism Requires World War, Yes or No? A single important counter-example would be enough to refute this somewhat crude and general statement. So what about WW1?

I am to argue that Imperialism, Geopolitics, or Strategic Doctrines -be it Mackinder or Wolfowitz, at least in WW1 were predominant to the Private Profit Motive, which we may use to define "Capitalism" here.

Funny thing is, I started out to disprove *"Capitalism Requires World War"*, writing and thinking about WW1 and now have to admit that it is —at least—halfway right.

What I came to realize is, that whereas at least two parties are needed for peace, only one, unfortunately, is enough for war. The US backstop of Britain was profit-motivated. Would the official and unofficial leaders of Great Britain have let WW1 happen without this US backstop?

Possible, but not probable.

Admittedly, capitalism played a role in WW1, and a decisive one in the US. There Capitalism was the big war motive: Though interest rates were not sensational, US war loans were profitable to banks as creditor risk was transferred to the US government later on. This was easy, as Rockefeller and Morgan controlled the government. And real profit margins were in supplies and ammunition (look at what DuPont´s stock price did after 1914).

That was common war profiteering by US enterprises – and these things have always happened, even long before capitalism was invented. Granted, those enterprises were controlled by Morgan and Rockefeller interests. But they did not start the war. They backstopped the British war initiative and made sure a Federal Reserve was around in time to backstop them if needed.

On the other hand, all European powers, the Middle Powers especially, ran existential risks in entering this war. They would only enter out of necessity, or perceiving chances to be much bigger than the risks. Granted, that allowed stupidity and short-sightedness as co-motives. But we know from their correspondence that most of their decision makers were dimly aware how horrible this war could turn out.

The only Power free to act or not to act or even to stop the war was Great Britain. Its strategic war planning and its motives were not primarily financial; i.e. they had not much to do with the Financial System or Capitalism.

In Europe Capitalism did NOT require WW 1:

1) Though Britain´s financial position was weakening through trade deficits, it only recently had conquered Transvaal in a brutal way, getting the biggest gold mines under control.

2) The important banking houses were quite internationally organised, f.e. Warburgs everywhere. Most bankers at least in Europe were against war. German, British and Jewish bankers got along splendidly.

3) The gold standard system was international, very solid and with clear rules and had brought great prosperity in a cultured, though somewhat nationalist atmosphere.

4) The control of oil in Turkish controlled Arabia and Kurdistan was a strategic issue for the English fleet. But a compromise about Bagdad-Bahn had been found between German and English banking houses in Spring of 1914.

The British were acting out of their Mackinder Doctrine, and thereby "putting the lights out on the continent". It was not Capitalism, but its older brother: Imperialism. Lust for Power precedes and dominates Lust for Money. Power, if it wants, gains money in an instant, whereas Money has to spend itself into Power much more slowly and with great care.

On the other hand: are those two not eternally intertwined? Can we take those two apart, as if its separation in language would mean separation in the real word and treat them as different things, when they indeed go together like yin-and-yang?

Appendix WW1:

So much goes back to WW1—which explains why so many lies are still taught about it in history classes—so we must understand the forces it unleashed. War, even offensive war, in 1914 was considered a very legitimate means of geopolitics.

The ruling British clique, a group around Lord Alfred Milner, began a rapprochement with France and concocting war against Germany starting in 1906. By 1914 the British had all the ducks in a row.
Motives were diverse:
a) Britain wanted to weaken at least Germany, if not all Continental Powers, and the oil areas controlled by Turkey.
b) France sought Alsace-Lothringia and colonies.
c) Russia, Italy, Serbia and Rumania sought expansion.
d) Austria-Hungary had revenge against Serbia in mind.
e) Germany´s Generalstab, with time working against it, in summer 1914 felt—probably correctly—that it had to prop up Austria-Hungary and help it take one adversary out: Serbia.

If Russia and France would go to war over this, then better earlier than later, when Russian offensive abilities would further improve. The exact timing of the war the British left to events, with Serbia and Russia first driving Austria-Hungary to war and Austria-Hungary dragging a desperate Wilhelm II with it. Britain only showed its cards after German troupes had crossed Belgian borders.

The British Foreign Minister, Lord Grey, had it set up nicely: Britain in the beginning only supplied a sea blockade and a few divisions in France; so "the lights going out all over Europe" meant a great weakening of all continental powers: the hostile ones, Turkey, Germany and Austria-Hungary AND the allied ones, France, Serbia, Italy and Russia.

Where things went wrong was that German military prowess, showed itself to be even stronger than anticipated, as the Reich, Austrian-Hungary´s and Turkey´s weakness notwithstanding, was able to stabilize or even win on many fronts: France, Russia, Tyrol, Rumania, Serbia, Macedonia/Greece and Palestine,

Contrary to the first expectations one could gain by looking at a world map, WW 1 would have ended with a stalemate or even a German victory—had not American money and ammunition, and later troupes given the decisive advantage to the Entente powers. So despite the nearly optimal set-up, the British had to mortgage their empire to the US to gain a costly victory, as all parties were in the end bankrupt at least in a traditional, non-fiat-money sense.

Before and after 1914 promises were made and many were kept in Versailles: The US got spectacular war profits against what we now call vendor-finance, the war debt was coupled with the reparation issue, was mainly defaulted upon, restructured or forgiven, and led to an inflation-deflation spiral.

France got Elsace-Lothringia from Germany and Syria from Turkey, Russia was promised a stronghold in the Balkans and Constantinople and (got a Bolshevik revolution and civil war instead), Serbia was promised Bosnia/Herzegowina and Italy got Southern Tyrol and Triest, Rumania got Siebenbuergen.

Now to economic motives: there are some to be found. In 1914, the prior dominant British economic position was already weakening as Sterling was undermined by British trade deficits. Germany was an upcoming power, whose language was then spoken by 5% of Earth´s population (100 million out of 2 billion), with a superior education and progressive social system producing superior technology. Just think about it: Without war, the first atomic weapon would most probably been developed by German scientists, many of them Jewish, in a Hohenzollern German Reich. World history might have taken a totally different course.

One might conclude that WW1 destroyed the foundation of the international gold standard; but the system worked pretty fine before 1914 except Britain losing some gold. So what? Britannia still ruled the waves, Canada, Australia, India, many parts of Africa were part of the Empire. Oil was discovered as a strategic energy source but the main owner, the Osman Empire, was a backward empire, militarily weak with suppressed minorities everywhere hoping for escape.

Granted, before the last hot world war (1914-45) one can see **a weakening hegemon**, Great Britain, feeling primarily endangered by an upcoming power, Germany – but there was no financial necessity coming out of a broken financial system.

Also, we may find a little justice in history, as British Power was not increased by WW1, but decreased as its gold went to the US and war loans put the US in the creditor position and put Britain into a junior partner position.

The lessons for today:

So again, did capitalism require World War? Hard to say.
The other way around the question is easier to answer: **World War requires debt-capitalism, at least the FIAT money one.**

Central banks were there to finance war; one of them was arguably created for it: the New York Federal Reserve in the winter of 1913/14.

The reintroduction of the gold standard into a world poisoned by war, reparation and debt was bound to be unsuccessful and ended in a defla-tionary bust in the early 1930ties and a second leg of the Great War, now called WW2.

Could the central banks of the world have inflated away the debts in the 30ties? The professors, especially Bernanke, argue "yes!", forgetting that this was already tried in the 20ties, leading into the 30ties. The experi-ences of Weimar 1919-23 are also not to be recommended. Anyway, in the eyes of the decision makers—the bankers, deflation was a lesser evil 1929 to 1933, and some banks with their lifelines to the Fed did profit quite nicely from others drowning.

War is a horrible enterprise, profitable only for a few and a catastrophe for mankind. So after the slaughter of 1914-45, in Nuremberg, offensive war was outlawed. So war was made to look defensive from then on — which at least quintupled the lying about it. The Gulf of Tonkin event led to the Vietnam War and in the end required Nixon to move away from the Gold-Exchange Standard in 1971, opening the next degenerate chapter of FIAT finance up until 2008, with only a short Volcker counter move in the early 80ties.

Now here in January 2016 we are in extra innings, many powerful people in Washington are promoting war against Syria, Iran, Russia and even China, forcing other countries to take sides: Venezuela, Brazil, Egypt, Jordan, India, Thailand, the Kurdish tribes – they all get thrown into conflicts which are bound not to end in one generation. As happened to Europe in 1914.

The wars of the 20th century were very profitable for the US establishment. They gained enormous power world-wide. War never reached their own shores. They lost a few soldiers — compare that to 20 million Russians and around 10 million Germans dead. And what were a few bombs on London compared to Dresden, Stalingrad and Hiroshima? Also, WW2 was the last time the Anglo-Saxons could superficially argue they led a defensive war of good against evil, with the Japanese attacking first in Pearl Harbour and Hitler getting into Poland.

So, having suffered no meaningful losses, and not having experienced war´s destruction of morals and society since the Southern States´ rebellion 150 years ago, and most importantly, 99% of the population being exposed to it only via Hollywood´s Fairy Tales – why not go for it? The Neocons are at it again. Economic and financial sanctions (still an act of war), a putsch in Kiev, the shelling of civilians in Donbass, the shoot down of a Russian jet in Syria – all to provoke the Russians to do something stupid, while risking WW3 and total extinction — for Europe at least. Europeans now shudder when they see US belligerence on TV: McCain, Hillary and all the mad generals and ex-generals — are we all supposed to be annihilated because they love war so much?

As WW1 turned not out as planned by its Mastermind Great Britain, neither might the Neocons be able to confine war to Eurasia. So what is the real motive?

Geopolitical doctrine à la Wolfowitz? Or is it done to conceal the bankruptcy of the West? Or does it lead to the final bankruptcy of the West?

These questions are crucial.

John Nikos

Well, which were the three events of the 20th century which shaped the world? If we step back from the euro-centric view, we would have some answers that may help us understand the present juncture and avoid a Third World War.

1) The October Revolution of 1917 — World War I did play a crucial role in bringing about conducive conditions for it, but the independent role of the forces which worked for the revolution was the prime factor. The Revolution quickly captured the imagination of people all over the world who dreamed of better conditions for the vast majority of people. The ideals of the Revolution influenced national liberation movements all over the world — this influence, and the consequent efforts to bring the vast masses of peasants and workers into the fold of those movements made the national liberation movements truly mass movements.

2) The Second World War — the turning point of which was the Battle of Stalingrad, not the D-Day Landings. The outcome of the war accelerated decolonisation, greatly increased the prestige of the socialist bloc among the nations of the world, and enabled the newly independent countries to chart out an autonomous path of development.

3) The collapse of the socialist bloc. The collapse of the Soviet Union spelt the end of a significant experiment in human history, and entailed a huge setback for the efforts of humanity to build a world different from the world where all gains of development accrue to a minority. This helped intensify the assault on the people launched by the likes of Pinochet, Thatcher and Reagan in the 1970s and 80s, and ultimately led up to the current predicament where social security has been whittled down even as Europe has 11.7% unemployment with 25% of the workforce in two countries (Greece and Spain) rendered jobless.

Over the Rainbow   *******   **Jun, 2014**

The superficial mind dangerously glides over the different intersections of politics and economy in different places. Markets are a tool of totalitarian states in Russia and China that are meant to further the ideology of the state. Feedback from citizens is quite limited. In Europe the state mediates the connection between capital and citizens to stabilize national identity, such as in the film market. In the US the state and capital effectively compete for varying levels of public influence. The tribalism is not the same in these places, either in its mechanics or goals. Without a more focused discussion of terms of debate and concrete analysis of particulars, they end up making dangerous myths about *power* in the world.

Invaderdan

China is as the USSR was in 1945. While not wanting to underplay the achievements of D-Day, it's worth remembering that we were up against 58 German divisions, while the Russians were fighting 228 divisions. The US wasn't going to immediately fight the Soviet Union after its alliance, given the Red Army had 4.8m troops mobilised in Europe at the end of the war I doubt anybody could have realistically fought the Soviet Union if that is what they wanted, as if there hadn't been enough death. Today, China has a multimillion man army; a population that would work itself to death if it was attacked; and Russia as an ally which is supplying the S-400 air defence system and would supply the A to Z of primary inputs required to wage unlimited and ceaseless war.

Quietly Spoken

Check your numbers. The US had a smaller "Army" at 3.4 million, but that does not include the "Army Air Force" which had 2.3 million, Marines (which were a relatively small force) or any British, Australian, or Canadian forces. Furthermore, the US had an equal number of forces in the Pacific Theatre, and annual arms production of about $42bn to the $16bn for the USSR, making army size almost irrelevant. In other words, no, the USSR was not that threatening and it took Roosevelt and then Truman to hold back the more aggressive US commanders from finding a military rather than economic source of compromise.

The unfortunate matter is that two of the countries who felt the most pain in WW2 have internalized the route to success in their national spirit as personal suffering, rather than the cooperation and integration that truly enabled victory over the axis powers. The integration achieved by the West in WW2 was so strong that it remains in the intelligence community even today, and would certainly return and expand today in the face of further serious threat. The cost of this integration was great, but the dividend was 65 years of relative peace through cooperative defence and industry. While this potential strength appears to have lost some gloss in the eyes of some, to abandon international cooperation for national gain holds the potential of long term economic isolation; of a sort that may be the only force short of direct conflict able to undo the greatness achieved in emerging and re-emerging markets.

*This refers to Germany and Japan and is central to an understanding of the Euro crisis. Korea was a tributary to China for several hundred years. Then Japan occupied Korea for several decades. Now the Koreans are in a race with themselves to prove—to themselves—that they're second to no one—making society an unlivable place where everything becomes a competition. The result is the highest suicide rate in the world. These historical experiences led them to internalise the route to success in their national spirit as domination over others. As such, cruelty and bullying are rife which forces the weak to disfigure themselves with plastic surgery while all social actors strive to accumulate symbols of status and position in a ceaseless struggle for *respect;* which often descends into naked domination over the other.

The S-400 air defence system is an extremely potent weapon. Designed to counter, negate and destroy NATO investment and production of stealth fighter and bomber technology; the new fleet of F-35 fighters will cost the US $1.51 trillion. As a rule, defence of one's own territory is far cheaper than the addition of offensive capabilities. And finally, any major war will ultimately be a war of attrition or resolved by thermonuclear warheads. The composition of armaments is of secondary import, as demonstrated by the Vietnam War – whereby the humble machine gun wore down a superpower.

Paul A. Myers - USA

Let me offer one principle on how to mediate the tension between cooperation and conflict: risk reduction. This is the big hidden lever of economic advancement. It should work as well during the next hundred years as it has for the past half thousand years. We're one generation of skilled public leadership away from realizing its potential.

At the beginning of the mercantile and capitalist age, two mighty risk reduction techniques evolved: first, the joint stock company and, second, ocean cargo insurance. With these two innovations long distance sea borne trade blossomed and resources were organized under common management to undertake vast commercial projects.

During the Great Depression, Roosevelt applied risk reduction techniques to public policy on an unprecedented scale (as did the social democratic movement worldwide in general). Deposit insurance and bank regulation took huge amounts of risk out of the payment transaction and commercial loan processes; the securities acts made American capital markets the biggest, the most efficient, and generally "best" in the world, the Old Age Security Act brought retirement security to ordinary working Americans, Fair Labor Standards acts took the "race to the bottom" pressures out of hours and wages practices (see big banks and financial firms exploitation of "interns" to understand the dynamic at work), and then the big federal mortgage guarantee programs.

In world affairs, the US pioneered the use of vast alliance systems of countries to establish and preserve world order and peace. NATO was the crowning achievement among alliances while the United Nations and a host of other agencies pioneered practical international cooperation. The period from 1932 to 1952 was a Policy Golden Age.

In particular, the federal housing programs were the backbone of the great post war prosperity. This was the House that Roosevelt and Truman built, and this was the House that Reagan, Bush, and the Clinton neo-liberals systematically went about dismantling by putting catastrophic levels of risk back into the financial system.

These "leaders" didn't understand that taking systematic risk out of the economy is the goal of good public economic policy management. Instead, for cheap profiteering reasons they put unconscionable amounts of risk back in. But "they" understood enough to throttle reform in its cradle when they occupied the commanding policy heights of the Obama administration, the first non-progressive Democratic administration in over a hundred years. You have to go back to Grover Cleveland to finds its antecedents, and the same dreary slow growth economics. So we continue with the privatizing of social profits and the socialization of private risks because that is what the Big Contributors to the modern Democratic party want. So yes, cooperation by all means. But be sure to put broad-based risk reduction measures to work if you want future economic pay-offs for all, and not just a few.

Pepin

If however nuclear weapons prevent another World War and Central Banks prevent financial meltdown; in other words if we will not experience a big economic re-set where concentrations of capital are destroyed; then we are headed for the Middle Ages 2.0. A world where a small section of the population owns almost everything, where growth stagnates because of this, where long term interest rates go to zero for several hundred years because of this, and where the price of any asset that produces a dependable yield (such as London housing) goes to near infinity because of this.

Jan Smith

Seventy-years ago Keynes was defeated by the Americans at Bretton Woods. He had proposed an international body, sustained by international cooperation that likely would have prevented the international thrift race, hence the global saving glut, hence stagnation and instability for the foreseeable future. He asked the other nations to cooperate in founding this cooperative institution but he didn't get it from Henry Morgenthau, the Wolfgang Schauble of that time. Amazing Keynes. He had just one case of global economic disintegration to study (the one normally dated from 1914 but should be dated from the late 1870s) and yet he knew how to stop it from happening again. Today's economists, in the midst of a second global disintegration, have yet to fully learn what Keynes knew in 1944. To all appearances, not even Summers knows, not even Martin Wolf or Krugman.

Stanislaus – Russian Viewpoint

The Bank of China and VTB have reached an agreement on settlements in their respective domestic currencies. That may seem to be a rather small development compared to the gas deal etc., but its implications can completely change the world of banking and investment as we know it. Not to mention the petrodollar as reserve currency. Gazprom is the only gas player capable of supplying major wholesale volumes to two continental markets due to its massive reserves, location of fields and integrated transport and trading solution. Pure LNG players are either not price competitive or can't match the volume.

China's leaders admitted during the Third party plenum in November 2013 that public anger over pollution is the single biggest threat to the communist regime. Thus, natural gas consumption is bound to soar. Currently, the biggest supplier of natural gas to China is Turkmenistan but Central Asia is a time bomb as it is likely to follow the Libya/Egypt scenario (China must know that well dealing with Moslem rebels in its Xinjiang Uyghur province) so the security of those gas supplies is questionable. Iran wouldn't build an overland pipeline to China (lovely Afghanistan transit anyone?) so it's a dearer LNG then and any maritime supplies are quite vulnerable in the case of a likely Sino-American war.

In any conflict, Chinese merchant ships might find it impossible to safely traverse the maritime trade routes across any Pacific Ocean outlet between China and its trading partners. Chinese trade could be embargoed from Pacific Ocean routes, and China needs a steady supply of oil, commodities and raw materials. Realizing this fact, China is certain to at least diversify into a new overland, more secure, transport corridor with roads, railways and pipelines via Russia. China currently pays $15 per mmBTU of Australian LNG vs $10/mmBTU reportedly proposed by Russia.

Dhako - Chinese Viewpoint

The larger question which we have been invited to indulge in here, concerns defining this word "cooperation". In other words, upon whose terms is the definition of that word cooperation made? Furthermore, as you may remember, Iraq was itself invited to "cooperate" with the US, in terms of a "regime change" when Saddam was running the show there. And, in fact, Bush explicitly told Saddam Hussein to "cooperatively" leave Iraq in 48 hours before the invasion of that country began. And, if he refused to "cooperate", then harsher measures would be applied to him and his regime.

This was the form in which the ultimatum was "delivered" on public TV, in America. And, of course, when Saddam refused to "cooperatively" leave his country, then it was only fair (from the west's view of things) to punish those who refused to get with the program, "cooperatively", as was the case in Iraq in 2003. Consequently, by all accounts that version of "cooperation" may or may not have been the optimum outcome for Iraqi people at the time. But, it sure as hell was the very definition of "mutual cooperation" (according to the Neo-Con's apparatchiks who were running the show in America during the Bush era).

Moreover, so long as other nations saw how the western version of "cooperation" singularly mimicked the notion of other people surrendering their national sovereignty to Western interest; or the notion of cooperation according to the Western play-book, being something that seemed to them as being nothing less than their saying how high they would have to jump, then I am afraid this silly argument about cooperation without defining the "context" of what one means by cooperation will simply be viewed as just another attempt to "disrobe" others of their national prerogative through woolly, and verbose words; when in fact, the hard power of olden empires (which used to compel others to "cooperate" with their overlord's empire) could not now be used on others.

Hence, this "soft-PR-game" of depriving others of their interests, while praising abundantly this concept of "cooperation", is like a man trying to sweet talk his way into your wife's sexual favours with, no less, your own consent. And, instead of his coming through the front door of your house with a cricket bat along with his mates, and instantly informing you, that, in five minutes he will need to see your wife naked in the bedroom, or else his "friends", with a decided look of menace about them as well as cricket bats to boot, will make short work of you; he starts telling you how beautifully and "cooperatively humane" it is to share each other's wives.

And, furthermore, he will say, that, although, he would have brought his wife to the party, he, of course, couldn't force her to come, since she was decidedly against the whole idea of "sharing caresses" with total strangers. Hence, it's only fair on a "point-of-principle" that you must cooperate with him on his desire to share your wife with you, since, if it were up to him, he would have already done the same thing for you, in return. And, if you, in turn, are minded to ask your wife if she wants to "share" things of sexual kinds with others, he will say, that the "notion" of asking one's wife's opinion about things of this kind, is not part of his definition of "mutual cooperation."

So, in a nutshell, this is essentially the sort of "cooperation" the West is after. Thus, it's unlikely to succeed any more than the old "empire-imposed-mutual-cooperation" did upon the natives the world over. Could it succeed now if some western powers tried these methods afresh? Just to show you how others will consider the last 100 years through their own perspective, let's take the Chinese view of the world. China's perspective is that for the entire past century China, through fits and starts, as well as various swerves, finally decided to a master her own destiny; or in Mao's famous words of 1949: "Chinese people have finally stood up".

Hence, to you China is an "assertive power" (or words to that effect). But China sees herself as essentially a nation that after the great humiliation of having a "colonial history", finally stood up for herself and for her destiny without the slightest concern as to how others saw her rise. Now, the intellectual elite of the West, do you see how you will never, ever, make China listen to your type of argument, particularly when you immediately start telling the Chinese that they have been "assertive" and that they need to "cooperate" with others?

For, in the final analysis, when anyone starts taking this Western centric view of China, and for good measure, start sermonising about what China should or shouldn't do, then the only outcome will be for the Chinese to say that, they do not recognise this description of themselves as an "assertive power". And, on the contrary, they consider they were acting merely to place China in her proper position in her sphere, which had been "denied" to her through the actions of others (such as European empire building) and by her internal weakness during the previous two and half centuries. And, secondly, she will demand to know on whose "terms of cooperation" she is being ordered observe?

So, as you can see, even your most basic concepts will find no takers in Beijing. Much less, will China ever come round to viewing the world through the standard historical lens of which most Western commentators and elites alike, are so seriously enamoured.

Felix Drost   ***   **2015**

The analysis of an economy by economists, does not tackle social and cultural essentials vital to it.

China has significant cultural benefits over India. The Chinese are 'on board' with the government's program, they share the ambition often overtly. The decades of communism have removed layers of social and cultural complexities that would otherwise (and did in the past) hamper growth and adaptation.

India is very different; the various administrative layers in India are divided. Few cities invest in infrastructure. Public spending on education is very low; and hence and in contrast to China at this point in development, there aren't enough qualified workers to keep powering growth. The government is mired in red tape and mistrust, especially of foreigners.

Society itself is far from egalitarian, the caste system is disqualifying almost half the population from achieving status. It also adds a double layer to any organization where people of higher caste but lower rank in the organization suddenly seem to have and exercise decisive authority without requiring experience. Furthermore the BBC documentary about the rape case in 2012 shows just how strongly sexist society is as well.

There certainly are areas where things improve. But these conditions do not warrant any optimistic scenario. India will not change sufficiently to hop on a Chinese trajectory. There just isn't sufficient political impulse and power, and society tends to oppose change.

KKB

India today is at least 30 years behind China. China was able to enforce the 1 child policy; it is doubtful if India can do something similar. India needs to control its population, including its fast growing Muslim population. This will prove contentious.

The quality of general population needs to be addressed. The poor, who are mostly uneducated, tend to have more children. They can neither provide their children adequate nutrition nor provide sufficient mental stimulation and proper education. The result is that a large segment of malnourished children grow into adults where they under-perform mentally and physically.

Infrastructure building needs a strong watchdog. The Public Works Department (PWD) is quite corrupt. Only a portion of the allocated budget gets utilized for infrastructure building, the rest is pilfered. The rate of GDP growth needs to be several times the population growth, in order to make a dent in the level of poverty, especially in the countryside.

Nation building requires discipline, transparency and a willingness to work hard over extended periods of time. Can India do it? Sure, but building moral character, especially among the corrupt elites, will not be easy.

Gluke   *******   2013-2015

The Chinese have been playing Pakistan for some time now and the Pakistanis seem to oddly continue to regard them as their closest buddies.

China failed to provide any assistance to Pakistani in any of their wars with India. Even in '71 when Pakistan was dismembered and Nixon desperately appealed to the Chinese to show some movement on the border to rattle the Indians, the Chinese held back. During the Kargil conflict, they advised Pakistan to return to their side of the border and quit making trouble - and poor Nawaz had to run to Clinton to find some face saving way to extricate himself. Not to mention $50 billion dollars in US aid - all misspent of course.

Even the Afghan intervention which Pakistan constantly harps on — the reality is that it was Zia's idea all along. He was the one who started the policy of training mujaheddin to fight in Afghanistan. He then managed to successfully get the US involved, but ran the show himself with the US role confined to providing arms and money. Of course the arms and money went all over the place. But you can hardly blame the Americans for that. The Americans were of course foolish to get drawn into Zia's poisonous schemes.

Yes China did develop Gwadar for them. But the Chinese also incredibly have a free trade agreement with Pakistan!! Why would anyone manufacture anything in Pakistan when they can do so in China and freely import it into Pakistan. Not sure what the Pakistanis were smoking when they agreed to that. So the only rationale for this odd Pakistani attachment to China is that they gave Pakistan plans for its nuclear weapons and missiles. And for Pakistan, such military matters are more valuable than anything else. So while the poor Americans were spending $50 billion in hard cash to try to buy Pakistani friendship, the Chinese managed to do it on the cheap by breaking their NPT and missile control obligations!!

Mkain

As a Pakistani, I can confirm that most of Pakistan's problems and challenges are not of India's making. They are the result of incompetent, corrupt leaders, an inability to separate church and state, an unwillingness or inability to exercise civilian control over the military through constitutional means and by using parliament. The myopic policies, following the Soviet Afghan invasion and the eagerness to embrace the American agenda for the region has landed them in this morass. They have no one to blame but themselves. The population crisis is another example of a nation that is enslaved by its religious tradition and seems trapped in doctrine.

Gluke

Change the name to Egypt and you get a similar scenario. The combination of overpopulation and environmental degradation intensified by global warming should result in grinding political crises in the future across the region. Do not be optimistic about Pakistan doing anything about its population problem. There are parts of Pakistan that refuse polio vaccines because they view them as a western plot to reduce the fertility and population of Muslims!!! So Pakistan actually witnessed growth in its number of polio cases this year. So good luck with actually telling them to reduce their fertility and population!!! As Nehrus said, "Population control will not solve all our problems, but without it none of our problems will be solved."

Trutheludes

It needs to be investigated how far Pakistan's deep Islamic sensibilities militate against use of contraceptives. In traditional semi-literate religious communities of South Asia there is a mistaken belief that children are born as per God's wishes which should not be interfered with. There is also a conviction in labouring communities that every child is a potential earner of some income for the family.

To curb over-population, all such archaic notions need to be countered by provision of modern secular education, which is practically non-existent in Pakistan. State financed school education for the poor in this country is virtually in a shambles, and the void is invariably filled by Madrassas to whom birth control is an anathema and which impart mostly a narrow sectarian Islamic education, more suited to grooming of Imams for mosques or even of Jihadis.

MKain rightly talks about Pakistan's corrupt and dysfunctional politics; it would be naïve to expect from it any reforms to pull the country out of the malaise in which it has been caught in. Lastly, consider comparative indices of Pakistan and Bangladesh, one of the salient of these is strength of currencies which are a kind of a mirror to respective economies. Pakistani Rupee is 103 to a US$, whereas Bangladeshi Taka is 77. Both diverged from the same level in 1971 when Bangladesh seceded from Pakistan.

Proclone

Just as an independent Scotland was France's foil against England, Pakistan is China's foil against India and the US wishes India would be its foil against China.

Dhako - Chinese Viewpoint

Another day and another dark thought about what China means to the world order, according to the FT's writers. Perhaps, our FT scribblers ought to simply spare themselves these regurgitated arguments, since, they seem to share a deep drop of diminishing credibility; and therefore simply say, that we in FT (as well as our sister publication, the Economist) have decided to wear our bile of anti-Chinese ideology on our shirt sleeves.

Consequently, they ought to add for good measure, that, anyone who saw fit to peruse our missives about China must be prepared to be emotionally manipulated and have their intelligence insulted along the way, in equal proportion.

Now, having said that, let's deal with the overall situation in an orderly fashion. And, that is firstly, China, unlike Saudi-Arabia which has bank-rolled the bulk of Jihadi ideology around the World, while US look the other way and indeed never said so much as "Beep!" till 9/11 happened to them, has never had any state policy to support openly Jihadi foot-sol-diers, as the US supported the Afghanistan's Mujaheddin against the Soviet Union. Furthermore, let's recall that it was the US which had even encouraged Saudi Arabia to financially support any free-lance Arab Jihadi from the Middle-East who wanted to go to fight the godless Soviet com-munists in Afghanistan.

And, of course, the blow-back against that particular American policy, which was a foolhardy action, is what we are dealing with now. Furthermore, while we are at it, let's also add that the late dictator of Pakistan, General Zia ul-Haq (who died in a plane crash) was the original villain who started the Jihadi viper nest in his country.

And it was, of course, the American's Carter administration, with Dr Zbigniew Brzezinski, who was President Carter's national security adviser encouraging these deadly policy moves, which has inaugurated the notion of using Pakistan as the ground level from which to launch a Jihadi agenda against others, even if the US thought the likes of Osama bin Laden was their friend against the then Soviet Union.

So, I do not see why the western's mouthpieces should have the temerity to speak ill of China's relationship with Pakistan in conjunction with the support the former gives the latter in defence issues, when in fact the western powers and Americans in particular have been the authors of the greatest geopolitical calamity in which the State of Pakistan has been party to; this at the expense of all concerned.

Secondly, Pakistan today, is by all intents and purposes, a singularly failed state, which is a danger to itself as well as to others. But, still and all the same, the ledger that needs an accounting for being that, since 9/11 and the beginning of the war-of-terror, whereby the US's foot-print in Pakistan has been the greatest by any measure: what has that policy—in beneficial terms - brought about to Pakistan, or to the region, or even to wider-global security?

And, since, by every measure you could think of, the US's policy in Pakistan has been nothing but a walking tragedy to Pakistan as well as being a self-inflicted wound to America itself; then, at least one can say that the Chinese policy on the other hand has been nothing less than constructive in comparison to what the US has wrought in Pakistan since the days of Dictator Zia-Ul-Haq.

Thirdly, in-terms of the nuclear issue, the idea of giving the Chinese the "rap sheet" of being irresponsible when it comes to "helping" Pakistan obtain knowledge in these areas is also over-done. And, it's over-done, since the Chinese have what could be called, at least in the old fashion-sense, "raison d'état" vis-à-vis India, which in turn necessitated the idea of giving these weapons to Pakistan (or the knowledge of it). And this, in turn, is no more incredible than the idea of remembering how UK's Macmillan government got the Polaris Nuclear deterrence from Eisenhower's administration; so long as the strategic alliances of UK and US were lined up in one direction against the Soviet Union.

And, since, it's unlikely that Pakistan would fire it's nuclear armament at India without the "explicit nod" from China (even if there is no "formal treaty" between China and Pakistan, particularly of the kind that exists between the US and UK on the other hand) then I do not see why there is so much gnashing of teeth among the western powers at the thought of seeing Pakistan having the means to level her inferior land-based forces against India with her own Nuclear Deterrence, in the event of a military confrontation.

Or at least why there is no reason to believe that the "MAD" (Mutual Assured Destruction) strategic posture between India and Pakistan that has been established with the help of China towards Pakistan, is any different from the Warsaw pact nations and NATO's countries that have had that strategic reality to contend with between themselves. And, lastly, that would be the case, since the strategic Nuclear posture of Pakistan vis-à-vis India could be said that it's "analogous" to the idea of having NATO's Pershing Nuclear and other theatre-based nuclear missiles in order to counter-balance the overwhelming ground forces of the then Warsaw Pact had had in their favour.

Hence, unless your western's imbued cultural blind-spot precludes you from seeing that what is "strategic source" for the defensive "goose" of the West could be said that it's also a "strategic source" for the defensive "gander" of others, then again I do not see why you or anyone else should complain about the strategic nuclear alliance between Pakistan and China.

Realist

One minor addition: In the 1980s the US President gave annual certification to Congress to the effect that Pakistan was not working on a nuclear weapon (hence America turned a blind eye to Pakistan's nuclear program), to enable assistance from America to flow to Pakistan in the effort against the USSR in Afghanistan.

Kropotkin

Let us not forget about the invisible 800 pound gorilla — the stationing of PLA (Chinese) forces in Baluchistan, the upgrading of the Karakorum Highway including tunnels bored through the mountains to facilitate infiltration of rapid response forces from China into Pakistan. China has created a buffer zone of sorts now as well as a staging area close to the centre of turbulence, for China would be dismayed if Pakistan's nuclear material were to fall into the hands of the Islamist's. This is the classic Sun Tzu strategy of keeping one's enemy (threats in this case) close at hand.

Perhaps we shall see a Chinese 21st century version of "The Relief of Chitral" in the near future.

*Reader, Pakistan provides a striking illustration of how Religion can be used as an Imperial weapon and how national security supersedes economic security. Also note, that no one has proposed a solution to the over-population/habitat crisis.

Population of Pakistan (191 million), Afghanistan (31 million).

Make Justice   ***   Feb, 2014

Robots are here since long ago, and are mainly humans. There was a whole class of robots who facilitated the initial capital accumulation of the West, and were black robots: slaves, "imported" from Africa. Today robots are in Asia. More than 1000 died in Bangladesh last year when cutting, making, and trimming our cheap clothes. They were not repaired but replaced.

The coming of the artificial robots will not change the landscape of inequality as long as the underlying system is that of capitalism. Robots are there to serve the capitalist, whose inherent goal is to make profits, not to give jobs. Unless capital is turned democratic instead of oligopolistic as today, the intrinsic system trend towards concentration of wealth (and *power*) will continue.

Legal Tender

Farm workers were unskilled, the largest group of labourers before industrialisation and 97pct of them lost their jobs. Our current system uses the wealth of the few and the borrowing of the many (government) to provide a life without work for a large percentage of the population, who then raise children in dysfunction. They are not poor by any historical definition of the word and have more possessions, more living space and more free time than the average working class person in the 40s and 50s.

Their market wages (the rate someone would pay them for their unreliable work) are already far below social norms. Fortunately they are paid more not to work, while employers pay higher wages to equally unskilled (but more diligent) immigrants (higher than they'd be willing to pay the native underclass). In other words, the fears we have, have already been realised (many times in history) and the solution to pay the underclass has been tried for decades. The idea of raising more taxes and finding more assets to seize to spend more on the poor is also quite stale.

All of the above is simple social democracy. The challenge of social democracy (aside from it being an insolvent Ponzi scheme) is not technological change but rather how to improve the lives of the children of the poor so that they have the morals, the work ethic and the commitment to education to have a chance to escape the underclass.

More money has already been tried. Fewer children might help (paying the irresponsible and ill educated not to have children) but fundamentally we need a completely new welfare system. Until then we will repeat the history of human behaviour in a crisis: scorn your enemies, steal their money and pay your friends. This is human nature and I don't see the robots changing that.

HR2

We may not appreciate what is really going on here. We are witnessing human evolution as much as the switch from Neanderthal to Homo Sapiens. The fact that previous major evolutionary steps took place in the DNA, bodies and brains of individuals may mask us to this new reality. Evolution is being externalized and subject to human consciousness for the first time in Earth's history and before our very eyes.

We will either make the transition over the coming years and next few decades to a higher level or we will not and disintegrate into chaos or even disappear as a species. Yes it can be argued that what is taking place in this new machine age is simply a change from one form of Capitalism to another which would be profound enough. Except for the fact that for the first time in history the very meaning of human labour as a core element in human existence is being challenged.

It can be argued without fear of ridicule from any thoughtful individual that 50 years from now any and every form of human activity we label today as "jobs" from the most primitive to the most sophisticated will ALL be upended by robots and automation. The point is we either deal with the emerging future now or we don't. Society and its leaders and all of us need to address the likely future without traditional jobs as it is already clearly developing, or suffer dire consequences in the near and more distant future.

The ultimate questions are 1) how do we distribute society's wealth when more and more of it is produced by non human means, and 2) what will humans do with themselves to live productive lives in the absence of traditional employment.

Paul A. Myers – US Viewpoint

We are being conquered right now by public mediocrity on a vast scale. Robots having nothing to fear from human leadership.

Let's use California as an example. There's a huge amount of physical work that needs to get done. You can have the smartest logistics software in the world, but once that shipping container hits Los Angeles it enters the most screwed up logistics maize in the world. Tens of billions of dollars of physical infrastructure need to be built by human beings pouring concrete, laying rails, building freeways.

How does that work get done? By skilled workers who can read a blueprint, take a dimension and build something to spec. My contractor clients have been screaming for twenty years about the shortage of people who can read blueprints, who can multiply accurately.

What of the public leadership in Sacramento? The legislative leaders say public education is aimed at sending every child to college because we live in some sort of info age. However, elementary school children are not drilled on multiplication tables, don't learn long division, and don't master basic skills. And teachers who are wildly abusive of children are kept on the job. Is this effective? Is this just?

In Southern California, tens of billions of dollars need to be invested into interurban transportation. The Jerry Brown administrations and the Barrack Obama administrations didn't put one incremental dollar into this even though Los Angeles County had the highest unemployment rate for a major urban area in the country. Instead, we're all going to ride some High Speed Train through the cotton fields of the San Joaquin and look at all our taxpayer subsidized water at work for the millionaire agricultural interests!

So yes, tell us about our high tech future and the wonders it will bring. The public leadership laps up these panacea solutions like a Hollywood starlet whiffs cocaine. On to high cost alternative energy! A windmill in every backyard! An electric car plugged into every electrical socket.

Millions for fantasy, nothing for proven public works.

Adam Bartlett

Historically, states almost always make provision for displaced workers. Even classical Rome is a good example. Tens of thousands of plebeians were forced into almost permanent unemployment by the ancient technology of slavery. The Keynesian solution of public works programmes tended to be only used when progressives like the Gracchi were in power. But even in the most conservative periods, the State doled out handouts to economically displaced citizens almost continuously through Rome's rise and fall.

Treepower

If Keynes was right about an age of abundance, and that age is arriving in rich societies, why can't Keynesian economists accept the natural corollary: that prices of all goods subject to increasing abundance will have a natural tendency to fall. Obsession with positive consumer price inflation in such an age would only result in too much money chasing the things which remain scarce, resulting in constant financial bubbles. Sound familiar? A coherent approach to the abundance debate must include an acceptance that the so-called general price level will behave differently than in humanity's long age of scarcity.

Suomi Reader

Try suggesting that today's puritan workaholic culture is not good, and that intellectual property and capital (in other words "the rich") must be taxed more and the money spent on regular people (some would call them "the 99%"). I'm afraid we're not moving in the direction indicated though, seeing how the Anglo-Saxon consensus, in the media, think-tanks, political and business elites, has been to mock and deride repeatedly the French 35-hour work week, which should have been hailed as a major social advancement if we were to move away from the puritan workaholic culture.

And then to refuse any new taxation of capital, think for example of how the UK systematically vetoes any French, or sometimes French/German, proposals to implement EU-wide taxes on capital or banks. The problem is, no single country can implement this alone (as we've seen in the case of France), because that would make that country less competitive in today's global economy. At the very least, these policies would have to be implemented by the EU and the US simultaneously as two blocs. But I can't see this happening given that the US, UK, and to some extent even Germany, are absolutely opposed to these heretical French ideas.

Texas View

What this and many similar debates omit is the role the rapid advances in "Smart Machines" (aka Robotics) is playing. When we invented the cheap, powerful microprocessor and started connecting it to machinery we created a job destroying monster. If you look at US data, from post-WW2 until about 1985, GDP and total employment grew at roughly similar rates. From then on they diverged, with GDP growing faster than employment. This is about the time the Smart Machines showed up. Per Moore's Law the computing power of microprocessors doubles every 18 months while that of humans doubles every 300,000 to 500,000 years. As the machines get smarter, faster and cheaper — and the humans don't — they displace humans and the wealth they create goes to those who own shares of the companies which employ them.

One characteristic of this shift is that an increasing number of jobs lost have been in service industries not susceptible to outsourcing to lower cost countries. The examples are all around us — the bank tellers replaced by ATM machines, store check-out clerks replaced by self-service machines, company telephone switchboard operators, printing shop workers. Even the traditional 3 man garbage collection truck has largely been replaced by a single driver/operator controlling a hydraulic lift arm monitored via a closed circuit TV camera.

And these machines neither demand nor require paid holidays, health care, retirement plans; most can work 24/7 with only occasional maintenance down time. And the wealth they produce accrues to those who own them via their share ownership in the firms which use them, thus contributing to "Income Inequality." We have invented the devices which are rendering an increasing portion of the population economically uncompetitive.

Enetia Robson, PhD.   ***   2012

This question begs a better answer. Luddites did not object to the new machinery because there would be less work to do. They saw the factories as ousting self sufficient home weavers while despoiling the countryside and using ever more noxious sources of energy like coal. They weren't known as the Satanic mills for nothing. Luddites were mainly objecting to losing status as homestead owners who worked for themselves and having to work for factory owners who could control their working day and rate.

Technology in the 19th century might have increased productivity but it did it by destroying an older way of life where many goods were made independently on a small scale. Funny isn't it that the main dream today is to make one's pile and then find a small holding somewhere and raise bees?

Vasastan

We are all out of work by now, if looked at by early 19th-century standards. A far shorter work week, a large percentage of the population in full-time schooling, and an even larger share drawing checks for retirement, unemployment, or disability, are all factors that reduce the total number of hours worked by the population. The trend will continue, and in the next decade or so we are likely to see a further shortening of work weeks as a response to unacceptably high unemployment even for highly educated workers.

*Anthropologists estimate a two and a half day work week for hunter-gatherers; work was seasonal for agrarian economies and paid labour was mostly by the job in pre-industrial economies. Machines were very expensive from the beginning of Capitalism; then the need for a return on capital called for 12-16 hour shifts, six-seven days per week. Children at the age of 5 were used and there are records of them being tortured. The subjects and serfs of those countries that industrialised later were spared the worst of it. Records from the late 19th century indicate an average work week was over 60 hours and is now 33 hours in the US.

The US economy was militarised from the early 1950's, which then required women workers and caused intense inflation. War output does not increase living standards. Nowadays, the Netherlands stands at 27 hours, France with 30 and Germany is lowest with 26 hours. China adopted a 5 day week in 1995. In contrast, a worker in a North Korean labour camp puts in 112 hours per week.

Felix Drost

First, let's not assume that what was true in the past is true in the future, that just is not a given one can bank on. History has shown us that indeed, technology leads to an increase in productivity and wealth. Why of course it does, otherwise technologies wouldn't have been implemented. What history has shown as well is that it is those who own or master the new technologies accrue most of the wealth, while those that don't lose their jobs.

Second, let's not gloss over the huge social dislocations and disruptions that have occurred in the past as a result of rapid technological change. The plough, the steam engine, indeed even the printing press have caused tides of unemployment; often young people who flocked to the cities. New jobs were eventually created but never by magic or default. Various revolutions and wars were powered by these dislocations as well. Western colonialism and imperialism would not have happened without masses of disenfranchised youngsters willing to risk so much boarding rickety vessels to far unknowns.

Third, let's not assume that increased productivity and wealth leads to increased demand. Most economists tell me that what's wrong with our highly productive economies is a lack of demand. The super productive Germans are saving, not spending. Where is the increased demand for goods? Rather, technologies have a deflationary effect, making everything less expensive. And with deflation lurking there's a real risk that purchases will be postponed only further. Also technology enabled China to become part of the highly integrated world economy and out-compete western labourers. Almost structural unemployment in various countries where industries have been wiped out is a result.

Fourth, let's not claim there are those who are lamenting the demise of particular jobs. I'd like to see someone in this debate who actually is lamenting that in particular. What we so-called 'Luddites' worry about is the actual social consequences of job losses already in place. There is no new demand, there are no new jobs. Jobs in fields we can barely imagine needs to be imagined first.

Soon driver-less trucks will ferry goods, driver-less taxies, trains and buses will transport people. Gone hundreds of thousands of jobs, hello hundreds of thousands of unemployed, ill equipped to imagine new fields for their skills. Several hospitals are rolling out robotic carts that transport medicines and food, replacing people. They're working on prototypes that can lift and transport patients. Augmented tools are helping surgeons do a far better job faster, allowing one to do the work of two. Robots are being developed to do minor surgery almost automatically.

Our societies are becoming ever more complex and highly trained and skilled individuals are necessary. At the same time, computers and robots are replacing all kinds of labour, increasingly highly trained and skilled ones as well. So we may be training people today for a job that is unavailable in a decade or so, and we cannot easily retrain them for perhaps even more specialized jobs in other fields. Sedasys, a robot developed by Johnson & Johnson, is replacing anaesthesiologists. Would you care to explain to all these medical professionals and those being educated over more than 10 year time frames that there are jobs in fields we can barely imagine?

This debate should not be about who is or isn't a Luddite, this should be about getting things in proper perspective and making sure that people who are going to or already have lost their jobs aren't going to lose all of their security and add to the growing ranks of discontents. Our society and economy must place humans first and the consequence is an increasingly re-distributive political economy as innovation makes production ever less the province of man but of machine.

It is about power rather than money. People do not willingly give up their power or wealth. Median wages are depressed (in USA especially) whilst wealthy people get richer. Indeed, the crisis was handled in such a way as to put the risk predominantly on the poor (poorer people more likely to default and thus loose assets and tax payers money was used to support banks, so that they didn't suffer from poor loans). The society is split between the investor and worker class (although obviously people working and saving for pensions fit into both classes).

The economy has slowed because money is no longer a means of exchanging goods and services, but an instrument of accumulating and stealing wealth. In Spain 50% youth unemployment didn't indicate a lack of demand, but that the money had been drained out of the system. In Greece people were reverting to alternative currencies as there was no money to exchange the goods and service which people wanted to exchange. The Euro had effectively stopped circulating yet people were prepared to work and there was a demand for this work.

I, like many people in the UK, bought a house because of fear of pension schemes (which had collapsed in the 90s). Where did this money invested in pensions go? Where did this money in interest paid on the houses go? It was funnelled to the wealthy. When I was working in Portugal my wage dropped so low that I couldn't even rent a room with my monthly income (and thus was forced to leave).

The free market is effectively being distorted to prevent wage rises for the poor by instead getting them to borrow and by making life cheaper (poorer food quality from mass production- esp. in the USA). It is effectively producing a slave culture to fuel a wealthy elite by ensuring that poor people are forced to take risks financially and to prevent them working their way out of debt. It is certainly well known now that one of the most difficult methods of becoming wealthy is from working.

Until sustainable economics is seriously addressed, and the elephant in the room (of the necessity of capitalist systems to redress the tendency for increased wealth gap) we will be caught in boom and bust, because this is how we are fooled into stimulating an economy with money that we don't have, to allow further wealth inequality to be produced.

Rxex

Very insightful. But my take is a bit different. I don't believe "markets are being distorted to prevent wage rises for the poor" as if everything was a big conspiracy. There is no doubt that wage rises have been dismal. But the less affluent did not demand higher wages. What they demanded was simply to be included in the alluring world of consumption. They couldn't afford it with their stagnant wages earned in low-productivity jobs but they were happy to take it in the form of cheap loans and cheap food.

Everyone was on board with this arrangement because it kept the illusion that wealth was expanding and trickling down to all. The less affluent were happy with the handouts and the rich were pleased to see the social order was preserved. This is an illusion that has proven very costly to maintain. Therefore, cheap loans have been taken away from the poor (code name: "household sector deleveraging") along with low-productivity jobs (code name: "labour market flexibility", along with automation).

But the rich continue to accumulate wealth because they don't need to deleverage and their income and wealth actually benefit from higher productivity. Thus inequality becomes evident and widens. This is not a conspiracy concocted by evil, shadowy moguls. It is a built-in feature of capitalism. Demand cannot be created in sufficient size without debt expansion. And the truly amazing fact is that this is what the vast majority of citizens want.

I don't know what will come to replace capitalism. But when you look at thousands of years of history, it is obviously destined to vanish along with so many other societal arrangements. So capitalism will be replaced by something better, or worse. Remarkably, we may be approaching that transition.

Mozart

Let me help you along here. Rich plutocrats spend massively on candidates who further their interests. It's called bribery elsewhere, but here we call it "campaign contributions." The voters are fed lies and red meat, appealing to their basest desires. Most voters vote for very narrow issues they get excited about since most have no ideas on how the country and the economy works. Sorry, but that's the truth. The candidates screams "It's foreign aid that wrecks the budget. Cut it!" Foreign aid accounts for less than 1% of the federal budget.

"It's illegal immigrants that steal your job." It's US employers who want to cut corners and make a buck that offer that job to cheap illegal immigrants who steal it. Illegal immigrants just follow the free market—supply follows demand. It's also us who want $5 cases of strawberries and cheap chicken burgers. "Religion is persecuted. Abortion. They want to take your gun away...And so on."

The masses are anaesthetized with such nonsensical red meat all the while the bribed politicians pull the rug from under them. They have the power to install judges at all levels, even at SCOTUS who will do their bidding and who are patently partisan. Look at all the 5 to 4 decisions. That did not happen 30 + years ago. Money filters through everything; recognize this fact and society becomes explicable.

MarkGB

"...the slowdown in 1998 was triggered by the Asian financial crisis, that in 2001 by the bursting of a huge stock market bubble and that in 2009 by the western financial crisis." Martin Wolf, Financial Times, Jan 2016

You list a number of crises culminating in the three above as if they were separate events. Whilst I appreciate this is an article not a dissertation, events are far more interrelated than you suggest.

Personally, I do not believe the world evolves through unrelated events, and economic crises do not come out of the blue - 'This time is different' and 'No-one could have seen it coming' are two of the biggest lies that we tell ourselves, ranking alongside 'We have zero tolerance for unethical behaviour' and 'Your call is important to us' in terms of how utterly spurious they are. They are cop-outs.

This time is not different and people do see it coming. Unfortunately these people are rarely policy makers, who seem to have a vested interest in 'group think', and in the worst cases 'wilful blindness'. In my view the biggest exponents of this are the central banks. The tech bubble of 2001, the sub-prime bubble of 2007, and the preponderance of asset bubbles currently floating around everywhere, are the direct result and inevitable consequence of a relentless expansion of credit, fuelled by the money printing and low interest rate policies of our central banks — primarily the Fed.

We live in a complex economic system that evolves through the combined choices of billions of people in markets all around the world; people who make those decisions on the basis of signals from the market place. We have policy makers who think they can bolt together a few mathematical formulas, sit them atop an unproven and to my mind ridiculous theory called the Phillips Curve, and come up with a DSGE model that will tell us what the most fundamental price in capitalism should be — the price of money. This is absurd hubris.

The QE and ZIRP policies of the Fed, the BoJ, and the ECB have achieved a number of extremely negative consequences, amongst which are:

1. Repaired the balance sheets of the banks that the market selected for liquidation in 2008, institutionalising 'moral hazard' in the process

2. Facilitated a massive transfer of wealth from the poor/middle class to the rich

3. Brought forward demand, which produces deflation — Student debt and 7 year car loans are two of the latest examples of this madness

4. Pushed forward the day of reckoning for countless zombie companies, which under market interest rates would have gone bust and released their capital and resources for productive enterprises

5. Exponentially expanded the bubbles of debt floating around the global economy looking for a pin

On the other hand it has not done what was predicted by the Central Banks the 'wealth effect' and 'trickle down' are bunkum. Even some of the Feds are starting to 'own' this. Anyone who wants to hear an honest Central Banker should listen to Richard Fisher on CNBC just this week, explaining how the Fed front-loaded the stock market expansion of the past 6.5 years. He also, unsurprisingly, reminded everyone that he'd voted against QE3, and also talks about the Fed being 'out of ammo'.

We will have another financial crisis Mr. Wolf — it will be the trailing edge of the financial storm that hit in 2007, which has been delayed but not solved, by the continuation of the policies that got us there. It will manifest as a sovereign debt crisis that goes global — the carnage will be in the bond market. Whether it will be 2016 or 2017 I do not know — I'm amazed they have been able to kick the can down the road this long — but the can has now become too big to kick.

JMC22

Those negative consequences are ultimately because economists have forgotten, and politicians are ignorant of, the basic fact that the purpose of economic growth is to increase real per capita income, most particularly to increase real wages. The possibility of higher wages, often cited as a problem, is what drives business to utilize labour more effectively, particularly through better training and more capital per worker, such as robotics, which boost productivity. If Germany and U.S. are going to forget this and go only for higher absolute levels of economic growth, then the best strategy would be to forget about productivity and open the doors to unlimited immigration of all sorts, whether refugee or terrorist. A huge and growing labour force is what India has. You might check what productivity, real wages, crime and living standards are like in that country as compared to Germany.

KKB

The problem has largely been caused by de-industrialisation. Both the Financial elite and politicians of the Right who feared, irrationally, the concept of organised labour prevalent in large industrial concerns con-spired in this. The result was the removal of middle managerial and tech-nologically skilled jobs, jobs with a marketable value, from the relevant economies. So, bring back manufacturing along with automation and apprenticeships. The down/upstream value chain will create more jobs. Germany is a classic example. The US has surrendered manufacturing in many industries – Textiles, Footwear, Electronics, Personal Computers, Home Improvements, Metallurgy, etc.

There is a lack of strategic vision among the business elites in the US that turns a blind eye to the loss of technical manufacturing capabilities in the US. They unwittingly strengthen the manufacturing ecosystem in China. It is difficult to stay a super power when the country is reduced to a net importer. What is good for the corporations is not necessarily good for the country. Quantitative Easing and other Central Bank monetary policies will only help so far. Yes, the service industries do provide jobs, but combining the service part with the entire manufacturing value chain will be more effective. Instituting balanced trade, and building a robust and economically viable industrial base will address the job creation issues. This is not a private vs. public sector issue, as some ideologues may approach, but a comprehensive national policy issue.

BW

"As mass production has to be accompanied by mass consumption, mass consumption, in turn, implies a distribution of wealth.....to provide men with buying power. Instead of achieving that kind of distribution, a giant suction pump had by 1929-30 drawn into a few hands an increasing portion of currently produced wealth.....The other fellows could stay in the game only by borrowing. When their credit ran out, the game stopped." This was written by former Fed Governor Marriner Eccles who was a board member from 1934-51. Is history repeating itself?

Australian

It may be. Is it not staggering to think that economists believe 7 to 15% credit growth per year is sustainable when wages are averaging less than 3% per year? Do the math: It's not sustainable. Soon the average person cannot afford the average loan to buy the average house. Oh wait, that's already happened.

Is it that easy?

When the S&P 500 has doubled in line with the Fed balance sheet, how much "wealth creation" is productive and innovative and how much is State induced and unproductive?

Cathal Haughian

Reader, please note that debt is your future income brought into the present. It is also a promise to society that you will create value in the future. The compounding interest is a transfer of wealth from you to savers/creditors and bank owners/employees. Government debt is future taxes brought into the present.

One should also note that differential energy prices do not affect the global labour market. US energy is very cheap but energy-intensive industry obviously doesn't need much human labour power: the energy powers the work!

If a nation state, with its own currency, has an abundance of cheap primary goods then it will find it difficult to have secondary industry that adds value. Because exporting those primary goods raises wages and the value of the currency which ensures secondary industry can't compete internationally e.g. Australia. (These phenomena affect the Russian economy to a lesser extent because they have a larger population. Therefore, they can manufacture motor vehicles for their own populace.) The US is a continental economy replete with natural resources and a large population.

Consequently, it may be tempting to see its problem stemming from a broken education system. Secondary industry needs master craftsmen. Thus, mastery and excellence are civilising ideals. The origin of income is the production of something another human wants or needs at a price they can afford.

In the words of an American, 'As one of the first to recognize the nation's new competitive advantage in energy I must note sadly that the failure of our educational system has prevented us from capitalizing on our luck. Tragically, the United States is doomed to become a third world country, rich in energy and other resources but lacking in the core human assets that could allow it to remain a leading manufacturing power,' Philip Verleger.

Though that doesn't sound quite right. Let's see, the H1B visa program has seen the massive import of foreign workers who Americans are forced to train before surrendering their jobs. This abuse is done under the fabricated myth that American labour cannot do the work; but if this is so, then why are the Americans forced to train the imports, mostly from India?

America, China and Russia are essentially, indistinguishable: A ruling caste of billionaires. The world's three superpowers are collapsing from within which is unsurprising as they are part of an integrated whole that's collapsing. The cause of all of the economic crises that have delivered the world to this point is an excessively destructive form of capitalism that leaders in the free world refuse to properly reform. They and their retainers have too much to gain by it, and demand greater and greater sacrifices from us in exchange for the empty promise of a 'sustainable' recovery. The masses seethe with hatred and resentment while a new animal awakes that resembles Yeats' "rough beast, its hour come round at last".

.

With a Minimum Citizen's Income.

Edward S   ***   Nov, 2013

I support a basic income guarantee. Everyone in society has a right to be protected against destitution if only because everyone in society is expected to abide by society's laws. In fact, among the only people who would not be eligible to the allowance would be people serving a prison sentence. At present, it is agreed that society should meet the basic needs of prisoners. But the same is not universally guaranteed to people who are not in prison. Recently, I read that some prisoners in Portugal have pleaded not to be released precisely for that reason.

Nuages

I have been advocating a citizen's income for some time now. Basically, there are producers and consumers and in an agrarian, peasant economy, you had to produce before you were allowed to consume, so everybody automatically belonged to both classes. Now, with so much production automated, most people don't need to produce at all and in fact many are not skilled enough to do so anyway. But we can't seem to break away from the "don't work, don't eat" syndrome, so we create useless jobs in order to keep the number of producers and consumers in balance.

Many jobs these days are actually counter-productive, with hordes of people commuting into offices every day merely to send emails and give presentations to each other. So it would be better to recognise that lots of people are only needed to consume and they can rightly be paid to do nothing, rather than be wrongly paid to waste resources and create problems. I came to this realisation when my boss was sent on full pay gardening leave, after the company realised he was doing less damage at home than when at his desk.

Everybody Play Nice

What is the risk of a country full of layabouts? Really? How many people who earn the minimum wage say to themselves "Wow, this is all I could ever want from life?" Precious few. And they are unlikely to be innovative or economic high achievers. As it turns out, the truly creative people are often willing to work for a symbolic $1/year after they have made their fortune. Or should I rephrase: After they have been freed from material need. We live in a world where essentially every "very successful" person could simply decide to never work again — this goes for every Fortune 500 CEO, every successful actor or Formula 1 driver... heck: Madonna! And yet they continue to strive for the next $(100) million. The threat of homelessness and hunger is hardly a sound moral basis for encouraging participation in society. But it's also pretty obvious that it isn't even really needed.

Henry Law

This cannot happen without reform of other taxes, most which are effectively a structure of fines and penalties for engaging in honest economic activity.

Rlindsl

I have read the "mincome" studies and it seems plausible that this is a better approach compared to welfare, disability, and unemployment benefit schemes. Mental health issues and crime also declined in the mincome experiment. Further support also might be found in the correlation between GINI coefficients and upward mobility. The Nordic redistributionist economies have the highest upward mobility, the US is 19th in upward mobility with a full 50% predictability of income outcome based on the parent's income.

So other than the seemingly "unfair" aspects of paying people for no assured output, other than spending there are social stability and mental health effects to consider. Truly the shift from labour productivity to capital productivity is a social artefact that must be addressed in proportion to the impact of technology. This is a transition period where people will be idled and must find a vocation and access to resources. Mincome is no more morally egregious than continuing the current path of growing inequality. Of the two paths, one could lead to extreme social instability.

Clive Lord

The total price of all goods in the economy is always equal to the total income distributed. At any level of income, that is, it pays for itself. Assuming that lower incomes would be lifted more by the rising minimum income, there will be a slight re-distributive effect from top to bottom earners.

A far greater consequence would be the redistribution from lay-abouts with capital (aka rentiers) towards lay-abouts with none. The productivity gains wrought by automation have today mostly accrued to the former. It is unclear why that should be right. But it is certain that it is unsustainable. The immediate problem is the benefits trap. The withdrawal of means tested benefits creates a work disincentive. That means someone unemployed being no better off taking a low paid job.

The Citizens' Income is like a chess gambit, an apparently 'stupid' move which has the opposite effect to what seems obvious. It removes the work disincentive. You don't have to work, but for the first time since the Beveridge Report was implemented, you will be better off if you do.

By creating new industries and thus jobs.

Adam Bartlett   ***   Jun,   2014

Here are four reasons why Silicon Valley fails to convince:
1) The geeks seem to believe in the made up story ahistorical 5th rate economists pass on to their less discerning students. As Rifkin and others show, actual Luddites rarely held a philosophy that machines always cause unemployment. Breaking machines was actually the least violent way they had to respond to the fact technological unemployment was making it impossible to protect their families from hardship.

By the early 19th century, technological unemployment had already been intense in many regions for over a century, how many decades were ordinary folk supposed to watch their children die from starvation before giving up on the hope that machines would soon bring new jobs?

Before the rise of mercantilism, ordinary people had little need of machine breaking, as the elites would frequently protect them from technological unemployment. There are dozens of examples of Roman emperors refusing labour saving tech—search for this quote from Vespasian: "You must allow my poor hauliers to earn their bread". Vespasian refused gracefully and even gave the inventor a reward.

But there are many examples of innovators being executed, sometimes with methods normally reserved for only the very worst criminals, like the Catherine Wheel. Even as late as the rule of good Queen Elizabeth I and James I, new technologies were still being refused, e.g. search for "Consider thou what the invention could do to my poor subjects. It would assuredly bring them to ruin by depriving them of employment, thus making them beggers."

Far from "Luddism" being an aberration, denying Technological Unemployment has been a fringe view for almost all of history. Thank God elites are once again seeing Technological Unemployment as a major issue. Technological Unemployment denial will soon be seen for what it is: An invented excuse to justify obstructing the massive state intervention that could have spared large sections of our populations from deprivation over the past 3 centuries.

2) Innovation undeniably deserves much of the credit for massive improvement in living standards from about 1860 to the end of the 20th century. But for the last decade or so, living standards have been falling except for the top few percent. Admittedly, there are different results depending on methodology. But it can't be denied living standards are falling for those in the lower quartile. Massive rise in the numbers needing food banks both in US and Europe etc.

3) Empirical evidence suggests it was only in the 20th century that is was generally an effective strategy to protect from Technological Unemployment with better education. In the 18th and 19th century, it was actually the better skilled worker who most lost out from automation. Again, this seems to be happening in the 21st century. A good 2013 paper showing the evidence for this is "The Great Reversal in the Demand for Skill and Cognitive Tasks". Unless you are in the very top few percent, good education is now of much less help in securing a well paying job.

4) And finally, if there's one thing that could turn whole populations against both technology and capitalism, it would be if the on-demand\sharing\cloud working economy continues to grow unregulated as some of its prophets seem to expect. Sure, not all workers are victimised, some benefit from the flexibility and accessibility. In the early days, pretty much all the platforms were good for their workers as well as customers.

The dark side became more apparent in 2014, where having built up a pool of dependent workers, platforms began to change in ways that took away much of what little autonomy and power the workers had. Some had the luxury of quitting, but thousands were trapped due to challenging labour markets in their locality coupled with expired benefits in the US and the despicable welfare sanctions here in the UK.

Those with the money have all the power in several of these platforms. Workers are publicly rated, customers are not. A complaint or two from customers gets a worker fired. Dozens of complaints against the same customer are ignored. In conventional employment relationships, where the boss sees the same person week after week, there's generally a limit to how exploitative even the more selfish bosses will be. Cloud working is non relational, with workers often matched to customers by algorithms for brief one off "gigs".

Even relatively decent customers drive excessively hard bargains. Most aren't trained project managers; they suffer from planning fallacy and other optimistic biases, persistently underestimating how much work a task will need. Economically vulnerable workers have to complete the task for the agreed price, or else not get a precious good rating, effectively working at well below the minimum wage.

Capitalistic economies, in global synchronization, have driven down the value of labour and re-allocated the released wealth to a tiny minority through the lens of technology. This was powered by revolutions in long range communication and logistical systems.

Dreams of new industries do nothing to detract from the need for radical solutions to Technological Unemployment, like Basic Income or massive public sector job creation.

Francesco Nicoli

The story is thus:
1) In the very long term, it is true that most people who lost their jobs to automation will eventually find something else to do. And it is also true that creative industries are some of the more attractive options. As consumer goods become cheaper, people will spend more of their revenues in creative production.

2) However, one concept is missing in this picture: TRANSITION. In the long term we will eventually find equilibrium, but what about the transition? The length of the transition is proportional to the re-skilling time required. During the 19th century revolution, the transition lasted about 25 years (from 1855 to 1880) and was coupled with a lower growth rate, higher unemployment, and worsening social conditions. And in that situation, the new skills to be acquired were not so complicated.

What if we face a situation where the new skills required for the creative-high-tech economy are simply out of reach for most of the people (after all, some individuals may be neither suited for top class engineering, nor for painting or singing?) In this case, you will face much longer transition periods; the issue is not whether we will eventually reach a long period of equilibrium, but what we should do to deal with a 50-years long stagnation characterized by high unemployment.

Skeptic

The Logic doesn't work: Let R be the number of existing human jobs made redundant each month by new technology. Let T be the average number of months required to train a person to do a new job.

Assuming an infinite supply of new needs and associated new jobs, the number of redundant people at any given time will still be at least R x T. If R grows over time (technology begets technology), and if T cannot fall below a minimum threshold (finite speed of the human brain), then everyone ends up unemployed. See Little's Law.

*Reader, if the disruption is massive enough, demand will collapse.

Harald Buchmann

Economists have turned Logic on its head. They print money to create higher demand in order to service the need for jobs. Any living species on the planet 'works,' i.e. creates the means of survival (including joy, fun, etc.) in order to consume them. Only 20th century economic theory claims that we should consume the means, in order to be "allowed" to produce them, i.e. have jobs. That we should consume more so we can work more.

Jobs are no longer a necessity to meet our demands, they are a substitute for what we really want to achieve: a useful distribution of the economic output (in this case salaries) and of the workload to create this output. To increase the demand and to allow for more production is not the point of what is necessary. The total output of the global economy is quite enough for everyone to live a well-off life. But as long as this output doesn't reach a majority of the people who exist in abject poverty, we need some super-consumers who absorb all excess output created by a heavily unbalanced economic system.

This is the trouble with a Calvinist persuasion in the 21st century. It leads to all this nonsense about the "undeserving" poor. It would not be so hard to swallow, perhaps, if memories of "Arbeit macht Freude" did not haunt.

Vic 79   ***   **Apr, 2014**

Please analyse the greatest experiment with income redistribution and equalization in the history of mankind, called The Soviet Union.

Analyse what led to the destruction of the Soviet Union or whether or not income equality was indeed promoting growth and invention (it was not — when you take out money worries from the equation, you need to come up with some sort of project to occupy people's minds, which in the Soviet Union was communist propaganda). This debate is so wrong and misguided when it does not include any analysis of the Soviet Union, did history not teach any lessons at all?

And then, what's wrong with envy? Isn't it driving growth? Speaking from personal experience of growing up in the Soviet Union — there was no envy, since everyone was roughly in the same situation financially with no opportunity to look different, but there was also no impetus for invention unless it was state-directed and copied from elsewhere. Why do you think China copies everything and does not come out with new inventions?

TCL

Please read Adam Smith's Wealth of Nations Book 5 Chapter 3:

"...And when, in order to raise those taxes, all or the greater part of merchants and manufacturers, that is, all or the greater part of the employers of great capitals, come to be continually exposed to the mortifying and vexatious visits of the tax-gatherers, this disposition to remove will soon be changed into an actual removing. The industry of the country will necessarily fall with the removal of the capital which supported it, and the ruin of trade and manufactures will follow..."

For social justice to work, you need:
1. To stop the rich from migrating. If borders are porous, then the relatively uninformed middle class will be the ones ultimately bearing the burden of the 'social justice' tax.

2. To ensure that governments are honest brokers. Given the state of public debt today, how can you ensure that 'social justice' tax receipts are

not conveniently applied to alleviate the public debt? Smith's Book 5 Chapter 3 is aptly entitled Public Debt.

If we are not careful, this can easily degenerate into a policy based on envy, coveting thy neighbour's goods.

* Say's Law asserts that aggregate production necessarily creates an equal quantity of aggregate demand; so gluts cannot occur. Unhappily for central planners, some men may increase the amount of money they hold onto; thereby reducing demand but not supply. And as we know from Volume one, the only thing that aggregates is bullshit (aka debt).

Marmora

The impetus to create a more equal Society in the 19th century was moral disgust and outrage at the idea that human beings could be destitute and deprived to the point of starvation in a Christian country. The physical conditions of all levels of Society have improved vastly since those times and due credit is deserved by all those who contributed to it through their activism and generosity usually against indifference but often against bigoted indifference.

The apogee of those sentiments was reached with the Welfare State set up to co-exist with an efficient productive economy from 1947. Both have constantly failed to achieve our expectations of them in spite of considerable efforts and good intentions. There are now 900,000 UK families apparently enjoying food aid in contrast to about 2000 a few years ago. The response of the indifferent that they should be allowed to eat cake, misses the mark because the hosts of unemployed, unemployable folk who are ill-educated and of little social use and a drain on public resources are a national scandal.

The denial of education, the endless tinkering with the education system, the creation of exam standards that fall far below those in China and in former Soviet Republics, and the excessive charges demanded by colleges and Universities must surely demonstrate how impoverished a provider Capitalism has become. There is no sign that things are due to improve and they were better when there was a mixed economy. And yet this kind of chaos can exist in the face of enormously expanded economic activity. A huge re-think is necessary not only on a national scale but also on an international scale as we devour resources unsustainably, all the time adding to lethal climate change.

It is shaming and demeaning for all that so many should either be condemned or allowed to live truncated meaningless lives imprisoned in a poverty trap with little or no prospect of employment and a liveable income or the self-respect to raise themselves out of their grim condition. In truth, the two go together because money is by no means the only answer. But by far the more important factor is inclusion, understanding and measures to raise the spirits and ambitions of these unfortunate people so that some kind of moral re-armament becomes possible.

What is growth? It is a purely economic notion; takes into account house price increases but disregards mortgage costs. It is a form of trickery which is really a recipe for complacency, a formula that allows much talk but is predisposed to allow a status quo to continue to exist which has long failed to offer what it promises and claims to deliver.

Pepin

Perhaps if the focus is purely on GDP there is a case to be made for going for redistribution. But if we look at GDH (Gross Domestic Happiness) all those champions of redistribution or equality (Sweden, France, Japan,...) tend to be at the very bottom of the global rankings. These super welfare states create a strong incentive for people to stay at home, collect a monthly welfare check and sink into a depression as opposed to forcing them to go out and make something of their life. Typically the people that are trapped by this system are those that have a weak character to begin with and tend to go for the easy solution. These countries create a vast 'underclass' of the unhappy, deprived of any chance to make something of their life and build self esteem. And this underclass then become the 'clientèle' of the socialist party: they feel fully dependent on government handouts. I find this quite perverse. Maybe higher inequality and lower growth are a price worth paying in order to give everyone a chance of self fulfilment and happiness.

Munzoenix

I can definitely see how if one rich person can forgo that luxury Prada bag, someone down the income poll can go to college with that money.

In that case, redistribution is better for growth (especially growth in human capital formation). But, I think governments have to deal with certain market imperfections. For example, a CEO can outsource jobs, but his job cannot be outsourced even if he is a poor manager (he is then given a "retention bonus" during bad times). Wages at the top are growing so fast because they can pay themselves irrespective of the company's performance. Some metrics of performance, such as stock price, can be manipulated. For example, companies borrow money (cheaply) to buy back shares. This obviously improves the return on equity metric (because there is less equity outstanding). It also boosts the stock's value (a benchmark to pay bonuses to CEO's).

This poses the question of where inequality comes from — talent or market *power*? I will be the first one to take my hat off and congratulate innovative people like Steve Jobs. But, should I be awed by an executive who fills the board of executives with his buddies who are certain to grant him a lucrative compensation package? The unions got busted so all the spoils can go to the top. In Japan there is so much shame when executives do not take care of their workers. This will obviously limit inequality at the start; that later redistribution policy can be minimal. In America, worker abuse (or even outsourcing) seems to be the hallmark of good management. Redistribution policies might then have to be starker. This is true in Latin America, too.

Additionally, advanced countries with more redistribution policies such as Germany and Sweden, have slower growth but seem to possess real exchange rates that continuously appreciate. Comparing the USA to Canada — the US has had better growth measured by its national statistic. But, if you assumed both countries had no growth since 2000, the Canadian incomes would be larger than US incomes simply because the Loonie has gained more than 60% on the US dollar since 2000. Evidently, whatever growth Canada has had seems to be more solid than the US, if not fast and evidently an illusion.

1776

Homogeneous countries like the Scandinavian ones tell us nothing about redistribution but rather highlight the benefits of like-minded polities and the impact of diversity on social cohesion. It is no surprise that the social problems that do arise in countries like Sweden are immigration related. That people can't openly acknowledge and speak about this is as much a problem as inequality and strips all scientific rigour from any argument. And I'm not saying that there aren't offsetting benefits. However, generous safety nets cannot persist in multi-ethnic societies. Humans have not evolved beyond the tribe and I see no evidence outside the elites that they want to.

Mypost

I think the first step should be to level the playing field. I was a believer in the benefits of the invisible hand. But in today's market the invisible hand is distorted — by regulations which make it very expensive to operate a small business, by capital markets which lend at almost free cost to big business but at prohibitive rates to smaller business. The whole system is favouring entrenched systems (regulation, taxes, access to capital), so how can the invisible hand operate?

Monopsony of the Press

My first observation is that in highly unequal open economies; savings-investments pour outwards, to developed countries, as unequal nations also often suffer institutional (and hence macro) instability as a result of their distributional problems. So if you're rich, you safeguard your savings abroad. This process is recursively negative for growth. **Secondly, why not mention the inverse side of the savings-investment coin:** consumption, the bedrock of the most dynamic economy in the world, the US. It is well known (I believe Keynes noted it as well) that marginal propensity to consume is higher at the lower end of the income distribution. And, given that firms invest only if they estimate that their future output is likely to be consumed, re-distributional policies provide demand-side support for local investment. This is recursively positive for growth. It is absolutely incredible that the world is finally waking up to such a reality.

BRR

There are three kinds of national demand — out of income, out of borrowing and out of foreigners. The third is ruled out globally as a transfer of demand. So if borrowing stops, the answer must be out of income. But when borrowing stops incomes decline. The answer is more spending out of the same income. How? By transferring income from chronic savers to hard-pressed households—Redistribution.

MarkGB

However, no amount of tinkering with this debt based monetary system will fix the problem of inequality. A fiat system requires ever increasing debt in order to continue. This one has lasted for 40 years and it is way past saving by money printing, income redistribution, or any other tinkering, however clever it looks on a spreadsheet. We live in a gigantic Ponzi scheme which needs to be continuously fed. This is financial gravity we are dealing with, and you can't deny the fundamentals with clever tricks.

A great opportunity to restore sanity was presented in the US in 2008 when Lehman went down. The US government could have allowed the market to complete the de-leveraging and creative destruction. Instead they propped up their pals and their own jobs. They could have temporarily nationalised the banks, allowed the shareholders to be wiped out, negotiated a haircut with the bondholders, protected the depositors, fired the management, and prosecuted the CEO's for any and all illegality. Then, they could have cut out the poisonous 'assets' and ring-fenced them, allowing the bad stuff to die over time, using anything that proved to have some value to reimburse the tax payers. Then they could have sold the cleansed banks back into the private sector.

Whilst all this was going on, our wonderful 'leaders' could have got together and said 'hey guys this isn't working is it?' - How about we sit down and reset the system, creating sound money to trade with. You know the sort of stuff that we had before Tricky Dicky reneged on US debt by closing the gold window. It'll mean we won't be able to go to war by printing counterfeit money, we won't even be able to ensure our own positions with electoral bribes we have no ability or intention of honouring—yes unfortunately it means no more guns and butter. I know, many of us are going to have to get a real job, but we must all make a sacrifice…'

The rational thing is for governments to reset the monetary system consciously and deliberately. I believe this is too much to hope for, and isn't going to happen. The politicians have too much to lose and lack the courage to tell the truth to populations which, for some strange reason, think that folks like Janet Yellen and Mark Carney are in control and know what they are doing. They aren't and they don't.

So, as well meaning as redistribution is, redistributing the counterfeit will not help. Unfortunately when the system does come down, the people who have worked hard, followed the rules and saved for their retirement will be the worst hit. A large proportion of their retirement funds will be largely held in useless government paper, put there by money managers who think it is 'safe'. Meanwhile the looters and the skimmers will have stashed enough away in real assets out of harm's way. The politicians and central bankers will say there was no way of seeing it coming.

Fiat systems create debt and cronyism. Equality is not on offer.

L'anziano   ***   Apr, 2014

I was highly suspicious of this Piketty brouhaha from the beginning—especially when he immediately became a darling of the leftist establishment. Thankfully I didn't pay much attention to it as I was busy working in the real world. Rognlie's point has the benefit of being intuitive and quite interesting in what it reveals about the way leftist economists like Piketty think. Socialists always assume that capital, once accumulated, is irrevocable. Anyone who has actually lived by their wits in business knows this is patently untrue. Established companies die. Shareholders go bankrupt. Established technologies are disrupted. In fact, Clayton Christensen of Harvard may have proved Rognlie's point a couple of decades ago, in a different way, with his work on disruptive innovation. 'Depreciation' is actually a very crude way of describing the risks to capital valuation once accumulated.

* These academics are disagreeing over the rate at which workers can be replaced by machines. (Rognlie thinks the rate of substitution is low whereas Piketty thinks it's high.) If the rate is high the capitalist will buy more machines to sustain their rate of return. Thus, capital returns as a share of income will grow at the expense of labour's share of income. And so capital accumulates for the capitalist. Surely no one would care if more plants, R+D and start-ups were financed. Alarmingly, economic data proves conclusively that capital is accumulating only in the housing stock. This means that homeless labour is being priced out of the market for shelter and must return earned income to the rentier as housing rent. Power relations of this nature pose a grave threat to social continuity. Housing depreciates though the land it is built on does not. So land is irrevocable. That's why they're buying Land. And its value can increase due to nearby public works, a lawful and ordered civil society, etc.

Risk Strategies

Piketty's work bears an uncanny similarity to Karl Marx's "Das Kapital". Update the language, replace Bourgoisie with middle class etc. and you have Piketty.

Some comments are frightening in their similarity:
"The class-struggles of the ancient world took the form chiefly of a contest between debtors and creditors, which in Rome ended in the ruin of

the plebeian debtors. They were displaced by slaves. In the middle ages the contest ended with the ruin of the feudal debtors, who lost their political power together with the economic basis on which it was established. Nevertheless, the money relation of debtor and creditor that existed at these two periods reflected only the deeper-lying antagonism between the general economic conditions of existence of the classes in question."

Karl Marx—**DAS KAPITAL**

Ealing

It is predictable that the plea for greater equality should be treated as a socialist curse by many contributors. I'm no socialist, but the growth in inequality threatens capitalism, the only system with a proven long term record of improvement. If the rewards for effort and success continue to become evermore imbalanced, there will be trouble ahead. A simple statistic will illustrate this: In the US, from 1947 to 1979, productivity rose 119% while wages rose 100%. As a share of the total wealth, the top 1% share rose from 9% to 13%. In a stunning example of deterioration in equality, from 1979 to 2009, productivity rose 80% while wages rose 8%, and the top 1% now has 23% of the total wealth. If anyone believes this trend is "good" or believes that this doesn't threaten our society's future, I think you're mad. And repeated insistence that any attempt to tax the wealthy at a graduated rate will be "unfair" simply doesn't stand up to the facts.

Sanjay Saksena

What has been overlooked is the fate of societies which focused on equality and followed economic policies aimed at discouraging the accumulation of wealth, societies which did not allow the market process to function. We know that communist and socialist economic ideas have been tried in dozens of countries after the War and it is nothing short of remarkable that in each and every country, ideological promotion of equality has brought forth misery and misfortune to the populace. You only have to compare the erstwhile East Germany with its western counterpart and the modern day China with the pre-Deng China to understand that societies with greater economic equality are not preferable wherein the focus is on division of the cake rather than allowing more bakeries to function efficiently.

In India, there was a time when the rich were taxed in excess of ninety percent. That may have resulted in greater equality (doubtful) but it certainly led to millions of people being condemned to grinding poverty. The hard truth is that the rich capitalist may be a bad guy, but without him you do not make progress. This is what is intrinsically difficult to comprehend—the idea that bad guys can produce outcomes which are beneficial to society. If economic inequality is the price we pay for ensuring there is food on every table in the land, it is a price worth paying.

There is a larger point. Freedom and democracy require the market process to function smoothly. So while it may give rise to economic inequality, it is not clear the alternative is philosophically more attractive.

Martin Klevstul

Sanjay Saskena's comment is extremely interesting, and reminds me of Nietzsche's critique of "the faith in antithetical values" in Beyond Good and Evil (Part One, Section 2). As Nietzsche said "With all the value that may adhere to the trust, the genuine, the selfless, it could be possible that a higher and more fundamental value for all life might have to be ascribed to...selfishness and to appetite."

Latina View

It would be less worrying for inequality were home ownership rates rising and not — as they currently are — falling. Falling ownership rates clearly point to further concentration of wealth (capital accumulation). So, what relevance does a variation of one particular asset class holding (e.g. shares) have on overall wealth accumulation? Only as much relevance as it affects the totality is the answer. If the shares holding is steady but the housing holding is rising, the totality of accumulated wealth is increasing. As far as I can see, Piketty hasn't been disproved at all. The reason that the trend towards wealth concentration — which began its current phase in the 80's — has accelerated since the financial crisis of 2008 is that government protection of the financial sector (bank bailouts, QE's, loan guarantees, etc.) didn't allow asset prices to fall to their natural level, more in line with incomes alone, and not income plus debt, as was — and still is — the case.

If an economy is built on ever expanding levels of private debt that functions to boost asset prices — when, concurrently, income growth is lagging productivity gains — then those who could access credit with ease, the increasingly wealthy, will always be increasing their share of the overall asset pie for the financial benefits of the gains in productivity accrued to them.

It's a myth — propagated by vested interests — that the poor would have suffered more from a collapse in asset prices in 2008 than the rich; the reverse has been historically true. That myth brought about the erroneous government reaction back then, they did totally the opposite of what they should have done, they saved the providers of credit, and therefore guaranteeing asset prices remained out of sync with incomes. So, if the current trend towards wealth concentration is to be reversed, one of two things (or a combination of both) must occur: Asset prices must fall or incomes must rise. And for either of these two things to happen (without massive state intervention) private debt availability must be severely restricted in certain categories. I see no other way out; if you think otherwise, please explain.

Londoned

In my approach to such matters one piece of research does not "disprove" another in some final sense, any more than Piketty "proved" his hypotheses. Piketty raised issues, provided data and an explanation of the data in terms of a theory. What a counter article can do is to raise questions about it, the data, or the theory which may or may not be damaging to it. For instance, in relation to Rognlie, capital's share of income could remain the same but with a high (and deflationary) savings rates it could still snowball itself into an ever higher concentration of wealth which is what seems to be happening, and which is what Piketty focused much of his analysis on. In a situation where the top 0.1% of US wealth owners now own 22% of US wealth and the bottom 90% own 23%;

I would say we have a wealth concentration problem, not just a distribution of income within labour problem. I don't see anything that overturns this reality, but I am open to counter arguments.

I also think it's interesting how much attention is being paid to this counter of Piketty which feels to an outside observer rather like desperation. Piketty's work, as he would be the first to admit, is limited by how little data we have on wealth rather than income. And I see nothing that suggests that the return on capital does not generally exceed the rate of growth of the overall economy. Any counter data? The difficulty is of course that much snowballing of wealth does not show up on income stats. If a Neo-feudal landlord with land in the family owns a big chunk of central London, his wealth could grow very large without showing in any income stats unless he sold the land and if he is clever he will find ways to conceal the rental income via reinvesting/snowballing it.

And the return on capital is one element, though asset price inflation as per QE seems to me to provide a way that wealth inequality grows fast, even if the real rate of return on capital aka the production of real goods and services through its use falls. Upton Sinclair said it well: "It is difficult to get a man to understand something, when his salary depends on his not understanding it." This neatly encapsulates the treason of the clerks of the economics profession, especially the economics professors sitting on the boards of reckless Wall Street institutions destroying value while they said nothing.

Piketty is pretty clear on the limits to what we know about wealth distribution and based on recent experience his projections for 2030 (of the top 10% owning 80% of the wealth being achieved, up from 70% today) on US wealth distribution are well on the way to being met on an accelerated basis. Piketty's argument in a nutshell: either reform the tax system to reverse the snowballing inequity of wealth and income, or face the four horsemen of the economic apocalypse: war, hyperinflation and revolution.

*The name of the fourth is not known but he's the one that shorts your currency into a hole.

Legal Tender   ***   2010-2015

Let's begin by appreciating *thee beginning* before we contemplate our future. The original vocations of the human species were hunting, gathering, child rearing, alliance building and slaughter. The "pay" was nutrition, shelter, safety and furtherance of the gene pool. Somewhere along the way someone got the brilliant idea to give people gruel in return for menial labour and loss of flexibility and independence, and we got farms, canals, pyramids and cities. Alliance building and slaughter also became paid positions. Child rearing is one of the original jobs, unless you only define "job" as following someone else's orders and time schedules in return for gruel.

*Reader, please note that this original model was disrupted by the Black Death, the plague that ravaged Europe between 1348 and 1350, killing about 50% of the population. Such a huge devastation represented a phase transition from the old system of feudalism and effective slavery, to a new system where people had to take responsibility for their own livelihood, and importantly – they demanded to be paid. The market was born out of the death of the old system and wealth began to accumulate in Europe, assisted by new knowledge gained from Jerusalem. The next phase change was in 1709 with the birth of the Industrial Revolution.

Latina View

When the neoliberal revolution of the late 70's installed the concept that productivity gains ought to be retained almost exclusively as profit by businesses and not shared out equally between employees (extra income) and employers (extra profit) the seeds of the current malaise were planted. As income for the majority has stagnated, a privileged minority has begun to acquire all the assets. This slow but inexorable movement towards uneven acquisition of assets — and the inevitable economic gridlock that follows such hoarding — was masked by the explosion of personal debt, which still allowed many to access assets. When the capacity to repay such debt (to acquire assets) was saturated because of long term stagnant incomes, we arrive at where we are today.

Acetracy

Historically in such a low interest rate environment we should have seen employment rise, incomes rise, investment in capital and infrastructure and inflation. The fact that we hardly see a blip in any of these for the past 5 years is the fact that low interest rates are only being enjoyed by hedge funds, speculators, private equity, etc. - not the traditional borrowers like small businesses. Yellen, Bernanke and Greenspan are all products of the Friedman's monetary policy theory which assumes that tweaking interest rates will run the economy (foot on the accelerator).

Fiscal stimulus is ignored in favour of just monetary policy. These past 5 years show the rise of financial engineering since the 1980s has absorbed available capital (that could have been invested in infrastructure) shifting income and wealth to the financial elite. Couple that with the outrageous pay packages of the top corporate echelon while pensions are gutted, healthcare is pushed off onto the employees, and many of these corporations spend more on lobbying DC than in Federal taxes. The USA is beginning to look more and more like France under the Bourbon kings.

Mysterion

There is no social contract. Pushing up asset prices by reducing interest rates redistributes from the young to the old, from the poor to the rich, from workers to capital and from those who consume to those who save. If the old respond to this absurd 'wealth effect' and increase their consumption (as we apparently desire them to do) it is as if that expenditure has been added to the national debt — it must be paid by the next generation. Real wages for the under 25s have fallen so far that they are now back to 1988 levels, asset prices are at record levels and we have massive unfunded liabilities on the horizon.

E. Scrooge

There is a simpler way to explain the working poor. The real reason is pure unadulterated greed, and in a number of corners. But the buck stops at the president and chairmen of the boards. Either you pay your everyday people a decent wage or you do not. But, before most answers yes, we do; put it in terms of your entry level admin assistant, engineer, accountant, salesperson, then against the mid level managers, than against the total compensation package of your top five corporate officers. I suspect the top five will take home multiples of all of the combined incomes of the majority of their employees. Charity begins at home, at the corporate home, lest we all be Bob Cratchits, with no Mr. Scrooge to see the light. The base or lower half of the income pyramid does the heavy lifting of the economy; they do the majority of the purchasing. They can only lift so high with such limited support.

Agwisreal

There's more to this story than greed. The US manufactures more stuff than ever before. It just does it with fewer workers. Automation does not make the nation lose the capacity to make stuff. Quite the opposite, the downside of automation is that it breaks what used to be the tie between factory production and middle-income spending power. Now, the fruits of the production go to those who are responsible for it [nothing new here] but that responsibility rests with the engineers and software geeks who coded the robots, with the managers and designers who told them what to make, and with the investors who risked their savings for all that. And finally, with the workers but there aren't as many of them as before. Fewer people, producing more, so earning power is lopsidedly concentrated compared to back when.

AllergicToBS

Problem is we've used every trick in the book to turn future income into current capital gain. Including:

a) Reduced the discount rate to zero (impact on bonds, pensions, house prices)
b) Ended generous final salary pension schemes, leaving the burden of funding their huge deficits on current and future staff
c) Created housing price bubbles around the world
d) Asset prices generally at record levels, driven by money printing rather than revenue growth
e) Off-shored many jobs to max out corporate profits
f) Concentrated most of the wealth in 1% of the population
g) Made students pay for their own education
h) All major economies heavily indebted which places an onerous burden on future taxpayers.

Those saying young people should get more involved in politics are off target. They would still be climbing up a very steep hill, when you look at the macro-economics of this. When you mortgage the future as heavily as this last generation has done, then anyone who hasn't participated to date is at a huge disadvantage.

John Bruce

Perhaps Mother Nature can inspire optimism in our future. My premiss is that from little acorns great oak trees grow - and in an economy 'in the blink of an eye' in contrast to in nature. Think Mond and ICI (1m directly or indirectly employed at its height) or Dyson, today, whose personal tax paid, is enough to support both houses of Parliament, and then there are his hundreds of engineers' et al. And the premiss is that you don't pick winners but bet on a self selected 'qualified' field, in the sure knowledge that some will win or get a good place. For the rest, cut funding as they fail at negligible cost (in the greater scheme of things).

The qualification is simply that the person has a patented product they wish to make for export—then the State simply hands over, on demand, what is asked for, and sits back. Some companies will in a few years be employing people generating c£145,000 pa GDP (IMI's 2013 figure).

This 100% funding (nothing matched or it doesn't happen) merely emulates Dyson's bank, who gave him £600,000 to make Dysons. It was brave of him; when all about him thought him mad – "Who needs another Hoover?' No one would license the technology until forced to by his growing market share. But that is what Growth is all about - realising an unlikely dream. Economic Growth is not primarily about how many new jobs or houses there are, or HS2 [none of which earn overseas] - the premiss is that the only growth that matters is in overseas earnings - it is the sine qua non all the rest. Without doing that, all economies default when debt over tops market appetite.

The argument is a no brainer in an 'ingenious' society. We are ingenious; the UK fathered the industrial revolution. It's in our blood now, as then.

One merely has to re-iterate Professor Christensen who on 'News Night' BBC TV, on 20 September 2013, told us, essentially, that all economies decline and fail unless they earn more abroad than they spend—it is simple Adam Smith dicta. And that if you wish to increase overseas revenue streams and the private sector won't or can't invest then the State has to do so 100%, or not get the new revenues—it is simple Keynes dicta.

The Professor lamented that in the USA commercialisation of Innovation (patented, disruptive game-changing new technology and products) had declined by 2/3 in 40 years, while here, in the UK, we have not managed to commercialise a single Innovation (so defined) in 40 years—not one. When asked why by Mr Paxman the Professor answered quite simply "you don't fund it". Our decline through oil, selling off the family jewels, then debt and more debt into QE is patent. We are broke and have no means of earning more from declining global markets - however much more finance is given to struggling companies. This is why the working poor multiply in the US and UK.

In fact, it may be that in a decade less than half a dozen 'dysons' emerge. It is not simple to invent a new technology or a new SATNAV. But that is the difference between earning enough and not long term.

We have had nothing 'new' for generations.

Cathal Haughian

Style is another word for beauty; it is used in mass marketing to manufacture desire. I can only speak for myself, but beauty seems so well and frequently used in mass marketing. If we let the choices of others speak for them, then '*Beauty is in the eye of the beholder*' is proven false by the ubiquity of iPhones.

Every product has *Substance* and *Style* properties. The first washing machine had a substantial impact on productivity. Every iteration since has improved *Style* over *Substance*. They look nicer and using them a more pleasant experience but most efficiency and productivity gains came with the first version. To my eye, the first version was ugly but every iteration since has added aesthetic value, and I can no longer see ugly washing machines at the marketplace. It bore an aesthetic disvalue to aesthetic value, from ugly to nice? The entrepreneur's dream, the idea, was realised by the first version. The form it took was ugly and then it became nice? Perhaps all objects have an aesthetic property with beauty just one inherent possibility.

The 20th century gave birth to a huge variety of new products which improved living standards via productivity gains. Nowadays, improvements in *Style* are increasingly dominating economic activity with ever more dollars spent on marketing.

This is due to a slowdown in the discovery of 'new' knowledge applicable to the human condition. And most importantly, the rate of entrepreneurial activity shall slowly decline during such slowdowns. Living standards shall have a tendency to stagnate as productivity stagnates. Payments to the unemployed are best during periods of rapid gains in new knowledge since they act as a bridge between jobs.

During this present slowdown, a *basic citizens' income* is more appropriate for economies with fully developed infrastructure. This idea can stabilise and encourage *faith and belief* in the nation. A *basic income* is an unstable idea in and of itself. It must be supported by *limited immigration* and *mandatory public service* that disciplines and provides a purposeful life to the citizenry.

How God made beauty a property of the World is a question best answered by silence.

Paul A. Myers   ***   Apr, 2013

To have your example emulated is the highest praise.

With regard to her prescient remarks on a single currency and the overall European Union, one can say that these points and their intellectual descendants will figure into what is probably coming: a major redesign of the architecture of Europe.

With regard to privatization, the first wave often has stunning success because it flows capital, talent, and resources back towards the productive. Thatcher rode this wave. Free markets, when truly competitive, are great at optimizing the employment of resources. This optimization function is too sorely missing in much of today's Europe and America due to excessive economic concentration across almost all sectors: we have monopolies, oligopolies, national champions, consortium, an unbelievable level of rent seeking (supported by both right and left political wings), various protections from the more competitive and productive, and a worldwide elite that has set its wealth and income beyond national reach through offshore tax havens and tax avoidance strategies conceived by the most devious lawyers in all the advanced country capitals.

To go to a top-drawer political fund raiser in any national capital or financial capital like New York is to go to the Hookers' Ball, the glitter of arriving in your own motorcade after the helicopter dropped you on top of a nearby skyscraper. A great deal of the charm of Lady Thatcher's memory is that she is such a remarkable "one off," not likely to be seen anywhere again but nevertheless a fount of worthwhile lesson.

Nicholas Sowels

The current "Great Recession" is no accident, and follows directly from the neo-liberalism of Thatcher and Reagan etc.

By dogmatically deregulating and privatising everything - not just nationalised companies operating in competitive markets, but all types of public services and above all finance - Margaret Thatcher and her political allies built the foundations of today's global economy. It is marked not just by massive inequality (both within the United Kingdom and the United States, as well as internationally). Today's advanced neo-liberal economies are also burdened with vast amounts of private and public debt as well as stagnating incomes of median income households.

The result is a vicious circle of stagnation, public indebtedness, fiscal austerity and more stagnation. Vast amounts of quantitative easing are only just keeping the show on the road, while providing cash to the wealthy who are now stoking up new asset price bubbles. As David Stockman (hardly a man of the Left) wrote in the New York Times (March 30), "When the latest bubble pops, there will be nothing to stop the collapse".

Last but not least, our neo-liberal societies today have put a price on everything, yet know the value of nothing (to paraphrase Oscar Wilde). None of this is surprising, just the logical consequence of cutting taxes for the wealthy, deregulating finance and cutting wages for the poor. In short, The Legacy of Thatcher.

Sanjay Saksena

Millions of people in the undeveloped countries owe an eternal debt of gratitude to Mrs. Thatcher.

Enchained by the socialist dogma of the likes of Mao, Nehru, Naser and Tito, over two billion people were condemned to live in abject poverty for decades. By convincingly demolishing socialism through firm action against militant labour, by promoting vigorously the cause of free markets and liberalisations, by undertaking very successfully the sale of government owned industrial enterprises, she demonstrated beyond doubt that there was a better way of running the economy.

The winds of change unleashed by her and Ronald Reagan; contributed to the demise of The Soviet Union and the ultimate defeat of socialism. The unleashing of entrepreneurial energies of the hitherto shackled populations of the undeveloped countries has seen millions come out of poverty and a rise in standards of living hitherto unprecedented. Never before in the history of mankind, have so many enjoyed so much prosperity as in the past two decades. Very few leaders can claim to have contributed to so much good for so many.

Man of Mode

"Living within one's means" misrepresented Britain's history. The history of invasion and settlement, inward and outward, is one of globalism.

Globalism does not stay at home staring at the hearth because it cannot afford the bus fare out of town. Globalism stands on the beach and knows the waves flow in and out across the world. The determination of small certainties, elevated to a world stage, does not equate to globalism on a world stage. Philosophically and financially, Britain has speculated to accumulate with money and human talent. A scholarship beneficiary with more talent than money is in no position to advise nations or individuals to live within their means.

Christian Wright   ***   **2014**

We are in phase two of the dissolution of England's inner empire. Ireland is long gone and Scotland is now in the process of delivering the coup de grâce. The deep-seated clinical denial is evinced by habitual reference to "rUK" - the fiction of a continuing union AKA empire after Scotland's departure.

That the UK is naught but England's inner empire is made crystal clear in the legal opinion of December 10 2012 (Opinion: Referendum on the Independence of Scotland – International Law Aspects), paid for by Her Majesty's Government, and adopted by it in early 2013 as the cornerstone of its official policy on matters constitutional and Scottish. In Part IV of that document we are informed that Scotland was "extinguished" in 1707 when it was absorbed by England, and that the titles "United Kingdom" and "England" are synonyms describing the self-same, continuing, unitary state.

So, let us not kid ourselves, the UK has never been a partnership. Rather it is a three-century old colonial construct sustained by patronage, privilege, and ultimately, force of arms. A stale confection now in irreversible decline and characterised by indebtedness, corruption, gross inequality, and ethnic bigotry. The best possible outcome for the people of England would be its summary dissolution and the establishment of a new system of decentralised government that truly is answerable to the electorate. It is beyond intolerable that all power is concentrated in the hands of a multi-millionaire ruling class that comprises but one percent of the entire population.

Job one for those who would look to fashion a more just and fairer English society should be the conscious deconstruction of this impediment of empire and the imperial hubris it sustains of England as an economic and military world power.

John Lilburne

The establishment pays too much respect to the past. They insist that the monarchy is a "guardian of national unity". But the evidence presented is of a nation that is not united! And write about the continuing possibility that Scotland will leave succeed. And then point to a great divide between the "southern regions" and the rest of the country. When I look at a system that includes hereditary legislators, a state church with some of its clerics as legislators, a legislative chamber unaccountable to the people, a monarchy whose members are paid millions more than bankers every year for doing very little, and a state-sponsored class hierarchy, I see an "establishment" that has nothing whatsoever to do with me.

I am alienated from a system that asks me to recognise "princesses" and "princes" as if I was a child. It might as well ask that I recognise fellow citizens as fairies. Nor do I respect a system that asks me to bow my head to what it would call a "lord" or a "queen". When they tell us that Elizabeth Windsor has kept the respect of "her people" I must reply that we republicans are not hers at all.

The problems this country faces will not be fixed by such nonsense as calling Northern Ireland a "nation" when it has none of the attributes of a nation and would not be recognised as such anywhere else. That kind of pretence is evasive and disrespectful of the people. The past deserves a lot less respect than suggested. If we are to change this nation for the better we can make a start by having the state recognise all of its citizens as equal citizens. No more free seats in the legislature, no more religious privilege, no more absurd feudal titles and no more monarchy.

Too much to ask, no doubt!

Mysterion

Modern societies are able to support ever more sub-cultures which don't have to interact or integrate with each other. Immigration or not, the mono-culture is dead. Unwanted fragmentation and division is just the flip side of desired diversity by the elite. Societies are subject to both centrifugal and centripetal forces. We've a big increase in the former— varied cultures, national attachments and religions are pulling people apart. The centripetal forces are fading - the days when everyone watched the same TV each night, read the same newspapers in the morning are over. Without a common culture with common reference points fractiousness is the inevitable result.

Barry Manga

In a centrally planned global economy the function of domestic politics is to provide the illusion of choice. In the UK the 2 main parties construct opposing narratives out of the same data. Whether this is growth, austerity, poverty, inequality, multi-culturalism, or whatever. The function of these opposing narratives is a polarised and apathetic population.

Any truly tyrannical action, e.g. the Iraq war, or GCHQ surveillance is met with wholehearted bipartisan approval as well as genuine social change such as withdrawal of access to free university education; choice is an illusion. The constant opinion pieces in the media are also symptomatic of this lack of genuine choice, dumbing down, very few facts, and the idea that people aren't interested in reality, just a version of it filtered through the editorial position of a newspaper. We are but a reflection of the US.

*Reader, please note that the purpose of this chapter is to explore the tension between Faith and Belief in representative democratic society and a Globalised economy. What can be learnt from above can be applied elsewhere, to Barcelona, Shanghai etc.

The original form of "democracy", a term misused to represent today's party-democracies, actually used "sortition" to elect officials, as Council members of ancient Athens were chosen from a random draw. This draw kept special interests from undermining intelligent decision-making in their governance—thus they were somewhat smarter than us in the design of their political institutions, or less cynical and manipulative.

The Athenian Assembly utilized democratic debate, where any citizen could speak and vote, while matters were put before this assembly after first having been drafted and reviewed by the Council members that were chosen at random from amongst the tribes which made up Athens.

Income tax or consumption tax is a cost, in that they tax all income and consumption equally without regard to differing supply or price elasticity. If you truly understand what taxes on income and consumption do to the supply and prices of goods not in fixed supply, then you would know that every dollar of tax collected from a non-land source costs more than a dollar in economic activity. This would lead you to want to exclude all income and consumption taxes on non-land items. This would mean that the only tax that could rationally be supported is a tax on land value. You then have the option of either taxing production just as heavily as a land subsidy or making the best attempt to accurately tax only the land subsidy.

Finally, land value taxation (LVT) actually makes land valuation easier because it inhibits the formation of land price bubbles, which accounts for most of the problems with assessing land year-to-year. Critics acknowledge how an LVT could stabilize land prices but then conclude that LVT cannot possibly measure land price variations, when it is land prices and their variations which are reined in by LVT.

John LVT

We must halt the Land Price Cycle for obvious reasons. No other method can do this effectively other than reclaiming the economic rents accumulated in the land. Economic rent is when there is no enterprise or costs of production. In short, others made the wealth, and in 99% of cases it was made by economic community activity. Those who appropriate economic rent, no matter where the rent was created (not all occurs in land values), are "economic freeloaders".

The knock-on beneficial effects of reclaiming economic rent from land values are far reaching. Boom and busts will disappear which is an inherent part of the current flawed economic system we all suffer under. Freeloaders and land speculators, who harm enterprise, will be pushed to the margins or eliminated entirely. Stability naturally arises with productive enterprise having a firm base to operate upon.

Taken to a full implementation, reclaiming economic rent can eliminate taxes on production (income tax) and trade (sales taxes). This simply means, we use commonly created wealth to pay for common services, leaving private wealth in private pockets. Currently, we do exactly the opposite; we use privately created wealth to pay for common services and commonly created wealth is appropriated by private individuals or organisations.

Halting the land cycle is the most basic and first step to any effective long term economic reform.

Henry Law

There is a difficulty in principle, in that all land value is in reality "from here", because it has to be continually sustained by the presence and activities of the community. If, for example, the pumps in the sewerage system stopped working, large areas of London would be worthless swamp within days. It would be easier to replace all property-related taxes, including Council Tax, Business Rates, Stamp Duty Land Tax and Inheritance Tax with a unified tax on the annual rental value of land i.e. ignoring buildings. This would have precisely the effect needed to damp out future speculative price bubbles.

*Buildings can't be taxed as this would discourage renovation, repair and general improvement in the housing stock of a nation.

John-Geonomics

Taxing houses is like taxing your dishwasher (a capital item). Taxing the land makes sense as it soaks up community created wealth that crystallizes as land values. The location of land is known to the inch. The tax cannot be avoided. Greece has income tax officers who stop people on the streets. Taxing land means the Greek government gets all the revenue they need and rich Greeks cannot move land to London.

General Economist

The cost to buy a house should be the same as the cost to build a house. Everything above that is unearned profit, monopoly appreciation of a fixed asset (the location). Why should some people monopolise what is by nature shared by all? Owners cheer when the city invests in a neighbourhood while tenants weep at the increased rent. Though, both classes paid for the investment. Hong Kong has got rich by realising that the state should only sell leases to land, not the freehold.

Benji

The UK's private debt is projected to rise to £2.26trn (in today's money) in 25 years time. Of this £1.68trn will be secured loans on land (location). This is the price we pay for allowing land rent to become capitalised. A 100% Land Tax drops the selling price of land to zero. So, if the services we share together were paid for by the value we create together, our private debt would be £580bn. Or about a quarter of its projected value. Capitalised land rent and taxes on work and enterprise both shrink GDP. So there, two birds can be killed with one stone.

These are the sort of fiscal choices our politicians and economists seem incapable of even discussing. Hence, the next credit fuelled housing bubble and bust is a certainty.

***

The situation is grave. That's why I don't say this light-heartedly, but I think it should be said nonetheless:

George Soros made it clear in "The Alchemy of Finance" (1987) that the debt situation became quite unsustainable already after 1982, and has been sustained only by a symbiosis of governments, central banks and commercial lenders, acting in a balance-of-fear type of environment. The banking system has been on the brink of collapse since then. Finding this out must make one slightly depressed, looking at the mountain of debt we have managed to amass mostly after the 1980s. PWC measured UK total debt to be 500% of GDP in 2012, no soul has had the courage required to measure it since.

The problem lies mostly with the human tendency to avoid short-term pain. Any top politician, or central banker, who would come out now would most likely cause a crisis. And proving a counter-factual is very hard, as we know, so this person (or institution) would need to take an unbearable amount of blame. Many still blame the Fed for what happened in the 1930s! Sure, mistakes were made, but mistakes will always be made.

Let's contemplate the detail, when personal debt started growing at a faster pace than personal income, it gradually replaced income as a source of demand, and so, it has to end in tears. A boom first, followed by a bust later, as the discrepancy between income and debt growth must mean that the debt burden will, sooner or later, become unserviceable. If much of that debt has been allocated to asset purchases, it will cause a financial crisis, as in 2008.

If left to unravel without state intervention, a financial crisis will collapse asset prices and bring them in line with incomes once again, not income + debt. And we can hope to start all over again. Unfortunately the myth that non intervention would have caused more pain to the poor than the rich was sold to the public in 2008, debt was jiggled around from one sector (financial) to another (state) as though, by magic, that would alter its overall level. Of course it didn't, it simply meant that the poor were made to take on the losses and asset prices were protected.

The private sector is intended to be fallible, otherwise the price mechanism would not work and it would be pointless, and the public sector is intended to be infallible, and so imprudence is hidden but the costs are real. It has been intentionally constructed that way; it's not some freak outcome or vestige of truth. The bailout of Wall Street was imprudent, the cost far too great, and so the real reason for printing money was hidden.

Unless it is accepted that demand must be tied to income growth, and not extra debt, we're never getting out of this one. The concept that higher bank lending — in an era of stagnant incomes — is an encouraging sign for the economy is a ridiculous one. More ridiculous still are Western governments (last 6/7 years) trying to bolster the banks in order to get them to do precisely that, lend more. The current disconnect between high asset prices, stagnant incomes and increasing, overall debt levels, is both economically and politically unsustainable.

And what is the ultimate result? There is no housing market for our young workers. The first rung of the property ladder only existed when wage inflation was higher than house price inflation. Those days are gone, well and truly. For not one politician or homeowner has the courage to see asset prices fall — as they assuredly would without endless money printing and zero interest rates. The result is a suppression of the natural market forces which would grab back property from overstretched speculators and see it distributed at sustainable prices to the productive young.

The market for money itself would correct stratospheric house prices. Then prosperity would settle on those who produce in preference to those who already have.

Why did the State do this? Because it cannot create growth. The root cause is the inability to create growth in the face of demographic changes. So instead they synthesized it. Aside from some Germanic nations, the West is slowly collapsing for she has been running at a loss for decades and successive governments have sought to shore up money creation by printing through housing. This point is central to an understanding of the crisis and highlights the enormity of what's about to happen. It is common to think that money printing began after The Great Financial Crisis.

In actuality, neo-liberal economies such as the US, UK, Ireland, Australia, etc. were printing money for decades by providing an excess of credit money to purchase property. For example, affordability measurements for mortgage applications used to use the primary income as a benchmark but this was changed to total household income. This permitted evermore future income to be sucked into the present for the purpose of consumption. This was money printing by sleight of hand. Thus, living standards dropped for the young while the elderly who owned property enjoyed a bonanza.

The West is now in a worse position than before she began this as the current monetary policy exacerbates misallocation of investment.

The establishment is therefore highly unlikely to let supply match demand (as it did in Ireland) as it will mean the collapse of house prices and the UK (and interconnected) banking systems and with it the West. I therefore posit that they do not want to remedy the shortage of affordable housing and therefore reject all suggestions as to how to fix the problem as meaningless. Alas, the dominant class did not envisage Brexit and the possible geopolitical consequences for asset prices in the UK, in particular, the property market.

This tragedy has several stages. It began with hubris, "The masses won't understand how we've shafted them" with the bank bailouts. Then David Cameron sets the stage for stupidity, "Let's give the peasants a chance to upset our apple cart!" Followed by madness shouting, "We'll have full access to the single market, outside the jurisdiction of the European Court, no payments to Brussels AND control of immigration!" It appears the mainstream still cling to denial. Let me explain why our beloved political mainstream and its shoddy EU project has lost its appeal. It's because the mainstream is not moderate — and most Britons are moderate. There are real extremists in the political mainstream — they have power and they have abused it mightily.

Allowing the bankers to devastate the public accounts with bailouts and thereafter leaving these culprits completely unscathed was an extremist choice. Engineering the financial suffocation of the entire Greek population so as to crush a popular vote was an extremist choice. Removing elected prime ministers in Italy and Greece and replacing them with unelected functionaries was an extremist choice. Allowing over a million migrants in to Europe was an extremist choice. Wage suppression in Ireland was an extremist choice. Permitting Germany's excessive trade surpluses whilst punishing everyone else's budget deficits was an extremist choice. Pension cuts were an extremist choice. Mass unemployment was an extremist choice.

The reason these catastrophic choices were made was precisely because mainstream parties have colluded to keep these barbaric policies safe from electoral retribution by making them effectively bi-partisan or sealed off behind a treaty wall. The normal process whereby democracy flushes out bad policy (and bad policymakers) has been terminated. The mainstream deliberately locked the voter out.

"But all of this is just the price of globalisation," sigh the well shod insiders. The masses were disrobed of agency to combat the 'manifest destiny' of the EU and globalisation. Now the insiders stand aside and watch in horror. The populists may have been made by the mainstream — but they clearly have no agency to unmake them now....

Those hoping for a rational and indifferent divorce must have looked on in horror at the tragedy unfolding in the EU parliament — scenes of gloating and ridicule. There shall be no adolescent stage in this tragedy. Laughter that sounded so childish was baptised by a kiss of death. We have witnessed attitudes harden, "The City, which thanks to the EU, was able to handle clearing operations for the Eurozone, will not be able to do them," the French President said. "It can serve as an example for those who seek the end of Europe... It can serve as a lesson." Ambitious people pursue opportunity rather than a place in the status qou. The talent in The City shall have no qualms in moving if income is elsewhere. You can write a contract under English law in Frankfurt or Paris just as well as in London. The immediate goal, it would seem, is to destroy the UK.

So Boris 'the dog that caught the car' scampers away. This is now Eastenders on acid ... as project fear becomes project reality. And now, the stage is being prepared for the next act, will prices in the property market slump and crater the UK's financial systems? The cracks have already begun to appear, three more UK real estate funds — following the example of Aviva and Standard Life — have just halted redemptions as they were running out of cash due to large withdrawal demands. Perhaps regulators should have wondered how an open-ended fund — whereby retail investors can demand their money back at short notice — would work with assets like property that take much time to sell. Yet another example of mis-selling by The City.

And so the tragedy unfolds ... though perhaps the politicians on the continent, that lust after revenge should first ask themselves, "Why did Britons vote to leave and can the panic be contained?"

That is very doubtful. Europe is in desperate need of moderate policies right now.

Contributors: Archimedes, Latina View, Peter Golovatscheff

If you start off either with a fundamentally wrong basic assumption in seeking to understand something, you will never analyse it correctly—unless you realize that your starting point assumption was wrong.

If you seek to understand the movement of planets near the sun, but your starting point is that they all revolve around planet earth, then the movements of those planets will never make sense, seen through that lens of total misunderstanding of the basics.

Similarly, all the stuff written about the Eurozone — what the ECB or the EU, or whoever should do — is a totally useless waste of time, because all such analysis starts off with the totally false assumption that the purpose of the euro, and the Eurozone (and the EU) is to confer benefits on the member countries.

This is a total fallacy.

The EU and the euro are controlled by Germany: if you don't understand that, then go and do something else — but don't waste time writing nonsense which fails to understand this 5 year-old basic starting point fact. And for Germany, the function and purpose of the EU and the euro is to benefit Germany.

End of story. Read it again and again — thinking not about what politicians say the function of the EU and the euro is — but what the simple facts are about what has happened with the EU and the euro. If you see a planet going round and around — and you know that it does that — then that tells you that it is orbiting something, even if you can't see it.

And if you look at what interest rates have existed historically in the euro zone, and what the ECB and the EU actually do — ignoring what they say — then if you have half a brain, you can see that Germany totally controls the EU, the ECB and the euro for its own benefit: specifically, for its sole benefit. Again — if you want to delude yourself, and imagine that anyone but Germany controls the EU and the euro, fine: but don't fantasize that starting off with a lie is going to get you any understanding of the EU or the euro. Therefore, for all those pundits to say that Germany should accept higher inflation to benefit Southern states, or the

ECB or EU should do this, that or the other to benefit countries other than Germany is just plain stupid.

Germany has taken control — directly and (particularly) through its proxy, the EU, and through the euro, Europe. It's done extremely well out of both the EU and the euro — and it's going to keep it that way, for as long as it can keep either or both entities intact. And it will prevent the collapse of either, if humanly possible, because they have been the instruments of Germany becoming incredibly rich — and more powerful than it has ever been.

A.Lex

Forget the economics and look at the facts!

We are at last witnessing a growing admission of the real causes of this failed experiment, the Euro. Ex. German Chancellor Gerhard Schröder claimed in 1998 that the introduction of the Euro would result in his words "a renaissance of German economic dominance in Europe". Germany would keep wages and costs down and thus achieve a dominant competitive edge over the other EZ countries who could no longer devalue within the common currency; German exports would be boosted through the EZ and German companies would acquire companies in the other countries weakened by the introduction of the euro.

All this has come to pass!

Schäuble's delicate reference in a recent FT article of 3rd November 2013 to "fiscal and structural repair work", otherwise known as enforced austerity in other nation states, dismissively generally referred to as PIIGS and peripherals, is the direct result of the virtual devaluation of some 25% to 30% within the "common currency" engineered by Germany in Agenda 2010.

This beggar thy neighbour policy crippled and virtually destroyed the domestic markets of those unfortunate countries which will now experience many years of poverty for youth and elderly, many living on the bread line. Is it so surprising that Germany now flourishes with an unbridgeable competitive advantage? Excellence in engineering, efficiency, production techniques and dedication alone are not enough to create such a massive divergence, which only became possible because of the "common currency" acting as a straitjacket!

The large growing permanent current account surplus increasing net exports at the expense of nearly all other countries increasing net imports with a now global effect, which Germany proudly continues to defend, is obviously unsustainable in the long term. It is not only the inevitable result of the Mercantilist policy but also of the German long time obsession with exports, a studied policy of Economic Imperialism which partly dates from Bismarck's time.

Hope Springs

There's little discussion of the point that Germany may be deluding itself about its asset-liability position, and that its reluctance to leave the Euro may have something to do with the wish to avoid reality in this respect. A country doesn't just get wealthy through exporting. It can also devote its efforts to internal investment in productive physical assets and productive non-physical assets such as education and organisation. This latter may be the ultimate determinant of how wealthy the people become. The German culture seems to find this investment natural. So does the Chinese. Differences in these matters will shape the world in 50 years time.

Ultimately, when faced with cheap labour, you either have to skill up somehow, or charge less. This fundamental truth is hardly ever discussed. "Skilling up" is shorthand for all sorts of supply side capability, much of which cannot be created overnight and much of which requires institutional frameworks and cultures that can take generations to come into being.

Olaf von Rein

"Faced with cheap labour, you either have to skill up somehow, or charge less. This fundamental truth is hardly ever discussed."

The supposition being perhaps that Italy, say, has not liberalized its economy enough to keep up with productivity growth in Germany or China, say? There are certainly a number of supply-side reforms around the Med that would help. And that's what Germany's crisis resolution is trying to bring about. In spite of herself, Merkel has become the Thatcher of the EZ. Thatcher, we remember, literally battled it out with the unions in Wapping and elsewhere. Compared to that, Merkel's crisis management can almost be described as "consensual".

However, the way I look at it, your question has far wider relevance. This is not about Italy vs Germany but increasingly there is a problem that some of our citizens will not be able to "skill up" — no matter how much education we throw at them. And as robots take over more low-skilled work, there is increasingly little room for these people to carve out a living. We end up with this dichotomy that in aggregates we are wealthier than ever, yet an ever increasing minority of our people lead really quite deprived existences.

"There's little discussion of the point that Germany may be deluding itself about its asset-liability position, and that its reluctance to leave the Euro may have something to do with the wish to avoid reality in this respect."

With reference to Germany AG (limited corporations, not the sovereign)? Yes, of course. There is no question that Germany AG would like to avoid marking down the various financial claims on the periphery. This is the tragedy of the German people: They believe that it is possible to store money over time — yet it cannot be done. The word "to save" is so stupidly misleading, it ought to be banned. So when a German "saves", he really forces some agent of his to sink the money into one ill-fated venture or another. Greek bonds, for example. And years later, when those Greeks don't repay the money, it turns out, ex-post, that all the graft put in years ago was for nought.

Still, the mark-downs will come — in EUR as much as in DEM.

Euro

Why are German surpluses a symptom of an under-performing economy rather than competitiveness? The German economy has a very weak investment record with investment having declined by over 5% of GDP over the past decade. This is visible in the services sector that is one of the weakest in Europe and has seen absolute declines in its productivity, leading to economy wide declines in productivity versus the US and the EU average.

Meantime export growth has relied on an unprecedented decline in the share of wages in GDP and rising savings. Wage austerity, of the relatively wealthier German worker, has allowed export companies to keep competitive prices while maintaining profits. Meantime, the weak domestic demand has directed business towards the export sector since it is the only profitable one as the latter is in addition being subsidised by Germany providing cheap loans to the rest of Europe to buy its exports i.e. German workers subsidising workers in the Club Med.

In fact, European debtors have been registering productivity gains that on average have been more than twice those of Germany over the past decade and have extended wage increases in line with those productivity gains when German wages have literally been stagnant to accommodate the competitiveness of their exports. German bankers have used the hard won savings of German workers; lending them abroad so the rest of Europe can buy German exports that remain competitive due to the Euro. Had there been a DM it would have appreciated and eliminated Germany's surpluses and their lending to foreigners. What did German workers gain out of all this?

Their savings are now residing with German "bad" banks (800bn) as non performing loans to the Club Med and Eastern Europe. However, Germans are being brainwashed to believe that this is the fault of the club med and are hardly aware that they run the risk of losing all their savings as current German policies risk generalised defaults or even the demise of the Euro i.e. they will get their money back as worthless new drachmas or pesetas.

Distant Observer

If Germany were not in the euro, the 'hidden hand' would have taken care of this entire problem on its own. Germany's currency would be at least 30% higher than it is being a member of the euro (conveniently held down in value by far less efficient national economies in the Eurozone). If Germany did not enjoy the massive benefit of being in the euro, its own currency would shoot up in value, and the other Eurozone countries and non-euro countries would be importing far less Germany products as a result.

At the same time, Germany's own strong currency — reflecting her economic success — would be sucking in imports at a far greater level, thereby benefiting other Eurozone countries, and many of the imbalances that are at the root of the current massive problem would have been automatically resolved. But for Germany of course, having a currency — the euro — which is artificially held down at least 30% below its true value is invaluable for its exports to the non-euro world; and equally, having the other Eurozone countries being permanently locked into a fixed exchange rate with Germany means:

(a) they can't compete with Germany, and thereby their own industries cannot recover; and

(b) that no matter how successful Germany is, a German car or machine still costs the same amount of money for a Greek, Spaniard or Italian — no matter how relatively unsuccessful those countries' economies are. And thus, the imbalances of trade between that country and Germany persist, and unemployment in those countries either rises, or won't come down.

Thus, this is not a case of 'how ridiculous' to criticize a country (Germany) for being too successful. What — instead — is ridiculous, is that the 'hidden hand' of the Price Mechanism, which would otherwise have automatically resolved this ridiculous situation of Germany sucking the life out of many of the rest of the European countries' economies, and preventing them from being able to compete. Germany is enjoying an exorbitant privilege of having currency which is more than 30% lower that it would be if they had their own currency — and the rest of the Eurozone is paying for Germany to enjoy that exorbitant privilege, in addition to being unable to devalue their currencies to compete with Germany. Germany should leave the euro — or the Latin countries should do so. It is that simple.

But of course Germany has fixed things so that short of some massive uprising of the populations of those Latin countries against the euro, that isn't going to happen, because they, together with the EU, have made sure that all EU countries' national governments are headed up by 100% obedient puppets of the EU — which is in turn controlled by Germany. And since Germany has no intention of giving up the exorbitant privileges it enjoys by using the euro, the other Eurozone countries' EU puppet leaders will keep the whole disastrous show on the road until it collapses.

Plato

Wynne Godley's prescient 1992 Euro-zone Structural collapse comes true:

"If a country or region has no power to devalue, and if it is not the beneficiary of a system of fiscal equalisation, then there is nothing to stop it suffering a process of cumulative and terminal decline leading, in the end, to emigration as the only alternative to poverty or starvation." http://www.lrb.co.uk/v14/n19/wynne-godley/maastricht-and-all-that

Why would the German's pursue this? Economic colonization! As Wynne Godley points out: "But there is much more to it all. It needs to be emphasised at the start that the establishment of a single currency in the EC would indeed bring to an end the sovereignty of its component nations and their power to take independent action on major issues. As Mr Tim Congdon has argued very cogently, the power to issue its own money, to make drafts on its own central bank, is the main thing which defines national independence. If a country gives up or loses this power, it acquires the status of a local authority or colony."

Forecast in 1992 and it came true!

Yet nobody listens.

Distant Observer

All very true. But you speak of the loss of control of a country's own currency inevitably meaning that they become a colony as if that was something bad: that was the whole objective behind the euro in the first place. The euro was from the start primarily a means of massively increasing the political and economic power of the EU over EU countries — with Germany and France (but now just Germany) controlling the EU.

And the European peoples in large part still don't realize that they are now, for most practical purposes, part of Greater Germany. But of course it's very important that they don't realize this — and thus, they keep their parliaments and Prime Ministers and the like, so that the sheep should not realize that the power over their own countries' destiny has already been surrendered to the EU and Germany.

But the French people are beginning, finally, to realize that their President, and their whole country, is under the thumb of the EU gang and Germany. And I suspect that allowing the normal French citizen to realize that will prove to have been a terrible mistake for the EU — and in time, will lead to Marie Le Penn becoming President of France, and the whole edifice of the EU and the euro being brought down as the French leave it. If Italy doesn't beat them to it.

Econometrician

Germany is waging an ill-fated economic war upon the rest of the world and the consequences have been and will continue to be dramatic. To imitate Japan is to bring upon the Eurozone Japanese consequences with the added potential to destroy the EU. The Euro came upon without Eurozone binding macroeconomic coordination policy or mechanism. Germany took it upon itself to choose an aggressive export-led growth policy by reducing its relative cost of production mostly by constricting the growth of its unit labour cost. This strategy was successful because Germany had the discipline required to implement it consistently, but also because enough countries of the Eurozone went into the opposite direction therefore preventing the Euro to appreciate too much as a result of the German strategy. Proof of that is that up to the crisis the Eurozone had a +/- balanced trade position with the rest of the world.

The fact is China has implicitly acknowledged that 'my surplus is your deficit' and is progressively shifting its export-led focus to a domestic one. The fact is that the Chinese currency has been appreciating more or less in line with what US 'suggested' it shall. Unfortunately, while Germans obviously know how to produce high value-added goods, their ability to understand the ultimate consequences of their actions is not as obvious. Even more unfortunate is the inability of European politicians to understand what is at stake and to acknowledge the facts and tell the truth to their citizens.

All of the above is irrespective of monetary policy that has shown that by itself it is not a sufficient tool to correct such situation. In fact flooring rates for long periods with little effect to show for is an indication that a major structural problem is not being addressed properly if at all. It has also induced distortions that could ultimately help a deflation spiral to take place. Most European economists will never criticize European politicians for fear of retribution. Under German guidance the Eurozone is self-destructing.

Clemens F

However, the argument to blame Germany is flawed:

1) The U.S. is receiving the bill for the hallowisation of its economy in the 90's and 2000's. The focus on R&D and services only, leaving production to be outsourced to China, the then workshop of the world, is now demanding its toll.

2) Due to the nature of German exports (machinery, cars and chemistry), a consumption of more of those goods within Germany is difficult to achieve.

3) The current surplus is largely due to the fact that fuel prices sunk over the last years (prices were driven down by shrinking demand and new supply methods such as fracking in the US).

4) Up until today, Germany's labour costs were kept low and did not enter the circle of higher wages without higher productivity, which many southern European countries did. Why? Simply because the exchange rate of Deutsche Mark to Euro was too low, causing a severe loss of competitiveness within Germany, hence the regain of competitiveness has taken nearly a decade.

Bernhard Otto – German Viewpoint

When Germany is a weight upon this world, what is then the United States of America? I see it the following way:

1) The US has for many decades exported mainly newly printed Dollars. This was and still is the main export product of the US. There was nothing wrong with it in general since this was necessary to provide the world

with the growing demand for US Dollars, which is the "Worlds Currency", besides being the local US currency.

2) Now the US is printing more and more of these Dollars, many, many more than needed by the world economy. The reasons for this are manifold. One of the main reasons is the US fixating on military spending which dried out other sectors of the US economy.

3) Now the other major players in the world especially the BRICS, Brazil, Iran and others have decided that enough is enough since the print orgy of the US is exporting inflation to them: as this is the side effect of the export of the US Dollar (which functions as the world currency). The more the FED prints the more the US is exporting inflation to the world.

What the US wants first of all is that the Chinese currency, the Yuan, is rising in value and of course the Euro too, because this would cause enormous windfall profits for the US corporations as far as their international activities are concerned. The showdown between US/UK Empire and the parts of the world which do not belong to their empire is what we see now. The US desperately needs inflation in the world, huge inflation. The question arises: is inflation good or is it, as many see it, a confiscation of capital (inflation destroys capital) while the benefits all go to the US.

As far as Germany is concerned the US has to make a crucial decision. We can see this now with the spying scandal going on. This was no scandal at all. It is just becoming visible that Germany was not an independent nation till now but a vassal state of the US. The most important and best controlled and spied on vassal state. The US has more rights and power to do what they want than the German government. This was and is the case since the end of WWII.

Germany alone can never get back its full sovereignty as long as the US does not want this to happen.

The problem is, that Germany is very important for the US, but at the same time the centre part of Euroland and the EU. Therefore the question arises, how this thing is playing out? It is of great importance for Europe as a whole. Italy shares a similar fate with Germany, it is the "key" country in the Mediterranean. It is the second most important vassal state of the US/UK Empire.

In my humble opinion, the US should in this case "learn from the Soviet Union" not how to win but how to give up with grace as it let go of Eastern Europe as a whole. The US should let go of its part of the blunder from WWII and let Western Europe go so that they are free to do what they want. Everything else is no solution; everything else makes the problems only bigger.

The US can also learn from the former Soviet Union on how to get back on its feet once the painful transition period is over. Europe wants to be a friend for the US but no longer a vassal.

The US should respect this.

Aristotle   ***   2015

Nietszche called it "ressentiment", Durkheim called it anomie…
…when the dream is infinitely better and more real than reality.

Stan Justice

Germany once tried real austerity and it didn't work very well. In response to the world-wide economic slowdown of 1928 and the market crashes of 1929, the Weimar government's austerity plan pushed by Chancellor Heinrich Bruening at the behest of his conservative coalition included a balanced budget, the forced reduction of wage levels and social programs, elimination of the unemployment insurance fund, lowering of property taxes, agricultural subsidies (Osthilfe) to prop up the East Elban estate owners, the delaying of public works programs to reduce unemployment until the budget was balanced, resistance to additional taxes on the wealthy, and most insidiously, a behind the scenes agitation for a presidential dictatorship (can anyone say technocratic government?) to carry out these measures.

When the elections of 1930 were held in Germany, the campaign did not centre on the hyperinflation of a decade earlier, it centred around the conservative government's austerity measures. And what was the result?

Hitler and the National Socialists, who hammered away at the plight of the lower middle-class, jobless school leavers, rural villagers who depended on handicraft production and farmers suffering from deflationary commodity prices, polled over 6,000,000 votes and increased their representation in the Reichstag from twelve to 107 deputies while the Communists, recruiting workers disaffected with the failure of the Social-Democratic led trade unions to halt the slashing of badly-needed social programs they had long fought for, attracted over 4,500,000 votes and increased their parliamentary representation from forty-four to seventy-seven deputies.

Democracy in Germany died that Election Day; it took three more years to bury it. In the meanwhile, despite the gains by the two radical parties, the conservative government insisted on continuing with its austerity program, leading to even further aggregate votes and parliamentary gains by the Nazis and the Communists in 1932. Yes, Germany once tried austerity. Yet their leaders of today, stumbling about in the murky myth of hyper-inflation, seem to have forgotten history's savage lesson as they push the Eurozone's peripheral nations to adopt many of these same poisonous palliatives.

What is hateful to you do not do to your neighbours.

Felix Drost

Look at the increasingly rationalized and automated world-class capabilities of the German economy, there should be no contest that it will continue to grow and grow at the expense of other European economies who have no way to defend themselves and no mechanism to achieve similar productivity and, vitally so, scale. All Eurozone economies are profoundly exposed but are not sufficiently integrated with Germany to benefit; the German economy simply does not sufficiently scale outside its own cultural and linguistic area to deliver benefits to the entire Eurozone.

Now that the Euro is down so much vs other currencies, the German economy will further heat up. But we're not seeing similarly bright flares in other European economies. Even economies like the Dutch and Finnish ones that used to mirror Germany are not seeing much recovery and unlike Germany have been shedding many jobs, adding debt, seeing housing prices drop, etc. This de-facto devaluation vs. the dollar/yen/yuan may help some but it is lopsidedly favouring the German economy. As companies like Volkswagen are sitting on ever greater mountains of cash they will be able to invest and improve their competitive advantage only further. But these investments don't often enough take place outside Germany.

It seems to me a rather inescapable conclusion that the German economy has grown at the expense of other Eurozone economies. Those countries that could chart their own monetary policy such as Poland and Sweden are doing well. One would wonder how Italy would do if it had control over its own monetary policy, at the very least it would not be in denial.

We need to realize that the Euro was a terrible idea; we're still in denial over it. But the realization that a break up is even worse is equally important. We need to restore the transfers of wealth that previously were part of the ERM, the ability to devalue the currency at the time was that mechanism and did amount to a transfer of wealth because it changed the economic dynamics between economies. Such sharing of the wealth is necessary.

Anyway, we do arrive here at the point where in the next few years increasingly jobs are being replaced by robots. This is already part of that movement as Germany is turning into one of the wealthy rationalized and robotic production zones and has solidarity only within its own nation. If this is the future pattern, nationalism is about to make a return.

Risk Manager

Why did Germany agree to the Euro?

I should think they were amazed when the people they had been complaining about repeatedly devaluing their currency were now offering to lock their FX rate. Suddenly the Germans thought their export earnings were safe, but just beyond the end of their noses default is of course what they will get, eventually. There was a reason currencies devalued against the D-Mark. Permanent export surpluses are bad for both sides, just at different times in the debt/bankruptcy cycle, debtors first and for a long time, then creditors fast and hard in the denouement.

The Invisible Hand

The too clever EU leadership shifted a few hundred billion euro owed by Greece to EU bankers onto the shoulders of EU taxpayers, even though they knew the debt was impaired, to put it mildly. It is bad enough that the EU leaders swindled their taxpayers. It is even worse that they transformed a commercial problem between Greece and its bankers into a political dispute with unfortunate racist overtones between nations.

Looking at the balance of payments performance of various European countries in the period 1990-2013; which covers nine years prior to the Euro and fourteen years of the Euro. It's not easy to miss the inflection point. In 2000 there was a dramatic change in direction – Germany's export performance greatly improved and most of her other European partners suffered as a result. Between 1990 and 1999 Germany had a manageable trade surplus of between $15-60bn, almost immediately after joining the Euro Germany saw its trade surplus balloon to over $200bn annually.

This had a detrimental effect on the rest of Europe as France and Italy, who had been running surpluses, went into deficit and for other less well developed economies the effects were much more catastrophic! The total advantage the Germans have gained from the Euro so far has been about $2.5tn – that's a lot of zeroes! So when Greece wants to be cut some slack Frau Merkel should remember that her economy has been exporting cars, pain and unemployment to the southern members of the Euro-zone for the last 14 years and its time she got off the PIIGS back!

Teacher

The entire EU philosophy is bankrupt. So everybody has an idea on how to patch it, rather than do what is necessary: discard it. The idea of a common currency but with no Federalism of States is futile. Especially when the core government system of the member states is Socialism. The idea that all these sovereign nations will set aside self interest, the unique issues their own nation faces, promised entitlements, and everyone agrees to some kind of universal budget / fiscal / monetary policy...one size fits all...but without Federalism...is just plain asinine. Like so much else, the entire EU project was meant to be Bait and Switch. First start with a common currency, and promise it'll never go further than free trade. Then later, when in crisis, get everyone to agree to give up sovereignty and become the United States of Europe. Since that didn't, and likely won't, happen, then the project is a failure. Move on and get back to reality.

Charles Shillingburg

Mr Draghi expects hard reforms will raise potential supply; the extra investment will stimulate demand. This premise should be challenged. With LEAN embraced globally, consumer demand comes first, then supply. The focus is on only providing the supply needed to meet demand, not building up supplies. Investment is only required when demand exceeds the existing capability and capacity. Another premise of Lean is scalability. Therefore, existing production systems have built in capacity, so it takes longer for existing capacity to be exceeded (In some cases, industries have excessive capacity that would have to be absorbed.). Demand will have to significantly, consistently rise for firms to invest in additional capacity. In other words, they need to be able to better trust that increasing demand will be sustainable for them to add capacity.

Governments need to do whatever it takes to stimulate consumer demand to drive their economies. *Faith* in the future is a key component of this.

Dr. Hu – U.S. Viewpoint

Back to the imbalances that are the heart of the crisis:

But as some guy said, "If nothing changes, nothing changes." Thus, pardon me for sneezing at any assumption that the US consumer, outfitted with a (relatively) strong currency, will once again become the buyer of last resort, fuelling that great engine of global growth that will chug and chug and pull the entire world out of the economic doldrums. Our wages are flat, as they've been since the 90's. Our credit ain't what it used to be in the days of the housing bubble when many of us were sent five credit card applications to clutter our mail slots each day.

Many of us are still de-leveraging from the binge days. But nowadays we saunter through the aisles (and petrol lanes) of the local Walmart and discover everything is cheap again. Tough choices: Toyota or Subaru? Samsung or Apple? Sure, we'll consume beyond our means — so long as some accommodating bank dishes out the credit. But we're more apprehensive than pre-'08, glancing over the shoulder to make sure the transactions will clear. Our kids hold student debt in excess of their parents' credit card debt—no house for them!!

Meanwhile the global economy sputters, currency anarchy reigns, imbalances soar. China would love to devalue, but that would exacerbate currency outflows, inviting condemnation from trading partners and stressing all those corporations foolish enough to borrow in dollars. So they accumulate record current account surplus, but must sit on (i.e. "hoard") the excess dollars. Geez! Maybe old John Maynard was right: without some mechanism for adjusting currency rates to the real relative strength of economies (his 'clearing house'), "currency hoarders" will wreak havoc on the system of global trade. It's strange how the "neo-

Keynesians" ignore that aspect of the purported "Master."

So, the big questions remain. Can the Eurozone endure without Germany agreeing to run deficits for a long while as the Club Med nations "rebalance?"—not likely. Will China really follow through on its transition to a "consumer economy," also accumulating current account deficits for years while its financially repressed citizens catch up with their counterparts in Greece, Spain, and Germany—not likely.

More importantly, in a global economy roiled by the addition of 2 billion new EM workers (see Alpert, "The Age of Oversupply," 2013), can finance capitalism under the WTO regime create enough jobs to keep our younger generation gainfully employed and our tax coffers sufficiently filled to permit the continuance of civil society. There is no reason for optimism there either. Our global demand dearth is really a dearth of jobs – a nasty mismatch between the power of technology, a glut of willing workers, and the ability of the worker-consumer, in the aggregate, to buy all the stuff they, in the aggregate, can manufacture.

It is I believe an error to see the peculiar German obsession with the running of immense and highly destabilising trade surpluses as a feature of the country's economic policy. It should more correctly be seen as long-standing and central to German foreign policy, originating in Welhelmine insecurities prior to WW1, when Germany's financial firepower was seen as being an inadequate match to the strength of its armed forces.

To right this perceived imbalance, in the decade or so before 1914 Wermuth and Haverfstein, Germany's then Finance Minister, and Reichsbank President respectively, commenced a measured and deliberate policy of accumulating gold and foreign currency reserves well in excess of any reasonable peacetime requirement, with a view to reducing Germany's dependence on foreign creditors, and to provide it with the resources to finance essential wartime trade with neutral states, and subsidise its allies.

With the passing of the second and third Reich, any logic behind this policy has passed also into history, but this policy nevertheless has remained essentially unchanged for so long that the necessity and rightness of aggressive mercantilism is seen by Germans as being self-evident. Germans, in their ignorance, are proud of their gigantic trade surpluses, which have become a part of the German national psyche, along with their atavistic and myth-ridden terror of inflation.

In seeking policy change, we are therefore wasting our time in appealing to Germany's better nature, to its sense of self-interest, or even to its commitment to peace in Europe, and we can remain sadly confident that, unless forced to the brink, this central plank of German foreign policy will remain entirely unchanged regardless of changing circumstances, or anything else. Pity then the unfortunate Greeks who will remain as always from Artemis, while the Germans align themselves smugly with Mars.

Remember Lincoln

Greece should be out of the euro and as fast as possible. Conventional Economic theory does not take into account that people see what is going around and act accordingly. Nobody will keep their savings in a corrupt country and companies will not invest there if they are not privileged by the government. Germany and Greece cannot and should not be in the same economic union. Money will go from Greece to Germany in spite of all efforts against this movement. People know that a contract in Germany will be honoured and not in Greece. There is a lack of *confidence* and it is almost impossible to change this situation.

Zander

Unfortunately Germany understands only *power*, collaboration and cooperation on equal basis is simply not deemed important or efficient, only *power* is efficient. This means that Germans will never let go; let alone "compromise" to let weaker nations have their way. This is the main reason why weaker EU nations must leave the Euro.

Mr. Alexanderman

Mr Wolf et al,
If you money printers wanted a better world, you would seek to understand why Germany is more productive. That would be the focus of your quest for economic understanding. What you will find is that there is a reason why economics is a moral theory to the Germans. Wealth creation is a product of individual effort and character. Try putting that into your econometrics, and you'll be left babbling at the black hole in the theories put forward by the collectivist academic world. Step outside the non-science of economics, and seek a better theory of wealth creation and economic governance, because the world needs better solutions than the 20th century trash you are peddling.

* They say it's a moral theory; but Genghis Khan had a moral theory too; which rationalised wars of annihilation. Just because Germans are motivated by morality; doesn't prove that their goal is benign. Recall that members of the German parliament have suggested Greece sell islands and even the Acropolis. Three possibilities coexist: that they are in denial to the risk to their savings that have been invested in other Euro countries; or they have been seduced by the feeling of dominance that creditor status offers over debtors; or it's a geostrategic plan to increase relative power before the US/UK collapse with the goal of restoring full sovereignty. US forces are based in Germany, UK, Italy, Greece, etc.

Pepin

What is often overlooked is that Germans themselves are victim of these foolish policies. Germany is the biggest capital exporter in the world and most of this capital is very poorly invested. Specifically, as it is invested in countries that Germany is in the process of bankrupting. It would be good for Germany if its current account were to move back to balance: the country would be much richer. At least the average German worker could comfortably afford a Greek holiday again—which is no longer the case now. The current situation is barely distinguishable from producing all those excess goods and dumping them in the North Sea.

What is the point?

Realist

1. It seems to me that some of the basic truths may be roughly as follows: the good Anglo-Saxons happily exported most their engineering-"outsourced" the dirty work. The new knowledge and "industry" was finance. Universities and the job market extolled "Finance", not engineering. The financial sector provided the jobs to the budding "masters of the universe". "Sound financial engineering" provided the easy credit to generate demand for goods that others manufactured. A rather happy outcome, until the 2008 financial crisis came along.

2. Germany stuck to engineering, in education and work. The result is that it produces first class manufactured goods that no one else does, and high class financial chicanery is not the daily routine. German manufactured goods are actually in demand, and just not in hi-tech goods- even the German saw blade (to cut the wood) sells at a premium price and is actually bought.

3. Just where do we expect to find the sources of US surplus. It has a "defence industry"- a euphemism for killing machines; and sells all this junk allegedly to the petro-monarchies. Perhaps something may be possible there. On the other hand the United States has availed every opportunity to increase its deficit, nothing like a good solid war to ruin the external as well as the internal current account!

Executive

Germans are just playing the Capitalistic game to its extreme: They have been squeezing their own labour force (salaries cut) during the last decade, a policy what I would call a "Beggar your Workforce" strategy. The Euro was just a means to eliminate the currency risks involved in that strategy and make it easier to recycle the surplus into the periphery countries. The alternative of "expansionary" policies is not less harmful, not to say hypocrisy. QE (1, 2, 3...n) and huge fiscal deficits are just "Pseudo Keynesian" "PK" measures aimed to generate "artificial" demand. Why artificial?

Because no one is able to say how this demand will be financed. Moreover, no one dares to think of how long these emergency measures will remain around. It´s even worse: The PK measures are just inflating financial asset prices and squeezing the retirement plans. The only coherent answer to the German inner logic should be a new paradigm based upon the recognition that the genuine demand motor is the end (mass) consumer. The "problem" with that paradigm is that the consumer is, by coincidence, the mass working class—and in order to generate genuine and lasting demand, output should be distributed in a more equal fashion.

Olaf von Rein

In response to all: Imagine an economy that produced the best of everything in any quantity. You can raise internal demand in that economy to any level you like and it would still not import — continue to export. Germany is not that economy but it is a lot closer to that point along the Capitalistic continuum than the UK, say.

Miles   *******   Jan, 2015

The market reaction gives some insights: fixed income and equities are up on both sides of the Atlantic. After all, we have all learned that 1Tn in QE pushes up liquid asset prices. Some commodities were an exception today but they will follow through the purchases of index ETF's and other products as liquidity trickles into markets.

For sure the financial industry is as happy as can be: some banks close to bankruptcy were given a lifeline today (and some bonuses to follow), governments can keep financing existing liabilities without the urgency of reform, central bankers have proven to be the real policy-makers albeit (or because of) lacking democratic legitimacy and financial journalists their cheerleaders. The more serious question is precisely the one that should have been answered before going into QE: will the liquidity trickle into the real economy since we expect banks to start lending into the real economy? My answer is a question: whom would they lend to?

I just came back from Italy and have to say that even if you parachute 3Tn over Rome alone there simply is no way one can invest it profitably there. The reason is very simple: one cannot populate a basic CAPEX 10 year discounted cash-flow model.

First, we have an impossible tax, social and employment law situation as well as other peculiarities. I guess one would call it a Supply Side problem as is proven by the lack of new entrepreneurs or start-ups. Second, there is no market for virtually anything as many companies are (or are close to being) bust, incomes are stagnating or falling and uncertainty favours less excessive consumption; unemployment is rampant. That is a Demand Side problem. Third, there is no visibility over 3 years let alone 10 years: at what rate would you discount your (already shaky assumptions about) earnings? Nobody can assume rationally that interest rates will remain where they are — and especially not in southern Europe where loans are effectively subsidized today.

What will be fiscal policies given the high deficits, what will be monetary policy given the central banks are already all in, what will be the level of the Euro given all this intervention?

Given you can't invest profitably there is no private demand for credit and there is no credit supply since few investment projects would pass the initial risk checks of banks. So the choices are we leave investment to governments, i.e. banks buy an equivalent of new government bond issues to finance fiscal policy or they keep the cash which will eventually find its way to the liquid markets. The first option seems far-fetched because governments are busy financing existing liabilities instead of new fiscal expansion, so it will be the second.

So do we have a Supply Side problem? Yes. Do we have a Demand Side problem? Yes. Do we have uncertainty? Oh Yes. Can liquidity solve any of this? No, on the contrary it blurs the future as it distorts prices and especially interest rates, exchange rates, liquid assets. Usually, after all is said and done and QE hasn't worked — except in the asset markets — financial commentators ask how come the world doesn't invest in long-maturity projects and durable goods.

Well, try to do even the most basic discounted cash-flow model and see what liquidity did to solve your uncertainty and Supply and Demand side problems. You will find it is a great subject of debate for bankers, economists and commentators. It also is of great use to those above, and to the top income makers. But it has literally no effect on the real economy directly when interest rates are 0 bound or indirectly through higher asset prices. So in a couple years time we will be back — those 95% of us who don't hold many liquid assets poorer but happily indebted — discussing the same topics as we haven't done anything except QE.

But who cares...we need to keep the show on the road.

Liberty is Replenished by Economic Opportunity

The conventional start of the industrial revolution is the 10th of January 1709, the place was Coalbrookdale in Shropshire, the man Abraham Darby. On that day he successfully tested a coke-fuelled blast furnace. Smelting iron with coke ultimately released the iron industry from the limitation imposed by the rate of growth of trees. Coke-smelted cast iron went into steam engines, bridges, and many of the inventions of the 19th century. Only coke smelting could produce the greater quantities of iron desired by the Industrial Revolution.

Before that day there was no measurable growth in output per person. It is a simple economic fact—until the Industrial Revolution economic growth was accounted for by population growth alone. And since that day a saga has unfolded, one where we've dug ever deeper into our planet's store of resources.

In the very distant past in the northern parts of Scandinavia salmon used to be the staple food. There was simply nothing else (almost) to eat. Hence, before industrialization, when educated people were sent there from the south (e.g. doctors) it would be written in their employment contract how many meals a week they did not have to eat salmon. That clause was also common in coal miners' contracts in Asturias in northern Spain. Lobster caps were common in fishermen contracts in New England.

Once industrialization came and poisoned the fish and sucked the rivers, fjords and sea clean, the amount of salmon declined drastically. Today's fat industrialized salmon have little in common with its sleek natural species (of which taste is clear testament).

In addition, the amount of feed that it takes to produce a given amount of protein for farmed salmon is about one half what it is for chicken, pork or beef. The primary reason is that fish are cold blooded, and warm blooded animals burn a lot of energy just maintaining their body temperature. To be exact, it takes approximately 4kg of wild fish to produce 1kg of farmed salmon, soaked in chemicals to kill sea lice and destroying its local environment. High levels of sea lice that crowd around the cages have a devastating effect on migrating fish. Juvenile trout and salmon heading out to sea past the cages are ravaged by the parasites.

The sea lice populations occur naturally but explode around captive, high density salmon cages. The wild fish are covered in lice when or if they stray too close. The lice destroy the fish's fins and will attack the gills. Worst case, the fish simply dies from loss of blood.

20 years ago, c. 30% of migrating salmon would make it back to their river of origin. Now the number is 6%. We don't really have wild populations of agricultural animals. Though we do have wild populations of fish which are under threat from practices harming the natural environment. The west coast of Scotland has lots of fish farms. Consequently, the wild populations of salmon have suffered in direct relation to where the new farms have appeared. On the east coast the wild salmon numbers are much better and there are no fish farms.

Fish meal production is declining rapidly as we are running out of wild fish to feed the farmed fish, so the most plausible protein source for farmed fish are soybean based / plant based protein concentrates. Though since salmon have not evolved to consume such a diet, there's a limit to substitution.

The problem is that the seas are mainly international waters and who can enforce what is not clear. Lots of countries have sold their fishing rights to the Chinese and Japanese who have no concern for fish stocks whatsoever—Japan would also (with Iceland) advocate whale fishing that would rid the world of whales—pretty much what China and Japan are doing with sharks, which are very much part of the ocean's ecosystem.

Closer to home in Europe a blind eye is turned to illegal fishing, such as tuna for instance. Sadly there is no concept of "limited resources" either with fish stocks or with other resources such as oil. When will the idea dawn that with an ever increasing population—because the subject of birth control is in many places deemed too sensitive—we won't have enough resources to provide for our current level of consumption?

Essentially, growth results from getting stuff out of the ground for less cost than would be necessary to have taken the stuff fairly with regard to the people living on the ground, the people doing the digging and the environment. More than a coincidence, surely, that periods of growth run alongside militarisation, colonisation, exploitation and, as we have seen in recent years, massive income inequality, banking fraud and gross moral turpitude on the part of the elite who purport to lead us.

"Value-added" services, such as taking in each others' laundry, have been an embellishment obscuring the reality of the basic model—which given adverse changes to the Natural System—will eventually prove to have been a zero sum game. What is the nature of economic growth? Exploitation of natural resources, including human.

But there are limits to exploitation.

Economic activity is, at the level of physics, the exploitation of energy—to manipulate and move physical things, to even think or breathe. You cannot grow economic activity without a growth in the supply of energy. The bursts in economic activity have coincided (been enabled) by massive leaps in the exploitation of energy (wood, coal, oil, nuclear).

The more energy we put into winning energy, the closer is the tipping point of the growth curve, and we are very close to that tipping point. Trend growth is already decelerating and will continue to do so. It is the ease at which we could use energy and other natural resources, which ultimately created the opportunity for growth. It is that simple. To some extent, human inventiveness may be a functional result of scarcity. However, whatever we do (which has some economic implications), we will need energy.

The energy balance of pumping and winning oil or gas has been substantially positive in the past (and is already less and less so because the cheapest oil was pumped first), but clearly, the energy balance of a solar cell is by far not that positive, even if we double its efficiency.

It is not that productivity growth shall fall; it is that productivity itself is doomed to fall—with the implication of increasing poverty amongst an increasingly broad part of global society. And we are not centuries away from that, it is in the present—US net energy gain from oil production peaked in 1974, with poverty as the ultimate result—for some citizens.

The link between energy and growth implicitly assumes a non-changing energy efficiency. Given the average waste of energy in business and private context, one could argue that peak-oil is relative. Though most systems are now optimised:

In the 19th century new technologies often led to declining prices and productivity-driven growth. Here are some statistics from the 19th century: Average railroad freight rates plummeted from 20 cents a ton-mile in 1865 to as low as 1.75 cents in 1900. Rockefeller's Standard Oil pushed down the price per barrel of oil from 58 cents to 8 cents. Andrew Carnegie drove the price of steel rails from $160 a ton in 1875 to $17 a ton in 1898. The effect of low prices energized the entire economy.

Unfortunately, since Nixon broke the link between the U.S. Dollar and Gold in 1971, it is no longer possible to accurately measure productivity gains, as the production of debt is now measured as producing. So we must rely on Logic, and Logic alone, to comprehend and define the present juncture.

The implicit assumption, thus far, is that technical progress is the driver of economic growth which derives from supply-driven growth theory. When growth is seen to be demand-driven the role of technical progress in the growth process is much more complex and contingent on other factors which drive demand growth. The problem of growth is not one of creating new ideas and generating technical innovation, it is, as Keynes long ago recognised, maintaining strong demand growth which not only embodies technical progress (in investment) but provides the profitable opportunities for innovation.

This problem highlights why population growth is so important to Capitalistic society. Ultimately, with respect to commodities, the total mass of desires and needs contained within society can be satisfied by mass production. This happened long ago in manifold markets—hence the policies of "planned obsolescence", limited warranties, immigration and export led growth via "free trade" were proposed.

When the Financial Crisis struck in 2008, the establishment's analysis of global imbalances was informed by a reading of Keynes, so they assumed an expansionary solution existed. Unfortunately, their Keynesian ideas did not apply to a world Keynes did not envisage—one of finite resources—especially one which had passed peak oil.

So reader, here's a question for you: Do you think we are going back to a period similar to the Middle Ages with no real growth and real returns on capital falling to zero?

Without growth and little need for investment, the real opportunity cost of capital goes to zero; in principle leading to increased competition any place where equity still returns anything above zero. This means margin erosion and return on equity eventually edging downwards towards zero. In the Middle Ages any asset that produced a reliable return (such as a central city property) had a price going to 'infinity' (and a yield close to zero). Strangely those crazy prices are back.

Sure, it's a bubble. But the superficial mind assumes it's **just** a bubble. Perhaps this is just us tumbling back into the Middle Ages. It was Marx who informed us that the evolution of private capitalism with its free market had been a precondition for the evolution of all our democratic freedoms. Is it not surprising that our rights, our freedoms and promises of prosperity are disappearing as the opportunities for free enterprise—provided by Mother Nature—disappear?

It would appear the tree of liberty and opportunity were planted in the same place. Such soil cannot be replenished by blood but by Man entering into harmony with Mother Nature.

The earth's resources already lag way behind population expansion. Regardless of our technology, population dynamics still control us just as it does field mice. The difference is that technology allows us to last longer in our habitat. Unfortunately that just opens us up to a harder crash. Already in many industrialized countries more males are being born. That's one of the signs of population/habitat stress.

Some unfortunately believe that technology will allow us to go on just as we have been doing. Those individuals really are just hoping that they can cash in on the status quo forever. Already potable water is becoming ever scarcer. The water table is dropping across North Africa. Even worse, something like 90% of the earth's population depends on the ocean for food. The oceans are dying, and drinking water will become the most expensive commodity.

We could have a thousand years and we won't "get it right" because there is too much money to be made by "the owners." They have no interest in change unless there is no more blood to be squeezed out. When that day comes, the change will be minimal because "change" cuts into profits. That's not a condemnation of Capitalism: it's how humans are in general.

The defenders of the status qou hope to vindicate Capitalism by measuring growth on a Purchasing Power Parity basis—and so by their preferred metric—the global economy just keeps on growing. But this ignores the very real costs of production which do not enter into the economists' value-added equations—so-called "externalities" such as resource depletion and environmental destruction.

For instance, Pan Yue, vice minister of China's State Environmental Protection Administration (SEPA), estimates that since 1980 environmental damage has cost China between 8 and 15 percent of GDP per year, which means that, once account is made of the heavy-metal contamination of vast swathes of farmland, the poisoning of 80% of groundwater, the ecocide of its river systems, the cancer villages and so on—**China has made no net addition to its wealth.**

When we take account of the fact that capitalistic development, especially over the last three neoliberal decades, has brought the world to the brink of ecological catastrophe, Pan's verdict applies to the entire planet, with a considerable degree of understatement.

When we evaluate the economy from a human perspective, rather than an economist's perspective, we are *already* living through an economic disaster and are inexorably heading to something much worse.

The technological "advances" are fascinating and keep the masses optimistic, but one of the problems is that very technology is what is allowing us to go way beyond the carrying capacity of our habitat. It is a two edged sword. All we can do is the best that we can in whatever circumstances we experience. We must do with less quickly or we will have to do with nothing.

"Technocracy" sounds great, just like Communism and Capitalism did. But like all economic systems they share one major and minor flaw—the greed and ignorance of humans.

All systems are corrupted by greed with the "goods" flowing to the top.

Do we have more than a decade? Probably not. For the loss of economic opportunity is not easily reversed and for many spells the end to their liberty. Since 2008, they have remained passive in exchange for cash payouts. We may be able to keep our societal arrangements together for another decade, but by then it will be too late to change anything—and ignorant men and women will spill blood—not in the name of liberty but over whatever opportunities are left.

Julian AD

Perhaps the developed economies stopped growing after 1970 due to a combination of:

- Ballooning of a welfare state that rewards 'victims' over 'producers'.
- Money printing by governments that devalues the savings and hence the investment capacity of the middle class.
- Increase of GDP that is spent by governments and inherently allocated unproductively.
- A preference for the best and the brightest to choose banking and finance as a career as opposed to productivity enhancing occupations.
- The emergence of 'lowest common denominator' popular culture that praises dysfunction, idleness, unhappiness and disfigurement.
- Decline in practising religion, organised or otherwise, to focus individuals on accomplishment.
- Growth of Political Correctness that prevents identification and rectification of productivity impairments by preventing discussion.
- Low birth-rate reduces the previous motivation of parents to provide for a large family.

A 4th Industrial revolution that may start us growing again could comprise mass produced mobile robots with Artificial Intelligence, or alternatively a new high-density power source that would enable personal air transportation.

Raging Wave

Prof Gordon finds that the 'third industrial revolution', powered by computers and the internet, has provided only a modest and temporary boost to US productivity — but much of this anaemic productivity growth is an illusion created by the outsourcing of low 'value-added' production process and service tasks to low-wage countries. As Susan Houseman found in a 2006 paper (Outsourcing, Offshoring, and Productivity Measurement in U.S. Manufacturing) offshoring, which is likely to be significantly underestimated and associated with significant labour cost savings, accounts for a surprisingly large share of recent manufacturing multi-factor productivity growth.

This points to a larger paradox. Economists measure 'productivity' by dividing total 'value-added' by total hours worked, in other words by the total exchange-value of all the commodities ('goods and services') produced and sold. But this is entirely different from the use-values produced by human labour, much of which (e.g. those created by domestic labour, boosted by labour-saving domestic appliances) are not sold as commodities.

Productivity advances that enhance the utility (i.e. the use-value) of a commodity may (and typically does) simultaneously result in a decline in their exchange value — ever cheaper and ever faster computers being a particularly relevant example. What all this means is that the perplexities and paradoxes of productivity can only be unravelled by distinguishing between use-value and exchange-value. This, of course, is the heart of Marx's economic theory. Read chapter one of volume one of Capital to find out more.

Duvin Rouge – French Viewpoint

Now go the next step and think about prices, money and value. At the aggregate level, total value is total social labour time. This is why growth in labour time (population) is so important to Capitalism.

Growth in labour time allows growth in absolute surplus value (the amount of labour time going to interest, rent and profit). Put a cap on labour time and profit requires a growth in relative surplus value (taking a higher % of the value created by a worker in a fixed time period). With productivity growth this can mean that the standard of living for workers in use value terms can increase even if they are being exploited more. But without productivity gains the class struggle comes into the open; that is, real cuts in workers standards of living to support falling profit rates. I wonder if we are there already.

*Reader, at the micro level, the value of a widget is determined by the market. For example, if you have a used BMW in Munich and advertise it, the market for used BMW's in Munich will determine its value. The price you paid to buy it is irrelevant. The cost to make the BMW is irrelevant. The number of buyers and sellers is relevant and so on. However, if we take a macro picture and wonder what is the value of all BMW's produced in Germany last year, it must surely relate to total social labour time required to make them.

Furthermore, when the citizen's of the US and Europe reduced family size so as to accrue wealth; immigrants were invited into their country because the capitalist system needed them, Germany invited millions of Turkish 'guest workers' that never left. This increased total hours worked.

The system had already lured women into the workforce so that option was exhausted. Children had been banned. This is the main reason why a four day working week couldn't be implemented under the current system. Ultimately, this is our Depression. Immigrants can't postpone the collapse due to automation of the labour force; they just add to the armies of unemployed.

Anise 60

Consumption based growth built Japan, and the US took the model despite the results in Japan. We are now at the stage where we do not know what we do not know and so there are no correct or insightful questions posed.

* Reader, try measuring productivity in the service/consumption sectors in London. For example, when the price of houses in London increased by 20% in a year; then the productivity of a realtor increases by 20% if all else remains equal. No agent will pose any correct or insightful questions because taxable volumes are increasing. The realtor just pockets his increased fees and keeps a low-profile. With respect to habitat stress, the cultures of numerous human groups have rationalised this unconscious biological response to environmental stress. Whereby male children are celebrated by one and all; and where a female foetus may be terminated, which slowly lowers the population size.

Teutonic Fringe – German Viewpoint

Let's start with what we know. We know the financial and monetary systems cannot create **growth**. Growth is created by entrepreneurs producing goods and services that other businesses and consumers see as cost competitive and desirable purchases. There's no lack of money. There's a lack of projects creating sustainable growth with a (risk-adjusted) Return on Investment comparable to that of investing in specific asset classes that don't create (sustainable) growth or investing in projects elsewhere, in particular in the B[R]ICs.

Free debt today will need to be rolled over tomorrow, at interest rates nobody can predict. There is no such thing as a free lunch in this world. Deficits send the bill to the next generation, just to avoid painful decisions today. As if the Greek debt crisis had never happened.

Excessive debt means loss of sovereignty or loss of borrowing capacity down the road.

Michael McPhillips

Significant demand can only come from the real economy but monetary policy is nurturing only the financial economy.

Sovereign debt in many economies should not be marked at zero risk in banks. Particularly those countries' owing nearly total GDP and when what the public sector owes to banks is marked for risk at the same rate as private sector debt; their banks, due to that burden on their economies are in no position to resource growth.

Thus, low interest rates reduce demand when those who spend are not earning more and cannot afford to borrow; when they're not earning more because of higher taxes and government charges. If they're not reversed and investment is not forthcoming, stagnation is inevitable.

The tax needs of governments are controlling prices and if we look to history for the consequences we need look no further than Stalin's Russia (circa 1937) where the top 12% or so of earners had around 50% of national income yet in America it was only 35% while the difference between the highest and lowest salaries in Russia was the same order of magnitude as that of America (around 50 to 1).

When economies are regulated to provide only for the needs of the State — as in wartime or under Communism — economies cannot produce the profits necessary for growth and prosperity because private property that underlies all workable economics is under too strong an attack. This is evident in developed economies when those with the secure jobs and working for the State almost all can afford to and do own property while amongst those who have to pay the taxes for them only a small proportion can.

This is such a confiscation of wealth that makes it impossible for economies to bear without excess debt, recession, and under-performance, not unlike that which brought down the Communist countries. Just like them, too many factories and businesses are uncompetitive, our goods un-exportable, outsourced for manufacture, or non-existent, and no one wants to invest enough to start again.

It was Marx who informed us that the evolution of private capitalism with its free market had been a precondition for the evolution of all our democratic freedoms. It is not surprising therefore that when taxes confiscate wealth and over-restrict the free market our freedoms and prosperous futures disappear too.

Daniel

What is the nature of the demand generated by government spending? Governments can create demand for goods and services, but that does not lead to economic growth if the demand simply gets more people shopping. Quite the contrary: it amounts to further destruction of capital, since the demand is based on more debt (government spending) being used to mop up surplus goods and services. Supply and demand are important parts of our economic system, they are not merely surface features.

Wealth production occurs in the workplace. New value is realised though sales, which produces profit. The profit represents growth and thus is also reflected in increased demand for goods and services. That result, however, is very different from the demand generated through deficit spending.

*Reader, at the monetary system level, Central Banks gradually lose their independence to set rates as the size of the government economy increases relative to the private economy. For example, if France were to have its own independent central bank; the rate would effectively be set by the government as it spends 56% of GDP (Cuba stands at 66%). Over time the economy mutates to serve the government worker, only the government worker can access credit for consumption, etc.

"The crash and the subsequent depression broke the confidence of a generation of political leaders. All the guff they had learnt about a new financial capitalism, self-equilibrating markets and the end of boom and bust was shown to be, well, guff. Seven years on, bankers are once again clinking champagne glasses. By and large, they got off scot-free. Not so politicians who believed their own propaganda and embraced the laissez faire Washington Consensus as the end of history. Capitalism survived the crash, but at the expense of a collapse of trust in ruling elites" Philip Stephens, Financial Times, Dec 2015.

I think this is a very important statement. Here are some thoughts on it:

A) 'The crash and the subsequent depression broke the confidence of a generation of political leaders'

Not quite—our political leaders abdicated responsibility for the crash because they didn't understand it, and didn't want to own their part in it. The crash was a result of decades of Ponzi monetary policy and 'guns and butter' fiscal policy, which combined to produce an unsustainable credit boom—which ended as credit booms always do - it crashed. In 2008, our leaders effectively sub-contracted the economy to a group of academics and central bankers, who have continued with the monetary side of it, whilst they themselves have been only too willing to squabble amongst themselves, arguing about what the band should be playing whilst the ship goes down.

B) 'All the guff they had learnt about a new financial capitalism, self-equilibrating markets and the end of boom and bust was shown to be, well, guff

Indeed, except they still don't get it. We didn't have self regulating markets then and we don't have them now—we have a system better described as cronyism. The misunderstanding of how market capitalism works, and its continuing abuse by vested interests was encapsulated by two huge mistakes:

1. Mistake number one was unleashing the banks from Glass-Steagall, effectively giving them casino licenses. This was a decision made by Pres-

ident Clinton on the advice of his Treasury Secretary Robert Rubin, formerly of Goldman Sachs and the Teflon coated Professor Larry Summers. It was a decision made by and for Wall Street.

2. Mistake number two was bailing out the banks in 2008 and effectively institutionalising moral hazard—this is very important—capitalism can ONLY work when companies are allowed to fail as well as succeed.

The mechanics of how this could have been handled are superbly described by David Stockman in his book: 'The Great Deformation - The Corruption of Capitalism in America'. In a nutshell what could have been done was this:

Lehman could have been 'ring fenced', the shareholders wiped-out, the bond holders given a haircut, the management sacked, anyone who committed crimes could have been prosecuted under the rule of law—meanwhile—the deposit holders could have been fully protected.

The junk could have been segregated and allowed to die peacefully or recover on its own merits. The good stuff could have been returned to private ownership with new shareholders and new management, and the world would have had a wonderful opportunity to re-learn the lesson of free capital markets. Moral Hazard would have been defeated not glorified.

C) 'Seven years on, bankers are once again clinking champagne glasses. By and large, they got off scot-free'

Absolutely. Glass-Steagall was 37 pages, Dodd Frank 14,000.

You can say, rightly, that finance is more complex now. I can also tell you, after 30 years in business, that when a powerful lobby doesn't want something, but is unable to block it, they slow it down, do all they can to remove its teeth, and make it as complicated as possible.

Wall Street even managed to put the tax-payer back on the hook for derivative losses just before Christmas 2014 when they wrote an amendment to Dodd Frank and got a few of their sheep in Congress to attach it to the budget just as the rest of the flock were leaving for their holidays.

D) 'Not so politicians who believed their own propaganda and embraced the laissez faire Washington Consensus as the end of history'

Again, spot on about the propaganda, except this is NOT laissez faire capitalism—these markets have been bent out of all shape by QE and ZIRP, policies which:

i) Enabled the casinos on Wall Street to leverage money to the sky and front run a Federal Reserve who clearly haven't got the foggiest idea of how real wealth is created in a real capitalist system and

ii) Enabled a clueless, irresponsible government to continue to kick the can down the road until an eventual crisis in sovereign debt and/or pensions forces the issue

Capitalism doesn't do zero interest rates Mr. Stephens, never in a million years would money be free in a capitalist system. It is however, an inevitable consequence of a government and a banking system clinging on to the debt sodden Frankenstein Monster they created in capitalism's name.

E) 'Capitalism survived the crash, but at the expense of a collapse of trust in ruling elites'

Cronyism survived and that is why there is a collapse of *trust* in ruling elites. Deep down people know that there is something badly wrong with the way our economy is being manipulated in the interest of governmental and banking elites. They may articulate it in different ways, but they are pretty sure about three things:

a) The geniuses that presided over the last fiasco are still running the show

b) Policy makers have done nothing to address the fundamentals, as evidenced by the still mounting piles of debt

c) When the system crashes again, which it will, they have a sneaking suspicion that it won't be the bankers or the politicians who pick up the tab this time either...it will be Joe Fourpack (he recently had to cut back from six)

Free market capitalism is not dead because it is a natural expression of people's desire to create wealth, look after their families and pursue their dreams in life. But please don't call this monstrosity by that name—call it what it is—crony capitalism and/or socialism for the rich.

German Viewpoint - German Mittelstand Company, CEO

But it is hard to define what "free market capitalism" essentially means, how it corresponds to the Financial System and if it necessarily degenerates into "crony capitalism". Can the assumed benign stages be maintained, or if not, reformed—and if yes, reform is possible, up to which stage of degeneration might that be? And how are the financial systems interlocked respectively in the economic system: as servants or as drivers?

On all of that we can draw ample evidence, not in a scientific way, but still.

Let us look at a few:

The most benign example might be the **German "Wirtschaftwunder" after WW2** up until 1990 when Erhard´s economic reforms went along with a very solid banking system. But it was certainly not free market capitalism. Banks were privileged and recapitalized from the start and then keeping equity stakes, board seats and generally a watchful eye on big industry. It was rooted in German economic culture after a specific, catastrophic breakdown – hard to draw general conclusions out of it.

Compare that to **Eastern Europe and Russia in 1990** where communism was supplanted by crony capitalism from day one. Some countries tried a comeback into more solid forms of capitalism, some with, some without hegemonic support, with more or less success on the way. Experiment is ongoing.

Russian progress under Putin might also be unique: a vast, immensely rich country in a period of high oil prices – once the oligarchs were in check, the wealth really could trickle down. But how will Russia cope with war and low oil prices?

About **FDR´s New Deal**: To me it looks like he slyly co-opted one part of the banking establishment against the other while saving the system by reforming it. The most interesting bit out of it is the Brown-Bothers-Harriman coup d´état against Roosevelt, how it failed and how this failure went largely unpunished - and then unreported by our great historians.

Glass Steagall was certainly a success. The abolition of double liability for bank equity might still be deplored, though. Also, Deposit Insurance is a very sharp, double-edged sword. Speculative finance was corralled out of commercial banking into a special reservoir, named investment banking, where it slowly blossomed until it broke out again first under Reagan and then mostly under Clinton.

London as city and Australia as continent will be a great example of what happens if you run a finance racket primarily on real estate for over a generation. Both draw on immigration as demographic and credit as financial inflator, both are still an ongoing example in primacy of finance over economics – where finance, with a service sector bound around it, is the only economy left.

Now, the **US in 2008 and Europe in 2011/12:** In both instances, there was enough popular support for reform but no political will whatsoever. All we can conclude is that the banks are in power, stay in power and the next big move, be it a bail–in, bail–out or currency reform, will be set up by the banks themselves. That does not mean that every bank will survive – the weaker ones again will be slaughtered to feed the politically better connected ones.

But above all, do not forget: Banking Power, since Rothschild´s times and most probably always, was interconnected with the Empires and Empire´s dirty doings—be it trafficking, espionage, blackmailing, freemasonry and intelligence gathering, war planning and finance and even darker arts. It was so much part of the Empire that it in the 20th century it mainly became the Empire, sidelining kings, nobles and generals.

So what is the nature of the Financial System?

It is a dark, imminent political one. How do you get reform out of, or some form of moral reason into that?

Wall Street Trader

They might not be able to articulate it, but deep in their limbic systems, the young know this life is over. I'll help their frontal lobe with this gem from Derek Foote: "Between 1945 and say 1960, when the dealing rooms were virtually closed – which you may be too young to remember – there were 4 of us in then MGT – now JP Morgan – dealing room and around 8 in New York – and say another 8 banks in London and New York – providing all the loans and liquidity that civil society and business in the real economy needed – at a time when the REAL UK and US economy was growing faster than at any time since 1960. Nowadays, with tens of thousands of useless traders, in several hundred banks in the City alone, not to mention New York, providing us a low growth economy and creating one of the largest casino and PONZI schemes the global political economy has ever known."

With the advent of money printing the financial and monetary systems became one beast feeding upon itself. Ask yourself: When someone with ideological convictions and no profit motive keeps trying to corner a market with unlimited money, should you buy in?

1. Central banks keep showing they will buy bonds and other assets at any price; indeed their actual objective is to drive prices higher (with various weak yet still unchallenged rationalisations).
2. Central banks also have no real limit to their purchases.
3. Market participants have a profit motive and are not all stupid.
   In this environment why not front-run them? Just buy and keep buying... It's one of the best one-way bets of all time and shows no sign of changing. The lower and lower rates which result also mean you can also get more and more leverage to keep buying more and more. With negative rates you may even be paid to borrow! And that payment will come from the savings of youngsters trying to put a roof over their head. Rates are negative in Europe and Japan went negative today. It's a perpetual money machine. Even better: as prices rise and yields fall, the central banks read the meaning as "signs of deflation" or some other nonsense, and respond by buying even more! You really couldn't make it up.
   Negative rates can only lead to more negative rates.

It's a turbo ponzi!

Acetracy

All the regulations in Dodd-Frank bill are easily circumvented by the big banks, off-shore financial entities, hedge funds, etc. because there is no way the government can effectively be a constant watchdog on these huge global institutions. DC legislative squabbles are merely a smoke screen. If the Administration, Treasury, and Federal Reserve were serious about reducing the risks of another 2008 financial meltdown, there is one simple step that can be taken: lower leverage. The Federal Reserve can easily increase margin requirements across the board on equities, bonds, commodities as well as all derivative contracts based on these asset classes.

Excess leverage has always been the culprit for crashes. What is scary today is that the level of margin debt on the NYSE is at an all time record high. Today's rock bottom, low interest rates have made leveraged carry-trade extremely cheap for traders. The US supposed 'regulation' of the big banks is merely a ruse to assuage the public ire. In reality financial engineering is still the major game on Wall Street.

B. A.

Catch all solutions like 'lower leverage' and higher capital ratios are not particularly smart. Such measures are the equivalent of sand in the gears. We need to understand better how come we ended up with so much risk in the first place. People still think of financial risk as if it was similar to earthquake risk. It's not. Financial risk is a function of existing positions, and existing positions are a function of what was thought to be worth adding to the balance sheet at the time. And that, in turn, is ultimately a function of how we choose to measure performance.

Compared to the real economy, complex finance measures performance in a very naïve way. In the real economy it is "revenue when certain, cost when probable", which, in my view, is a great rule. You have to sell whatever it is that you are making before you can talk of revenue. In complex finance, it's not the same. The unspoken rule is, in effect, "revenue when probable". That is what mark to model or mark to market consensus means. You have to convince your risk guys and accountants that by making reasonable assumptions in your complex mathematical model your 30 year product has a positive "mark to market" right now.

And if you can do that, you can declare it as profit right now (less some reserve, to make it look as if you are being prudent, you are not).

The big problem with "revenue when probable" is that it is too easy. The next thing you have is many people chasing it, and as that happens, what was probable initially will become increasingly improbable. What is a reasonable assumption when few positions exist becomes a completely absurd assumption when all banks stuff their books with hundreds of billions of it. Banks didn't exactly load up on risk in the hope of future gains, as a reckless gambler would, but rather because that hope of future gains had already hit the P+L, and was used as a basis for generous rewards for a lot of the people involved. The next thing we start blaming chance, bad luck, inadequate capital and all when in fact the cause of the whole thing started with the fact that declaring P+L was too easy.

We can learn a thing or two from the real economy. Maybe a car manufacturer can reasonably assume that he can sell his large inventory at a huge profit, but that wouldn't be a good rule. That can sound like a good idea, but it's much smarter to take it easy on the "mark to market" gains and let him sell the cars before he can show big profits. Likewise, complex financial products may look fantastic on day one based on what may truly look like very reasonable and prudent assumptions. But we should still accrue whatever profit we will make over the life of the product

In short, the best way to reduce the likelihood of a crisis is smarter performance measurement, not sand in the gears.

Change My Worldview

It's telling that you present no 'smarter' measurement. How about this: Economic activity can be thought of as a mixture of value creation and value appropriation. The ideal of innovation is that it creates a great deal of value for society, and the innovator gets to appropriate some fraction of this (this provides the incentive to innovate). When it comes to financial innovation however, the effort is expended entirely on appropriation, and the activities create little (or negative) value for society. Merton H. Miller made this observation in his 1986 article on financial innovation: "the major impulses to successful financial innovations have come from regulations and taxes."

This value creation/value appropriation logic applies to trading activities more generally: traders create value through the liquidity they bring to financial markets. But beyond a sort of threshold level of liquidity it is hard to see where any additional societal benefits arise; it becomes an appropriation game of the type Michael Lewis describes in Flash Boys.

So, perhaps, we can learn a lesson from the Communist Party in China. The Chinese State owns almost the entire financial sector. Superficial observers assume everyone evades paying tax in China but no one avoids the financial sector. No one avoids that tax.

Oregon

The most important advantage to society afforded by stripping private banks of their usurpation of the government's prerogative to create debt - the elimination of interest paid to banks for their magic money-from-nothing scam. A recent study done by Professor Margrit Kennedy shows that debt based money adds 35 to 40 percent in overall cost to everything anyone buys - and most of this siphoned wealth goes directly into the pockets of a very tiny minority. I submit that it is no exaggeration to say that interest paid to privately owned banks for the money they are allowed to create from thin air is the root cause of virtually every evil humanity is faced with today.

Here is an excellent article by Ellen Brown on this study:
http://www.globalresearch.ca/its-the-interest-stupid-why-bankers-rule-the-world/5311030

This is the engine that drives the growing concentration of wealth in the hands of fewer and fewer individuals, a phenomenon which in turn exerts a profoundly corrupting influence on governments and social institutions at all levels. The catch 22 Gordian knot we are faced with is how do we manifest the necessary reforms through political systems that have been captured by these very banking interests that will do everything in their power to prevent any such reform?

Tsotsi

The richest 0.001% either controls the media or are close allies of those who do. The damage is not done by the richest 1% per se: most of this group are wealthy on a global scale, but true influence is limited. Most of this group are simply content to not 'rock the boat'. The combined political influence of the top 0.001% and the ability to 'mind control' the rest of us means that there is little prospect of voluntary or peaceful change. The only event that has ever perturbed the über wealthy is World War. Even then, the top 50 to 100 families come out relatively better than the rest of us.

Adam Bartlett

The money powers at the centre of the neoliberal/neoclassical consensus don't really want a truly free market where they'd be exposed to significant risk. That's just an outer doctrine sincerely held only by those at the edges and some of their allies like fundamentalist Austrians. What they want, and have successfully achieved since the 1980s, is a fairly powerful state that governs principally in the interest of the capitalist class: socialism for the rich.

Paul A. Myers

The democratic political elite, operating with their economic policy deputies, have learned how to use endless state credit creation to avoid making painful structural economic choices. Credit creation becomes a substitute for meaningful policy reform. Credit creation tends to sustain consumption to keep the public in some form of comfort zone which will keep the elite in power. But the lack of policy action results in stagnant employment and significant youth unemployment. Incomes no longer rise. Neither globalization nor nationalism drives this stagnation but rather stasis in government policy making. In the EU there is not enough integration to mount unified and coordinated policy responses.

France and Italy hope for some form of external subsidy to keep employment afloat in what are moribund economies. Both countries cannot afford reform so they avoid it. Neither Sarkozy nor Hollande has put forth a credible growth plan. They can't face the trade-offs.

With respect to the USA, Congress believes—deeply—that there is a pain-free path to prosperity through "free" monetary creation by the Federal Reserve which is distributed into the economy through capital markets dominated by very large financial institutions. A powerful group of well educated, quite bright, highly articulate financiers has explained to Congress that a low-capital, high-bonus capital structure is the only structure that can deliver on "prosperity" and "jobs." And of course less capital and more bonus are part of "letting the markets work."

Why does this group of financiers dominate the public debate? Because these are the only people allowed to become policy makers and high officials in Washington. Lesser resumes are screened out. The mandarins conduct an in-house debate and call it a "public debate."

Who constitutes this oligarchy? In the US today, the oligarchy is drawn from a few dozen universities and grad schools, a few dozen financial institutions and their law firms and lobbying firms, and some captive think tanks. If you are not part of this group, when you get to the revolving door you find out your key card doesn't work. Homogeneity? This group makes vanilla ice cream look diverse.

As to Goldman officials calling clients "muppets," undoubtedly at the top-floor boardrooms across New York they call the Senators and Representatives "muppets" when they deign to ask if the retainers are doing satisfactory work for their munificent remuneration. And by the way, are you going to the reception over at the Clinton Global Initiative? Bob says it would be a good thing to do!

Global

Dimon 'runs' the only Bank with a capital base below the FED's viability threshold, $22bn below, despite having 42% of the entire US banking industry's tradable assets on JPM's book. Citigroup have 23%. This unmanageable oligopoly effectively determines FED monetary policy which supports the 'value' of these assets. Dimon wants no constraints on risk taking and has evidently now taken control of fiscal policy as well.

BTA2

The "financialisation" of the American economy is at the core of the crisis. The complexity of its legal and government system, only serves to divert economic resources to parasitical social classes: politicians, lawyers, accountants and financiers (bankers, hedge fund managers). These are the equivalent of the robber barons of the late 19th century, with the exception that the greedy goals of these at least resulted in real economic output (steel mills, cars, electricity, etc.) The current rentier class does not produce anything of any value; it is about pure wealth transfer without giving anything in return, almost zero economic value added.

The social instability created by these rapacious activities will eventually lead to a severe social discontinuity that will likely sacrifice the most cherished values upon this country was formed: individual liberties, of thought, action and religion. At this rate America will likely go the way Germany went with the Nazis, or the way Rome went after the split of its Empire. Our future generations will be looking forward to the American Middle Ages over the next 100-500 years.

Cynic

You just got to love the statement "*firms and markets are beginning to adjust to authorities' determination to end too-big-to-fail.*" Martin Wolf, Financial Times, Apr 2014

In plain English this means: we have done nothing and will continue doing nothing until everybody has forgotten about it and then we will do some cosmetics, give it a nice and flashy name and sell it to the public as a major reform through our usual propaganda channels. By the next blow-up those at charge will be off sailing into the sunset, those who had to foot the bill of the last blow-up will be gone and the new responsible will dish out statements like: "this time it is different", "no one could have known", "totally unacceptable" and (my favourite) "we gotta save main street."

* Reader, The Economist magazine reported on a looming housing led crisis repeatedly before the hurricane landed. Her Majesty was informed no one saw it coming which was untrue. Tellingly, The Economist did not contradict the establishment narrative that it was unforeseeable.

Praxis

There is a reason why "resolution authority with teeth" doesn't work; nobody resolves a bank in a panic. To do so would feed the panic.

"But what about credit?" I hear you cry, what about it? Credit is debt, and it just makes the rentier richer. If banks were allocating sparse capital efficiently to valid businesses, doing risk assessment, and taking the balance sheet risk themselves, (like Goldman did before they went public) then it may be more difficult for bubbles to form, and for the economy to grow unstable. Yes, growth would be slower, but it would be sustainable. This is not rocket science.

Farmman

Let us set aside the political, power and moral dimension and reflect upon the absurd operational nature of the financial system today. Having been hijacked by PhD economists of the central banks, determined to create inflation and so called growth continuously for decades via monetary policy. The result has been to create massive flows of credit underwritten by assets whose prices have been inflated by the flow of credit.

Many of these assets are so leveraged that the cash flow supporting the asset often are negative and require continual increases in the value of the asset to support the transaction. The value of these assets are as opaque as they were at the time of the Great Financial Crisis, in fact made worse by the suspension of mark to market rules.

So now we have Prof. Martin Wolf (and others) who seeing the problem totally ignore the cause. Why have banks got so big or interconnected that they destabilise the system. The answer is of course the crux of the financial system that requires continual credit growth to support consumption. The cost of this credit has become so great that currently any rise in interest rates from the record lows of today will stall the so called recovery. The BoE and the Fed are going to great pains to convince us that no interest rate will happen any time soon. Yet we are supposed to believe that the UK economy has returned to full health.

The truth, which has made a rare appearance in the pages of the FT lately, growth in GDP both in the UK and the US is not being driven by healthy economic production, instead the same ponzi scheme is operating now as it was prior to the GFC. In the UK it now takes not only a subsidy of the banks via TBTF but also a subsidy to borrowers via record low interest rates manipulated to remain that way via the BoE and a subsidy via Help to Buy!!

The assets of the TBTF banks are mainly housing and government debt, the cost of which is expected to be supported by the household sector, most of those households have a declining household income, in real terms, for the last couple of decades. The TBTF banks have become, thanks to the central banks, the rent seekers of our age.

The absurdity is that commentators, such as Prof Wolf, want to prop these banks up and even let them operate as a cartel sanctioned by the government, as if that's not happening already, and worse than that, looking through his blinkered view, thinks that this is for the greater good and the alternative must be worse.

Before I finish, I must add that writers such as Professor Wolf, write this stuff as if the science behind it is unquestionable, yet we have yet to really recover from the GFC, prior to which, Wolf and his ilk called The Great Moderation, even though many economists at the time, where warning of potential problems, and for their efforts where called, as in the case of Raghuram Rajan, now Central Bank of India Governor, then was of the IMF, was called a Luddite by none other than Larry Summers, all in the cause of healthy debate I guess.

Tulip

An interesting debate but it misses the fundamental, germane fact: private banks create currency out of thin air, and so debt is always greater than currency. The total amount of money/debt must either increase so as to permit existing debt obligations plus compounding interest to be paid back or the risk of default must be realised. Until we reform "money" creation in and of itself, all this techno babble from the Fed is meaningless. We will forever have this intractable problem because the system by its very DNA has to keep expanding (hence the tendency to ever higher leverage) otherwise it implodes. The continuation of ZIRP and QE (or whatever new name is conjured up) is evidence enough that governments know their actual insolvency would be crystallised if the cost of money was not manipulated by central bank "decree" or fiat.

MarkGB

Well argued, well written and wrong.
The first sentence is where the trouble starts: "No solvent government

will allow its entire banking industry to collapse."—Prof. Wolf, Financial Times, 2014.

Here's an unfortunate piece of information — most governments are insolvent. If we take the 'snake oil salesman's' definition of solvency then yes, they can keep printing money. But in the real world, a place that will once again reveal itself before too long — the US is bust. Bust is when you owe more than you make and have no prospect of ever paying it back — the US is bust, and no amount of kicking the can down the road will change that.

The US will never pay off its debt with money that possesses the same purchasing power that it had when it was borrowed, and has no intention of even trying to do so. Washington and the Fed are trying to inflate away the debt. Let's call it what it is — stealing. If your neighbour borrowed a bottle of Bollinger every Monday and returned a bottle of Asti Spumante every Sunday you'd get out of the alcohol lending business pretty quickly. Fortunately, the world will eventually tire of Asti Spumante irrespective of what the US prints on the label.

If Congress had any integrity, which is another way of saying, if it wasn't on the payroll, this could be changed. Failing the election of a few hundred Ron Pauls, and so long as Presidents pander to Wall Street bagmen like Hank 'I saved the world' Paulson, Timothy 'It was nothing to do with me' Geitner and Eric 'I've got a legal practice to go back to' Holder...nothing will change. President Obama had his chance, he blew it — he capitulated to the banks before he even got there.

This system is bust Mr Wolf. All the clever ruses and optimal control models in the world won't change that. The medicine is making the patient sicker. I've never been a fan of Lord Keynes, but the poor chap must be turning in his grave at the mess that his intellectual descendants have created. If he were alive now I suspect he would be shouting 'stop' at the top of his voice. I don't think he'd be sharing a cigar with Ben Bernanke and Paul Krugman, or any of the current crop of academics who, whilst very clever, are not terribly bright.

The Monetary system has three layers – the core is Religion and the unconscious mind – as they formed first. The outer layer is operational and intersects with geopolitics, it explains:

Why we need to beat Russia

We may see Syria as a testing ground for Imperial Power. Russia has tested our influence and shown the World it's wanting, so it's crucial to appreciate why and of what consequence.

Our Imperial weapons give definite form to our Empire. And nothing has shaped our Empire more than the FIAT. The deformation began in 1971, when the US imposed her Power to re-define the rules of the monetary system for her sole benefit. The ability to print IOU's in exchange for real value is more clever than theft as we borrow and do not pay back in kind due to inflation. Our enemies, adversaries and vassals must found their financial systems upon the printed dollar which they must purchase with hard earned money. That seizure has financed a vast network of military bases, bribery, assassinations, coup d'états and perpetual war.

What's not to like? All that Power without taxing the produce of the American people. So why have we lost in Syria? Let's begin by appreciating that the global "FIAT system" is responsible for our moral crisis and departure from virtue. As we embrace further the gods of greed — just listen to the masses cheer for Clinton and Trump — we must recall that virtue is knowledge of what is good. We are getting weak because we have forgotten what is good for us.

The root of this evil is our love of easy money, or FIAT money, defined by those with power as "wealth by decree" which places an arbitrary value upon "wealth issued by men" such that buying power has no natural governor, as it did when gold was freely traded along currencies in truly free markets. But whom, may we ask, has the power to decree wealth? And with such great power to do so, who can be trusted with such great responsibility? No one. That is who.

But nonetheless, governments and monarchies throughout the ages have been entrusted to *issue wealth by decree*. All have failed, because power corrupts, and absolute power corrupts absolutely.

So in every FIAT time line we see the more powerful become wealthier and the wealthy become more powerful, because it is they who control the issuance and distribution of wealth. Inequality of Wealth, therefore, always reaches its peak at the end of the FIAT time line. As social position offers more favours than purpose and production. What has happened is what always happens — you have a system politicized to such an extent that political access — and not profits from innovative new solutions become the core of the incentive structure.

Notice how productivity declined after Bretton Woods and later when Bretton Woods was abandoned. One of the problems of easy money, not the only one mind you, is the financialization of the economy. Financialization drains key human capital and generates malinvestment. Nuclear engineers are doing MBA's so that they can work as investment bankers! Trillions of dollars have been invested in real estate developments that provide no productivity gains. Easy money kept fracking companies alive producing an endless glut of gas that had nowhere to go but heat tar sands in Canada – what a waste!

This is the real economic evil of our current monetary system – malinvestment – with two insidious effects:

1)   A halt in fundamental scientific breakthroughs and
2)   The West, apart from Germany and Norway, has run at a loss for decades

If the common man had a say in all this, he would declare his modest holdings to be the pinnacle of wealth, by *his* decree. He will offer you his apartment for your mansion, his hot dog for your lobster, his bike for your car and so forth. If this sounds ridiculous, then think how absurd it is to offer stacks of paper for these same items, which (based upon the numbers and signatures printed upon them) you would gladly accept, by decree.

We know that paper is just as intrinsically worthless as the electronic digits they represent in a bank account. The issue here is who holds the power of decree. The little people never will. The monied men hold this power — like a parasite feeding upon any who design to offer value at the marketplace.

And that is the cut of the second edge my friends. That is the death blow. The Fiat produced a parasite — the financial sector — that in its greed is killing the real economy. So when we read about absence of opportunity with such empathy, know that the parasite suffers too, as the problem of debt reaches higher toward senior capital.

When we see debt piled on debt just to prolong the dying system, take note that a few monied men enjoy the fruits of this easy money for a time before defaulting ... and with no collateral to make lenders whole, many walk away with nothing more than an impaired credit rating — into a waiting system where debt is harshly devalued.

Monsanto can darken the sunflower harvest in the Ukraine, and Allianz can steal a few tranquil Greek islands, but the ambience is never quite the same as when hard working people had their just rewards, and goodness and charity and kind souls rejoiced — with compassion and cooperation — while loving the narrative of a life written by desiring only the product of their work.

The world this Global Reserve Fiat creates is one of misery and strife where evil and greed feeds upon the spirit, and the world becomes an immoral wasteland of modernity. The worker is discriminated against as all pressure and stress is heaped upon his future, as the law discriminates between debts held as an asset vs. debt held as a liability.

You see, reader, while we all hold "deposits" at banks, which is a euphemism for bank debt, only the lending class (and I use this term in the broadest sense) get to hold debt on their balance sheets as a wealth asset, whereas the little people hold debt as an obligatory liability. If there is a default, all the better as the law allows them to seize the "secured" assets as collateral. Is there a flaw in my thinking? Let us see...

You may say that banks are able to hold debt as an asset because they have the capital to cover that debt — to which I would say, "Really??!!" As we understand the nature of debt in this modern era of ageing debt, and the derivatives that attempt to hedge those obligations, this is simply not the case, as the lessons of Enron, AIG, Lehman, MF Global — ad nauseam — clearly prove. The empire of debt is hallmarked by misery for the masses though this is no accident, for a system cannot discrimin- ate in and of itself. Financial laws are written by and for the hidden agenda of monied men, how can we conclude otherwise? A few of which see war or systemic crisis as an opportunity to rewrite the social contract e.g. the tax payer takes over bank debt, see Ireland, Britain and soon Australia and the Eurozone.

Look at the workers as they make their way home on the subway, standing tightly together, neither wanting nor caring to utter a word to one another, their grey features melted by the stress of their "wealth as debt". Their one stint at consciousness ground away while vampire and zombie stories speak to their existence. Look at the once prosperous cities around you, like Detroit, or Camden, crumbling into 3rd world ghettos. Not exactly a world that the 1% wants to live in, but one they deserve, one of their making.

They can insulate themselves in the Hamptons for only so long until the sirens sound. It has always been this way, and it will always be this way, until man changes his nature by recognizing what is good for him.

Now, the East — China/Russia/India — challenge the Global Reserve Fiat. And when the dollar fails, and it will: For debt is the essence of fiat, and when it defaults, the system defaults with it. Fiat Debt is unstable for two reasons:

1) Because no natural ecosystem is able to sustain unlimited, continuous exponential growth — as all 100% fiat (debt-based) valuation systems require. More debt is required to repay existing debt plus interest. The basic operational problem is: you can inflate a system easily by issuing new "secured" debt against collateral and thereby increasing collateral value (think about mortgages as buying power to buy houses, pushing house prices up, collateral looks fine even if debtors cannot pay interest or principal — as long they can easily refinance or banks can sell recovered properties in a real estate market spiked by easy credit and demographics (like in the US from 2001-2005, or London and Sidney now). Easy credit can paper over affordability and to some extent demographics. Now this definitely does **not** work in reverse; you cannot even stop because once credit stops flowing, prices start to tatter; and in the latter stages even a decrease in the rate of increase might be enough to crash the system.

2) Because it is entered into and created so lightly, and it is based on the

assumption of a fixed future performance by an entity or individual. And when the 98% - their future burdened by intolerable debt, unemployment and declining wages — decide to walk away? The fear of that decision is why interest rates have been going down for decades, to make it bearable not for the good of mankind but to prolong the system. Until then, we watch this balancing act between debt pretending to be wealth, and wealth being treated as a "bad investment".

All performed for the benefit of gradually changing our definitions, as we evolve into a new equilibrium determined by the East. Their collective gold reserves will be large enough to re-price the currencies and free the markets. As we look at the precarious nature of our faith-based money, we must acknowledge the moral implications of "dishonest money". Seizure by decree, whether judged **just** by Constituted Power, is immoral. But the fact that *dishonest money* is so easy to create, control and redistribute helps one understand the wave of immorality that has swept over our world.

Paying tribute with labour and exchange rates is not enough for the empire of debt. Rather, its vassals must accept and embrace the ideology of the empire as well - "Wealth as Debt" and Globalism. It's their separation in language which causes the confusion –Globalism and Absolutism – for they are one and the same thing.

When Russia and China stockpile *honest money*, they attack our most potent weapon and father of our decline. Our Imperial weapon will die by both edges of its own sword, one being the contempt with which it is so easily created to bend the will of the world to its bidding, and the other sharp edge which the wicked are blind to recognize: The evil that sound money prohibits.

Will Russia and China attack the fiat dollar using overt enemy action? Possible, but not probable: as they can simply undermine "confidence" in the FIAT and wait upon the 2% to bury the blade. **The Dynasties of Wealth — Have you ever wondered how they hedge their holdings through turmoil?** The top 85 patricians of which own more wealth than the bottom 3.5 billion humans — will move first. The 1%, then 2% and whoever else left standing will be forced to follow through.

Only Gold has the history, depth, unique qualities, loyalty of the elite and transitional power to challenge any man, any nation, any system on earth, past, present and future. The Dynasties understand this, because they have both witnessed and authored this axiom across generations of asset accumulation.

When they vote, they vote with their ability to make markets, and then reap the profit from the market they make, offering favour to those who protect their interests. They easily control men through greed and are beholden to Gold alone. Gold transitions their wealth recycling system through change.

As the sand peters past the last curve of the hour glass the Dynastic hand is clear to see. So the Neo-cons need to beat Russia, and soon, as only Globalism can keep the markets enchained.

Power Intrudes into Every Human Relationship

America has become brittle in ways not seen from outside because our most important social **instrument** — money and the mint — has been deliberately transformed into an **institution** — the Fed and high finance — so much so that the social utility of money has become secondary to the agenda of those that own and control said **institution**. When we look upon events since 2008, their agenda is quite clear to see — the expansion of personal power, wealth and prolongation of imperial privilege — how can we infer otherwise? It's critical to comprehend the process that has led our nation to this unique juncture and what possibilities for reform exist.

All growth results from an organisation utilising resources. Thus, growth can only be expanded by increasing organisational efficiency or capturing more resources. When growth in production exceeds immediate needs the nation begins to store 'growth' as wealth, e.g. infrastructure, art, knowledge, etcetera.

The organisational structures of the United States—defence, education, finance, transport, and media—are as adept at capturing more resources as they are at avoiding internal reform. Their way of doing things has gone on for decades, which forces our security apparatus to capture ever more resources, via wars of aggression, bribery and coup d'états, so as to fuel expansion of the organization itself and overall growth.

We've seen this script before — it was written before WWII when Japan refused reforms of her political, financial, and economic organizations, insisting that higher standards of living could only be enjoyed by increased resources obtained by force from her neighbours. The United States enforced organizational reform of extractive 'institutions' after 1945 which permitted an explosive expansion in growth in spite of a sharp reduction in resources — land and slaves. German and Italian citizens enjoyed the fruit of similar stories.

Why do organisations expand at the expense of the society they were designed to serve?

1) Capitalism results in labour redundancy – organisations may be used to soak up the unemployed.
2) Capitalistic societies use "jobs" to distribute national income.
3) 1% of the general population are natural predators with a limited capacity for empathy and affiliation, morality is absent and their inner life is a wasteland which they seek to fill with power and sex. Strong and determined predators are attracted to concentrations of power and resources while the weak congregate around easy victims. It's amazing to think that no political or economic ideology recognises their existence and tendency to congregate around sources of power.

Familial, tribal, national and religious groupings are cherished world wide because they satisfy deep seated emotional and instinctual needs. Within such groupings, control and behaviour of the individual is guided by moral and reciprocal feeling. They tend to be happy affairs as an individual's psychic experience is all that he truly enjoys.

A chief characteristic of our Empire is that social rewards are externalized by way of wealth and money accumulation which reinforces particular behaviours – and control is enforced by militarized police forces and 'politically correct' social peer pressure broadcast by the media. The urge to accumulate status symbols is driven by deep-seated insecurity as the individual vainly desires and tries to attract a community wherein his inner life can be expressed — though sadly none can exist within a universal Fascist state. Concentrations of corrupt power fear those that associate and express thought freely, which leads to a growth in the surveillance state and control of the media.

Those that 'buy in' to the dominant ideology resent doubt sowed by those that 'opt out' for they have not relinquished their freedoms. Rather than loyalty to one's neighbour, the externalized 'self' pledges allegiance to economic or political ideologies and parties while those that yearn for self realization reject society, e.g. Occupy Wall Street, anti-religious movements, drug usage, etcetera.

Money in its proper form is an 'instrument' that aids in expanding civilised space and social welfare. Alas, after decades of feasting on the FIAT Dollar, the organs of our state are completely divorced from and indifferent to the opinion of the citizenry. For access to debt meant:

1) Everyone was prosperous.
2) The purpose of a politician became one of distributing unlimited debt instead of prioritizing who gets revenue raised by taxation.
3) Over time, expectations became warped whereby buying power and prosperity became a given and the entire purpose of government was lost to the populace.

We even had articles in The Atlantic magazine asking: "Is government relevant?" Of course not, with unlimited debt, who needs government? Plus there is the little matter of behavioural conditioning: in that in a system with a policy of positive inflation, debts aren't expected to be repaid. They are to be re-financed.

Access to banks (and the Federal Reserve Bank) became the key determinant of success in society. As debt is not neutral within society, the productive became subservient to those with access. Who gets access to it; who gets to "spend" it, who decides to create it. These matter as much as the debt itself. The answers determine power relations within "society".

Central planning via Fiat Debt creation caused a destruction of Representative Democracy because the crony-capitalist benefited from the political connections required to manipulate the "planning." The stimulus worked in the 30's because it was new. It worked in the 40's because there was a war. Its efficacy has declined over time as the social benefits were diverted to 'institutions' captured by the elite, 'institutions' which serve their private agenda, private most likely, because it's not benign.

For the sake of example, the Military Industrial Complex began as an instrument that furthered the welfare of the nation, though fewer and fewer uttered so as time passed by. Social 'instruments' that improved education, agriculture, energy, transportation, housing, finance, and policing have all been transformed by unlimited debt into expanded 'institutions' of power and privilege. The perpetually re-occurring and refinanced debt caused the corruption. The corruption is what kills our society.

Per the above, you cannot have a central state authority of debt creation and democracy. For nothing this centralized can be a Representative Democracy. History is not without a sense of irony as the United States government has transformed into a fascist organizational structure with a likeness to Imperial Japan, which the American people, at great cost and sacrifice, defeated in WWII.

Public 'institutions' or privately owned 'institutions' receiving public monies would be open to reform by the people in a Representative Democracy, which events clearly show is not the case. Have you seen any reform since 2008? Have you even heard a politician utter the word 'reform'?

No, all that's called for, by true believers and sycophants alike, is an expansion of resources to feed the beast. This is in spite of the fact that our organizations are demonstrably not fit for purpose:

A) Our military cannot win the contemporary battle-space
B) Our workers lack the skills to compete on the global stage
C) Our "news" media structure only highlights the lack of genuine choice in society, with five or six organizations offering only a version of reality filtered through an editorial 'position'
D) This list is endless...

Reform is possible, but not probable. The Federal Deposit Insurance Corporation (FDIC) manages receivership of failed banks and has a stellar record due to its efficient organizational structure. Wouldn't it be funny if the FDIC seized the Federal Reserve Bank of New York for insolvency? Wouldn't you love to see them fight their way in? Would probably be like the lobby scene from the Matrix. Don't think the Federal Reserve Army would surrender without a fight.

Since informed circles have ruled out reform as a viable option, we can see good natured people, who have 'opted out', congregate online with the goal of circumventing the corrupt 'institutions'. There is no finer example than Zerohedge which has successfully challenged the 'editorial position' (and propaganda) of the Financial Times and Wall Street Journal. Bitcoin circumvents the banking cartel. Bit-gold circumvents 'the Fed'. The defining characteristic of such countermeasures is a decentralization of power, decision making and organizational efficiency.

A civilisation arises from, is shaped by and rests upon a stable set of ideas. We are in the midst of a civilisational crisis because the FIAT Dollar is an unstable idea, which has destabilised the set of ideas that Western civilisation has traditionally rested upon. A crisis of civilisation will adversely affect all aspects of human life. We can see the Religious, Economic, Political and Constitutional realms of human life become 'politicized' because they are seen as part of the crisis that needs to be solved.

Even Art and the Intellectual realms are affected by the widespread frustration and discontent, with the assassination of artists by Islamic fanatics and slavish intellectuals abandoning principle to gin up the public for more wars of aggression. Family formation, child rearing, food aid and other instruments existing in the Social realm come under political attack. Distrust of the other becomes commonplace as every behaviour can be judged and meddled with for "power intrudes into all human relationships" as the crisis encompasses all aspects of life.

Only 'Fascist Empire' can accurately describe the resulting aggregate where smothered communities rail against their powerlessness and loss of sovereignty. Our Empire's need for ever more resources (and debt laden consumers) has fused together Nation States under a system of global aggression (NATO) - that has placed nuclear tipped missiles on Russia's border, forcing Russia to reply in kind. Our empire is hallmarked by Global corporatism, where debt is held as a wealth reserve asset and all manner of moral hazard, spectacle and illusion is unleashed. But the question arises — is this really the "U.S. Dollar"? Does it represent only the debt of a single nation? Or is it the Global Dollar, a fiat which holds no sovereign or national alliance at all — much like those who abuse the privilege of its issuance?

These questions must be asked, because we know that no member of the dollar faction, at the systemic level, truly believes that taxation of the American people will ever fulfil the obligations denominated in this currency and its derivatives. We must, at this point in time, accept that the old adage of a currency being "backed" by the future production of a nations' people has become obsolete, and that instead, it is the future production of ALL labouring classes world-wide which now back it.

We have printed the FIAT to buy elections, topple regimes, arm the incubus that became ISIS and facilitate other such evils. So the *political* advantage of our Global Reserve Fiat has been weighed and "outed" by the emerging system led by China and Russia. The repudiation of this backing is in fact the essence of the competing system which has the potential to transition our crisis into a civilisational collapse for several Western states, e.g. Greece.

Foreign support for the dollar has been discussed yes, and it is being withdrawn, yes. But we must understand that this withdrawal represents our enemies desire to free their working classes from the obligation to pay future promises which continuing support would imply. Their tribute to our global empire has ended. So we should not see them as our 'enemies' in the traditional sense of the word, they are only hateful to our distant and faraway elite that purport to lead us.

This competing system is driven by a singular idea: *that big investment ultimately yields big outcomes.* China's international investments create domestic demand while improving long-term overall productivity. Her investments in energy corridors across Central and South Asia to the Middle East will lower the cost of an important import; allow substitution of low-grade polluting coal with natural gas while similar investments in transportation corridors across Central Asia to Europe will create a vast infrastructure of almost inestimable future value. Complementing these efforts are China's Silk Road maritime harbour projects across South East Asia, the Middle East and into the Mediterranean. China is "going international" in a very big and profound way and on a scale unappreciated in Washington DC.

The DC power elite seem to take solace in America's massive military spending. However, a look at where China is truly putting resources highlights that China is building its future pre-eminence upon commercial and economic power – the real geopolitical fuel of the twenty-first century. China has an "Asian landmass" strategy that is unprecedented and will make them the predominant power across a vast stretch of territory. These types of investments—a vast web on a massive scale—lead to full spectrum economic dominance.

So one should see China's strategic adjustment is not so much to transform, magically, from a producer to a consumer model but rather to a balanced and harmonic model where each country's resources and expertise are used wisely to balance production and consumption, within a larger regional economic system that gradually indemnifies debtor economies to irrelevance.

When the dollar is used so egregiously to undermine the sovereignty of the nations that indirectly support it, the people will instinctively learn the truth through the moral response by their leaders. President Putin and Secretary Xi are under immense pressure but they enjoy overwhelming support from their people.

As the global reserve fiat dies, it dies a thousand deaths, and a thousand different masks of deception are slowly removed:

➢ those of the compromised courts – who judge corporations to be people

➢ those of the compromised press – who call bribery "campaign donations"

➢ those of the compromised politicians – who governed while Wall Street cut the throat of American workers

➢ those of compromised academia – who call one another Doctors of Philosophy while selling their students into debt slavery

➢ and most ironically, those of NGO's like the so called "National Endowment for Democracy".

It is beyond contempt to see such "morally upright sounding" names given to these nefarious agents of global empire. This is to perpetuate the illusion of the good shepherd for "democracy", while in truth these façades are (nearly universally) agents of financial fraud, regime change, wealth appropriation, sabotage, death and destruction. This is one of the more despicable aspects of the FIAT dollar, such that it rewards terrorists, saboteurs, and puppet dictators in countries where the currency is gladly accepted, to undermine the sovereignty of its own citizens.

Gold is the hope that has been fulfilled in epochs past when men ushered in the darkest ages of the past with the fiat. Perhaps gold is a gift from God that regulates the power and greed of men and their printing presses (and those benefactors closest to the levers). Though make no mistake, be neither nostalgic nor naïve, for theft of Gold requires violence, examples of which exterminated entire nations in South and Central America. Gold should simply be seen as an anchor that helps to keep commercial and governing customs honest; it cannot make immoral men moral.

Some sacrifices shall be made as we pay our final respects to the Fiat, but to be rid of the corruption that absolute power enables will, in the long run, be in the best interests of all people, and of all classes.

Confidence in the Future Evaporates

We may see globalization as a political/economic/social value system (as opposed to an organizational system) because "values" extend from the socio-economic/political realm into our moral, and of course spiritual realm. While organized religion may have its faults and graces, and clearly our values and beliefs extend there as well—globalisation does not fit Religion as defined in volume 1. In order to achieve a stable and coherent globalised economy all economic agents require a standard of exchange that they trust. You would need to suspend your intellect to trust in the dollar, when a trillion can be printed today or 2 trillion dumped by China whenever she feels threatened.

What is The Nature of the Monetary System?
It is an expanding and contracting cycle of honest money and trust to dishonest money and corruption. Yin and yang.

The cycle is about to begin again, and soon. For our "money" has no "labour time value", therefore negative interest rates can be seen as either an outcome of that recognition or a necessary precursor to it:

Confidence in the future utility of paper is the only real value that contracts hold, and all paper money is a contract exchanged today on the assumption it will have value in the future. And when **confidence** in assumptions made by the unconscious mind is shaken? That future can evaporate.

How has the Fiat regime remained stable since 2008? *Trust* and *gold* are related ideas that are timeless and stable in isolation. For both have an organic basis. And gold, being chemically stable, is available to the intellect and senses as is.

Belief is an emotionally laden state of mind; the emotional aspect cements the conviction in place. *Faith* in a nation or institution is the result of a cost/benefit calculation made by the intellect. Scientific output from the field of psychology informs us that the individual trusts family before tribe because they are genetically closer. My Chinese students, aged nine, inform me that they have differing degrees of trust. They trust their mother the most, and then father, grandmother, grandfather, and cousins. They also love their family.

Thus, trust and love are associated phenomena in the unconscious. Trust is an instinct that some nations invite the individual to indulge in, Christian nations in particular. For the Christian is commanded to love his neighbour. Religious rituals encourage this association, e.g. The General Instruction of the Roman Missal states: "There follows the Rite of Peace, by which the Church entreats peace and unity for herself and for the **whole human family**, and the faithful express to each other their ecclesial communion and mutual charity before communicating in the Sacrament."

This amounts to an injunction to greet strangers in the immediate vicinity as brothers and sisters by offering a sign of peace. In this way, by weekly repetition, the notion of a universal family of faith is inculcated in the congregation. The child is invited to associate Christians as family members. Christian Catholicism is inclusive at the unconscious level. *Trust* would have played an important capitalistic role for Christian proto-governments and illiterate subjects. A handshake or public word sealed an agreement. Thereby, *trust* aided Christian nations in the accumulation of wealth and power.

Mohammed advocated mistrust of family, which causes instability between intellect and instinct within the Muslim mind: Koran [64,14] - 'O ye who *believe*! Truly, among your wives and your children are enemies to yourselves: so beware of them!'

Trust has been partially eclipsed by *faith* in written contracts and *belief* in organs of state capable of enforcement. Though, *trust* still has a part to play within family businesses and when the cost of written contract is prohibitive. Trust in family or gold is a stable idea in and of itself for it has an organic basis. Trust extended to community or nation state requires support, these others need to be worthy of trust, or earn trust, by way of predictable and normative behaviours.

I have worked for organs of dictatorial, tyrannical and communist governments in Africa and Asia. An appeal to 'trust' from such governments would cause convulsive laughter [that may last all night.] Western nation states and their security apparatus continue to suggest 'trust' to the unconscious through secular myth, ritual, and symbols broadcast by their propaganda channels. For the sake of example, *'Father, I cannot tell a lie,'* is a falsehood, attributed to a young George Washington, perpetuated in American History classrooms so as to inculcate *trust* in the Secular State via secular mythology. 'Trust' is written on U.S. currency. Suggestions to 'trust' in the nation state and capitalistic society are a manipulation of instinct, per the above. These Secular Nation States inherited this modus operandi from the religious governments that preceded them.

Why do Western Nation States require *trust*? Because they are democracies that promise full participation in public life to their citizens. They require *trust* because they cannot afford transparency. Capitalistic nations are positioned within a globalised framework; they have enemies and competitors that would take advantage of transparency to undermine *belief* in the nation and undercut the nation's global corporate *power*. It is this *trust* in society, more than anything else, which has sustained the fiat regime since 2008. It has been badly abused and when it breaks so shall social continuity.

Mistrust advocated by Mohammed means democracy is not a suitable form of governance for Muslims. Christianity invited the individual to take ownership of the instinct to trust and extend it to others. The priest is called 'Father', the nun is called 'Sister', the monk is called 'Brother'. The *individual* is a Christian phenomenon, a grade of human able to choose Christian nation over kinship, able to choose goodwill to Mankind over familial feeling, able to choose public duty over familial loyalty.

The Christian is a communal creature. The *self* can only become *separate* by way of understanding. Those *separate* men bearing honest and trustworthy means shall flourish, as the time for honouring theft and dishonesty is about to end.

Appendix: Religion has historically affected the language and politics of the State. In Christian countries Church and State have in the past been so close that the Christian ethos has permeated those countries and their societies, even now that they are secular. And their secular citizens carry Christian values in their unconscious so that their normative behaviours are akin to Christian without the ritual. If you want to enjoy a real secular life join me at the heart of the wasteland—China.

Reader, please note that it's how, or for what political purpose, the religious text is used by those in authority that matters. All else is academic or personal. For example, the first Christians after the death of Christ, stressed parts of the Bible which we now overlook. They would barely recognize our religious life as Christian. The spirit of Christianity changed as the Mind came to know itself, and now religious authorities in Christian nations stress (or highlight) parts of the Bible that are in harmony with our present day moral grade and temperament.

Notice how the religious text quoted above is published and highlighted by present day authorities. Of course, the way you analyse religion is based on your experiences and mental cognitions. Since these are personal to you, religion is, at heart, a private affair.

Shia Islamic and Christian Catholic nations enjoy the benefits of a strict top down hierarchy of power—Religion—for they can easily change their 'message' as their nation gains new knowledge and understanding of the World. In contrast, Sunni Islamic clerics are quite independent of influence coming from outside their mosque and can advocate interpretations of the Koran which are at odds with political power at the nation state level—which reinforces tribal feeling.

Many thanks to the legend Roacheforque (USA).

And Who Led us into Our Unresolved Depression
Jun, 2014 – Oct, 2015
Chinese Viewpoint – Cathal Haughian

If you can't comprehend the micro then the macro is meaningless. The micro involves individual transactions and the macro is the whole Natural System. The economy never leaves the confines of the Natural System.

All economic growth depends on energy gain. Unlike our everyday experience whereby energy acquisition and energy expenditure can be balanced, capitalism requires an absolute net energy gain. That gain, by way of energy exchange, takes the form of tools and machines that permit an increase in productivity per work hour.

Thus GDP increases, living standards improve and the debts can be repaid.

Oil is the most energy dense source of net energy gain, except Uranium.

Fissionable metal ores and their refined metals represent a dangerous and security sensitive parallel energy economy of their own. Nuclear power cannot be dug up or drilled for, to be used almost straight away. It has to be made using heavy capital equipment — fuel processing plant and power stations — which are energy expensive, using vast amounts of concrete, metals for special pressure vessels and radiation hardened heat exchangers before the power even reaches a turbine to generate electricity. It is not the quick fix once thought it was because the energy has to be extracted first and the many dangerous toxic elements dealt with afterwards, before it is economically and ecologically viable. Once you have the potential to assemble more than a critical mass of such metals in a pure enough form you become a security risk. Iran is an interesting case in point. For this reason — fissionable metal ores cannot be traded as freely as oil.

US net energy gain production peaked in 1974, to be replaced by production from Saudi Arabia, which made the USA a net importer of oil for the first time. US dependence on foreign oil rose from 26% to 47% between 1985 and 1989 to hit a peak of 60% in 2006. And, tellingly, real wages peaked in 1974, levelled-off and then began to fall for most US workers. Wages have never recovered. (The decline is more severe if you don't believe government reported inflation figures that don't count the cost of housing.)

To mitigate domestic decline energy efficiency was improved in internal combustion engines and computer chips. These gains, though, can only happen once and most systems are now optimized. Also, while total do-mestic oil production declined, absolute net energy gain declined by a greater degree since the cheapest and cleanest sources were pumped first. You can pump all the tar sand you want but the capitalist system is only stabilized and expanded by net energy gain. Extraction of oil from tar sands does not provide the appropriate net energy gain, being too ex-pensive to extract against a background of the Saudi's pumping cheap oil.

What was the political and economic result of this decline? During the 20 years 1965-85, there were 4 recessions, 2 energy crises and wage and price controls. These were unprecedented in peacetime, and furthermore, in 1971, the Bretton Woods System collapsed. GDP in the US increased after 1974 but a portion of end use buying power was transferred to Saudi Arabia. They were supplying the net energy gain that was powering the US GDP increase. The working class in the US began to experience a slow real decline in living standards, as 'their share' of the economic pie was squeezed by the ever increasing transfer of buying power to Saudi Arabia.

Faced with a proud and well armed population during the height of an ideological war with Communism, the US ruling group found the temptation to leverage through the creation of credit money irresistible. The idea that lending and loans was a good thing in and of themselves became the ideology of the State.

The US banking and government elite responded by creating and cutting back legal and behavioural rules of a fiat based monetary system. The Chinese appreciated the long term opportunity that this presented and agreed to play ball. The USA over-produced credit money and China over-produced manufactured goods which cushioned the real decline in the buying power of America's working class. Power relations between China and the US began to change: The Communist Party transferred value to the American consumer whilst Wall Street transferred most of the US industrial base to China. They didn't ship the military industrial complex.

Large scale leverage meant that US consumers and businesses had the means to purchase increasingly with debt so the class war was deferred. This is how over production occurs: more is produced that is paid for not with money that represents actual realised labour time, but from future wealth, to be realised from future labour time. The Chinese labour force was producing more than it consumed.

The system has never differed from the limits laid down by the Laws of Thermodynamics. The system can never over-produce per se. The limit of production is absolute net energy gain. What is produced can be consumed. How did the Chinese produce such a super massive excess and for so long? Economic slavery can achieve radical improvements in living standards for those that benefit from ownership. Slaves don't depreciate as they are rented and are not repaired for they replicate for free. Hundreds of millions of Chinese peasants limited their way of life and controlled their consumption in order to benefit their children.

They began their long march to modern prosperity making toys, shoes, and textiles cheaper than poor women could in South Carolina or Honduras. Such factories are cheap to build and deferential, obedient and industrious peasant staff were a perfect match for work that was not dissimilar to tossing fruit into a basket. Their legacy is the initial capital formation of modern China and one of the greatest accomplishments in human history. The Chinese didn't use net energy gain from oil to power their super massive and sustained increase in production. They used economic slavery powered by caloric energy, exchanged from solar energy. The Chinese labour force picked the World's low hanging fruit that didn't need many tools or machines. Slaves don't need tools for they are the tool.

The US in the 1920s provides a classic example that chimes in with Karl Marx's thinking. The upper crust of society was under-consuming and under-investing in productive enterprises and chose to accumulate wealth and land. In the 1920s, as US agricultural production fell relentlessly because rural farmers were rushing to the towns to find work, yet industry too was failing. Steel production declined, construction fell, auto-mobile sales went down and consumers built up high debts using easy credit.

At the same time, in the 1920s the market in foreign investments boomed. US direct foreign investment averaged $150 million a year in the first half of the decade. It surged to $268 in 1925 and $600 million in 1929. Long term portfolio investment tripled between 1923-4, persisting at high levels throughout 1928. Meanwhile the stock market boomed. Charles E. Mitchell of the National City Bank provided $25 million in credit to stop the market's slide on March 25 1929. On September 18 1929 markets crashed.

The working class thus over-consumed relative to 'their share' of the economic pie. Huge amounts of credit had made working people neglect production in favour of speculation. This was facilitated by the provision of credit from the upper crust. The banking sector inter-mediated between the accumulators and debtors. Once the banks realised that the principal plus interest could not be repaid the system seized up. The run up to the Credit Crunch in 2007 is in similitude to those days though our Depression, per the above and below, has extra layers of complexity including profound geostrategic possibilities.

Without a gold standard and capital ratios our form of over-production has grown enormously. The dotcom bubble was reflated through a housing bubble, which has been pumped up again by sovereign debt, printing press (QE) and central bank insolvency. The US working and middle classes have over-consumed relative to their share of the global economic pie for decades. The correction to prices (the destruction of credit money and accumulated capital) is still yet to happen. This is what has been happening since 1971 because of the growth of financialization or monetisation.

The application of all these economic methods was justified by the political ideology of neo-Liberalism. Neo-Liberalism entails no or few capital controls, the destruction of trade unions, plundering state and public assets, importing peasants as domesticated help, and entrusting society's value added production to The Communist Party of The People's Republic of China.

Total prices can never exceed the value of total social labour time in a single country economy. Alas, prices have certainly exceeded the value of total domestic labour time in the US since the advent of Globalised Capitalism. How?

a) It's hard to compete with a free energy source

b) The Chinese kept manipulating their currency

c) Congress granted China favoured trading status

Prices in the US have since represented total present labour time of US workers and part of the labour time of Chinese workers. If your country is running at a loss then the retail price of an imported good is added to GDP as consumption but was partly funded by credit. Who do you think provided the credit? The difference being that when Chinese workers get old and draw down on their savings part of that *value captured* must be repaid or defaulted on.

This is understanding at the micro level: A US company can buy a t-shirt from a Chinese factory for 1 US$ and sell it on the high street for 10 US$, but if your country is running at a loss part of the purchase was funded by credit. 9 US$ was added to GDP as consumption but the part funded by credit was *value captured* that must be repaid. And most likely the repayment is owed to China. They want their value back, with interest.

Though this is a second order motivation. Their first motivation is power. Power is more important than money. If you're rich and weak you get robbed. The global economic system is not that complex. Contemplate the micro and build up from there. One household's income is another household's expenditure and vice versa. One country's loss is another country's profit and vice versa. A country goes broke if it runs at a loss for too long. Apart from Germany, the West has been running at a loss for decades. When the collapse happens it will be the creditors that call the shots.

This is what the Chinese and Germans comprehend and that's the long game they've played.

UK Viewpoint – Will Johnson

Rising productivity was an important foundation in the growth of workers' wages and state welfare (paid for by taxing profits) during the post 2nd World War boom. Much of the available data suggests that the problem today is not excessive productivity but low productivity growth. In any case, the fundamental determinant of inequality is not the character of technology but the political balance of class forces. The capitulation of both social democratic and Stalinist mass parties to capital over the past three decades has allowed a huge shift in global output from wages and welfare to corporate profits.

Wish lists of nice things that capitalists could do will get us nowhere. If they had any interest in limiting inequality they would not have brought us to where we are. The task of reversing the corrosive neo-liberal ortho-doxy of the twenty-first century rests with trade unionists and as yet dis-organised workers who must re-build the global labour movement: Not in a Stalinist of social democratic fashion but behind a programme of democratic socialist planning in place of the capitalist market.

UK Viewpoint - MarkGB

We are in a debt crisis that has been building for decades. The crisis even-tually erupted in 2007/08 when the subprime housing debt collapsed. The policymakers who had encouraged the housing bubble, responded to the consequences of their previous actions by...creating more debt... through the vehicles of QE and ZIRP. I.E: They kicked the can down the road. This process is similar to giving more drugs to a drug addict. It temporarily relieves the pain of withdrawal but it does not solve the problem. It is a temporary fix, which requires ever increasing doses in or-der to continue the illusion that it is working. Hence we are now being told that raising interest rates is too 'risky', and what is required are neg-ative interest rates, helicopter money, QE for the people, and a cashless society so that people cannot avoid the negative interest rates.

A chart of US debt shows the curve of the hockey stick was reached in the early seventies, when the last link to gold was broken by President Nixon, saving the government from 'spending' all of its gold in a vain at-tempt to keep it pegged at $35 an ounce. This should also have revealed the deception that governments use taxes to 'pay' for their policies of guns and butter — they don't — they use debt. Sadly, the penny has not yet dropped for a sufficient number of people. If it did they would wake up to governments' love affair with debt, and the consequences that this will have so long as they are allowed to spend our children's future.

The confidence that was badly shaken by the de-linkage decision of President Nixon and the failure of the 'guns and butter' policies that preceded it, was then bolstered by the Middle Eastern foreign policy efforts of Henry Kissinger, which resulted in the 'petrodollar'. From then on the dollar was backed by 'black gold', and as Professor Krugman admitted in an irritated interview that will eventually come back to haunt him—'men with guns'.

From the late eighties onwards Mr. Greenspan increasingly used his famous 'put' to re-inflate the credit markets every time it appeared that the bubble might burst. Since then, this 'confidence' has rested increasingly in the Federal Reserve. Not for much longer. People are waking up to the realisation that they have been 'had'. Fed policies are indeed a 'con'. When a critical mass wakes up, that's when this charade is over, not before.

In the meantime, don't expect a solution from central planners. Most of them don't understand the problem, and any that do would not care to admit it publicly. The economic theories that have been dominant since the nineteen thirties are based upon a misunderstanding of what caused the Great Depression. The only economist to predict the financial crash of 1929 and the depression that followed it was a man called Ludwig von Mises. You may wonder why more people haven't heard of this man? Isn't it strange that such a prescient fellow is relatively unknown? Actually it's not surprising at all. When you understand the real nature of the problem, the unpopularity of anyone pointing this out becomes self-evident:

The people who run the world like debt. The global economy is run by bankers, who make a living from packaging and selling debt. The bankers fund the politicians who give them the debt friendly policies they like. Both bankers and politicians prefer the academics that provide them with the intellectual credibility necessary to keep the credit expansion going. E.G: A perfect example of this was the repeal of Glass Steagall during the administration of President Clinton. This was a policy change that enabled a massive increase in casino banking and derivative trading, signed by a President backed by Wall Street, given academic credibility by Professor Larry Summers, an academic with a very poor track record, at least in the real world, but a very rich address book.

In summary, debt caused the last financial crash, and debt will cause the next one. I'll leave the last word to the aforementioned prescient economist, Ludwig von Mises, who wrote the following before the crash of 1929 and the great depression that followed. It is still as true today as it was then:

"There is no means of avoiding the final collapse of a boom brought about by credit expansion. The alternative is only whether the crisis should come sooner as the result of voluntary abandonment of further credit expansion, or later as a final and total catastrophe of the currency system involved."

German Viewpoint - German Mittelstand Company, CEO

It is and was always about the interlocking of confidence, power and empire.

Confidence that one would get one´s gold for dollars — broken first for *US* citizen by Roosevelt in 1933 and for nations by Nixon in 1971. Cutting this link to gold was cutting the external anchor impeding war and deficit spending. The promise of gold for dollars was revoked, **one** could only exchange a dollar for two times 50 cents from that moment on. A non-US-central bank could still buy gold on the open market, but it presumably would not come out of US gold reserves and soon cost much more. Also, it would expose itself in not playing along with international central bank politics decided upon by The Powers That Be.

Now even the "old gold" from the 1950s and '60s trade surpluses are not handed out to Germany.

One can still buy Gold in different forms and quantities and locations, so there is still a connection between the two and though no one would come to the idea to call it a "gold-anchored dollar", to some extent it still is. The price of gold in dollars (or dollars in gold) still matters psychologically, confirming or undermining confidence in the current FIAT system. Though one can see **confidence** like sand running out, the hourglass waiting to be turned.

Next is Power.

The Power to define the rules, 1944 in Bretton Woods, against the British then; to draw the reserve currency privilege from bankrupt Britain to the sole new world power, the USA.

Power to keep the gold *physically* in New York — tested first by De Gaulle around 1966. He sent a destroyer to get France´s gold home. On board it may have taken ill with something we now call "color revolution". The Empire's virus — released in 1953, Persia — broke out in 1968 in the streets of Paris and, not much later, De Gaulle was on pension and George Pompidou moved from Banque Rothschild to Palace Elysée.

The US had the power to *effectively* redefine "reserves" and they used it: Up to 1971 "reserves" of foreign central banks were mostly gold reserves at the Fed in New York. From then on any additional reserves would primarily be US government bonds held at the Fed. These reserves would be acquired by US trade deficits in the old-fashioned way but also could be mutually created *ex nihilo* out of Swap lines between central banks or from Special Drawing Rights *by* the IMF.

Now some central banks and Sovereign wealth funds (Japan, Israel, Norway, Switzerland, etc.) have moved reserves *from Government bonds* even into equities. One of the pioneers of this, Stanley Fisher as former head of the Israeli Central bank, now sits prominently on the Fed's board.

Motives are diverse: the Governor of a small Central Bank may seek to aid his Ministry of Finance by maximizing the financial return from his existing portfolio of reserves, thereby providing an unexpected source of foreign currency to the Finance Minister.

However, to the extent that these holdings are held by "developing country" central banks like China's, what it does reveal is the abject failure of many developed countries to come to terms with the rise of Asia. Rather than upset their mostly hedonic populations and explain to them the challenges that their countries face via Asia and China, and force structural reforms to allow them to compete, developed country authorities are allowing their national wealth to be slowly depleted and devalued, in a process that is too complex for ordinary people to understand.

So China's first order motivation would appear to be the accumulation of real world wealth while undermining confidence in the FIAT dollar. Their ultimate goal is full spectrum economic dominance (at least in Eurasia.)

What drives the Fed we must set aside word games and state plainly that the Fed has only one mandate: To protect and preserve the existing power structure as long as it includes the Big Banks prominently. And that power structure is not bound by borders on a map.

They're doing it because it enriches their client states and banks at the cost of the general public which has seen their savings watered down by the FIAT and inflation gains taxed by governments. Central banks can print fiat currency ex nihilo; and in the process use the newly printed money to buy the real assets of their choice. Theoretically everything and without limit.

They're doing it because they can. And because it protects and preserves the existing **power** structure.

And the Empire part: In 1973 geopolitics was brought into pre-eminent play by the OPEC embargo after the Yom-Kippur war.

Back in WW2, FDR and the Office of Strategic Services had set up **Arabia and Persia** as a geopolitical protectorate of the USA with Britain now as a junior partner, handing the oil areas to a few sheikhs and a shah, performed according to the usual divide-et-impera manual.

So the 'petrodollar' it did not start with Kissinger. The Nobel Peacemaker only activated it by "allowing" the Arabs to cartelize oil, milking US consumers and the surplus economies of Europe and Japan, recycling petrodollars into US and Israeli weapons, wars and dollar deposits at international banks, thus greatly expanding the Eurodollar market.

Saudi Arabia, the Gulf Sheikdoms and Persia — they were all added to the new dollar zone, guaranteed by half a dozen floating aircraft carriers, a landed one in Palestine and the CIA everywhere. And by the way, Big-Oil also made a bundle. So the dollar was from then backed by 'black gold' and as Professor Krugman admitted in an irritated interview "men with guns".

In the late 90s, with GATT and most favoured nation status for China the game continued with China and Emerging Markets constructing their monetary systems upon dollars earned or borrowed, building up infrastructure and export economies, again providing dollar reserves in a virtuous loop. *The Yuan-fix to the dollar (after a devaluation) in the mid-1990s put China into the dollar-zone.*

But now geopolitics has switched radically. Hard to say when though historians may point to Putin´s speech at the Munich Security Conference in 2007 or the beginning of his second presidency in 2011, or the choice of Xi Jinping as Chinese President in 2012 or possibly with the Russian-Chinese trade and defense pacts in 2014 — where they seem to have bound their destinies together, against the Empire.

Anyway, we now know the game has definitely changed. The Reserve currency role of the dollar is in question – as John Kerry admitted recently before camera. (What he said was astoundingly honest but as First Diplomat he may have better let that moment of truth pass.)

For some years now some countries are trying to get away from the dollar slowly while the USA tries to collapse their *financial* systems. In a paradoxical and hard-to-grasp way a simultaneous run into and out of the dollar has begun: Russia and Brazil are best examples of what happens *to you* if you have not enough reserves of a reserve currency you actually do not want to hold – but have to, because your monetary system is built upon it. Too much reserves and best case its value gets slowly or less slowly inflated away (**with zero or maybe soon negative interest as compensation)**, worst case frozen by US enemy act or decree (see Iran early 80s); not enough of them and your local currency comes under attack by the banks and hedge funds looking to short it into a hole provoking and causing (or being provoked and being caused by) capital flight and color revolution. Nobody knows what the right amount of dollar reserves should be under these circumstances, or more to the point, if such a right amount even exists.

So yes, there is a Dollar bear case that can be made.

The **Empire** will do everything to keep the monetary charade alive — including all sorts and forms of war: sanctions, blockades, assassinations, color revolutions, hacking war, kinetic war, orbital war and maybe even nuclear war — all while using the historically successful method of accusing the other side of starting hostilities *(while repeating the lie often enough)*. One could argue that we are already in the third or fourth inning of an international financial war and the events in Syria, Yemen and Ukraine suggest that we are in the innings of kinetic **warfare**.

What's next? South China Sea and the Baltic region as candidates for conflict, and perhaps Turkey, Thailand, Egypt, Brazil as candidates for civil war. All the undecided areas of importance in this Great Duel between competing systems may be decided by violence.

Humanity, once again, staggers toward interesting times.

US Viewpoint - Citizen 88

The seeds of the crisis were not sown in 2006/7. Years previously, using short term data of a rather coarse, macro-economic kind, policy makers and financial analysts formulated a policy solution to encourage savers (and perhaps more importantly their advisers, given the global changes to Pension Funds) to place their trust in speculative assets (which, particularly in the US, included housing, a fact well known to anyone able to read about the S&L crisis of the late 70's/early 80's, comfortably just outside the data observation period). The banks accepted this plan as their analysts told them that mortgages over the last twenty years had had a very low rate of default making them a "safer investment" than other forms of lending and because of that they could be securitised. The economic data set used to plot the financial trends involved was manifestly too short, too small or both.

This new policy encouraging speculative investment on the part of pension funds and large institution, along with the revision of Glass-Steagall, created room for derivatives and other practices. It was the practice of bundling speculative loans into supposedly AAA rated 'Collateralised Debt Obligations' overly reliant on housing as a security class at the expense of other investment options that eventually broke the system. Before that there had been Credit Default Swaps, financial futures trading and even spread betting allowed in what had been described as 'casino banking'.

These derivatives were traded around the world to other banks. This weight of money changed the operations of the housing market; a market that is still hugely important to the banking sector, the SME sector (how many business loans are secured by property) and the agriculture sector. In addition, repackaging mortgages for onward sale was complicated by the fact that the banks had secondary liens on property for loans which had been redirected into consumer spending. These new financial instruments seemed to be transferring wealth that was notionally locked up in future property values straight into the current retail sector, thus giving it a large financial interest in this new scheme's success.

The obvious next observation is that "growth" in spending and "rise" in asset values of that time, which today is wistfully hoped for as "when we return to normal", was not in fact normal. It was fuelled by credit, expected to be fully repaid and therefore a "safe investment" on an increasingly narrow equity base. A great layer of seeming wealth tapered down to a much smaller property, or real value and so became a classic pyramid inversion.

Here is a news flash: when consumers determine the value of assets and income receipts afford them current and future safety they will make positive consumption decisions. When they don't do so, spending will contract, unless they make more cautious decisions. When money is virtually free they will take it and treat it as such. This recklessly speculative attitude made solid investments hard to come by or assess.

Second news flash: when financial institutions determine the value of assets and income receipts afford them current and future safety they will make positive lending decisions. When they don't they will not. When money is virtually free they will take it and treat it as such.

Mr Summers and his fellow Generals flipped the equation when it suited them. Essentially they said: The man in the street leveraged at 9:1 e.g. a 90% mortgage (and this was by no means the average just an example) must give up their 10% nest egg (or whatever was left of it along with the utility of the roof over their head) to save a bunch of Harvard and other graduates leveraged at 30:1. Oh and by the way in case you had not noticed the leverage on the financial institutions balance sheet was borrowed from you, Mr Man in the Street, through your Pension Plans and Stock market investments. There you go. We circle the pyramid and the man in the street can take it both ways with a pineapple.

UK Viewpoint – Ravi

Who actually lent money and allowed sub-prime mortgages to be given? Who was responsible for creating dodgy financial instruments? Wall Street's compensation system was—and still is—based on short-term performance, all upside and no downside.

In 2005, the then chief economist of the International Monetary Fund, Raghuram Rajan, made a speech at Jackson Hole Wyoming in front of the world's most important bankers and financiers, including Alan Greenspan and Summers. He argued that technical change, institutional moves and deregulation had made the financial system unstable. Incentives to make short-term profits were encouraging the taking of risks, which if they materialized would have catastrophic consequences.

The speech did not go down well. Among the first to speak was Larry Summers who said the speech was "largely misguided". In 2006, Nouriel Roubini issued a similar warning at an IMF gathering of financiers in New York. The audience's reaction? Dismissive. Roubini was "non-rigorous" in his arguments. The central bankers "knew what they were doing."

US Viewpoint – Kronsteen

How about this for an explanation:

Rapidly increasing cost of home ownership (and much higher reported general inflation) directly affecting disposable income to the point where discretionary spending is no longer viable. Wages have not risen in real terms for decades, everything else has. It's really that simple — a zero sum game.

Chinese Viewpoint – Cathal Haughian

Traditional Western civilisation always promoted a purposeful life. The stoic sought knowledge of the Natural System whilst the Christian sought the means of forgiveness come the day of God's Judgement. A purposeful life results in inner traits such as discipline, patience, fortitude and encourages the formation of a well balanced separate self that engages with society on terms beneficial to the purpose of both parties.

Americans collected a lot of big houses and big cars so that their essence would be included in the collective self. US media is a well oiled machine that sold a lifestyle that celebrated status seeking behaviour and display. This resulted in a collective sense of self that desired envy and jealousy from other communal members. Rather than being aware of their *essence in action* they were aware of being looked at. Their ideology formed a false consciousness that presumed that the goal of a capitalist economy was the collection of wealth.

Capitalism is not about wealth, it is about capital and its continuous productive employment. It's productive because it has a clearly defined purpose for the producer and consumer. Increasing inequality combined with rising wealth in non productive assets is essentially anathema to a structurally sound capitalist framework.

Credit, leverage and liquidity were advertised as a given by the ideology of the State. The day before the credit crunch it was leverage that created the *appearance of liquidity* until liquidity begot illiquidity.

US Viewpoint - Vernon L. Smith, Chapman University, 2002 Nobel Laureate

Ex Treasury Secretary Summers' (and the policy makers') error was to suppose that bank bankruptcy (the judge is not the one to make "write-offs," the market does that via auctioning the mortgages) reduces the flow of new capital. It's the other way around: the new return on any new lending goes entirely to the new investors and does not have to be diluted by the claims of incumbent investors who were rescued from their hit, for risks taken that then failed.

Japan's sheltering of banks—permitting them to carry loans at their original book value after 1992 ushered in 20 years of lost output. Allowing this to carry on had left Japan stagnating till around 2010. Loans have to be serviced and so businesses paying interest on them wanted low interest rates. This was not possible without low inflation. Inflation then became lower because of a shortage of real liquidity for investment – real investment in enterprises which make or do things.

Sweden put their banks through failure, zeroed out their equity, and they recovered much faster. It is essential that incumbent investors take their loss so that balance sheets can be re-written and new capital flow set in pursuit of its full return. The political process will always protect incumbent investors to the detriment of recovery by preserving their claims on recovery profit, and thereby protect them from the de facto failure of their previous investments.

Chinese Viewpoint – Cathal Haughian

Important features of the system framework and operational model have disintegrated since the Great Financial Crisis:

A) All policies that resulted in the crisis served their sole purpose which was to enrich the financial sector. These included the outsourcing of America's industrial base to China, the Greenspan 'put' and low interest rates, repeal of financial regulations, subsidized home-ownership and university education and so on and so forth. Politicians of every hue and allegiance supported these policies including central bankers: "The management of market risk and credit risk has become increasingly sophisticated. … Banking organizations of all sizes have made substantial strides over the past two decades in their ability to measure and manage risks." (Ben Bernanke, 2006.)

B) The financial sector's share of domestic corporate profits rose from the low teens in the mid to late 1970s to hit a peak of 41% in the first decade of the 21st century.

C) In 2008, the IMF reported that a nationalization, cleanse and break-up of the financial sector would cost $1.5 trillion (or 10 percent of US GDP) in the long term. Since the bail out and subsequent concentration of political and market power the media has facilitated a public relations campaign to support the status quo: *"The government got back substantially more money than it invested."* (Ex. Treasury Secretary Prof. Summers in 2014, Financial Times). The government was $9 Trillion deeper in debt only 6 years after the crisis hit. It remains unclear if the US taxpayer agrees with Professor Summers.

Since the Crisis began, the heavily indebted have determined central bank interest rate policy — this represents an enormous transfer of influence from creditors/savers to debtors/borrowers. This is in direct contradiction of the operational model, for the system response to over indebtedness of individuals and companies is bankruptcy; more recently displaced in favour of 'extend and pretend' aided by near zero interest rates.

D) In addition, the marketplace deems the financial sector to be infallible. The financial sector is so concentrated that large banks are too big to let fail. The framework of the system was deliberately designed so that all privately owned profit seeking enterprises are treated as fallible. How and why should an infallible bank measure risk well? (The counter-parties of an infallible bank have no incentive to investigate whether that bank is solvent.) This ad hoc arrangement that began to evolve with Greenspan's 'put' became crystallized in 2008, and must result in system wide misallocation.

This unstable arrangement can only bleed losses.

US Viewpoint - Paul A. Myers

The failure to properly price risks has resulted in poor capital allocation and soggy international growth: too many copper mines and not enough new end use products. When one looks back at price charts of grains from the medieval era one sees that large price swings are the defining characteristic of free markets where prices move to clear markets.

In the modern era of state-sponsored financial capitalism, reducing price variation is sold as a virtue because a placid sea is seen as a safe sea by the state and its principal vassal institutions, the big financial institutions, which are mostly in the business of harvesting government-subsidized management bonuses. This also fosters the perception of control by the government. The answer is not less regulation but more. The real trade-off should be more capital being available for the financial intermediaries and less leverage for the customers.

Today, we have under-capitalized financial institutions servicing over-leveraged investors. The risks are multiplicative!

As to the government, how can it measure its success at ensuring adequate capital levels at the risky end of the spectrum if there are not significant price variations on the measuring stick? And if risks are not being properly priced, how can one say capital is being properly allocated?

Chinese Viewpoint – Cathal Haughian

Internal contradictions result in system disintegration.

We know that the underlying rate of return is now zero in the West. The rate of return falls naturally, due to capital accumulation and market competition. The system is called capitalism because capital accumulates: High income economies are those with the greatest accumulation of capital per worker. The robot assisted worker enjoys a higher income as he is highly productive, partly because the robotics made some of the workers redundant and there are fewer workers to share the profit. All the high income economies have had near zero interest rates for seven years. Interest rates in Europe are even negative.

Yellen foresaw the precipice but stepped back in September, 2015 even though rates must rise, for many systemic reasons but here's two:

1. The private pension system is nearing existential death due to the lack of compounding interest. This 'death' has been a quiet one. The purchasing power of their hard earned pensions is decreasing exponentially. All private pensions will be defaulted on when measured against the expected return.

2. The bargaining power of labour has evaporated in the face of free capital. Which places their share of the economic pie under unrelenting pressure. Something has got to give and my bet is the debt. How can US students repay their 1.2 Trillion US$ in debt?

A capitalist economy gravitates naturally towards a stable state where profit is guaranteed by price fixing via cartels, oligopolies or monopolies. Historically, all major capitalist economies have had to break up concentrated market power though this is impossible if the central government is captured by its agents. Agents of concentrated market power virtually capture or buy governments by funding election campaigns, buying newspapers and many other methods. The US is now a dominator economy. If rates are raised expect an increased concentration in market and political power. Fascism or Communism become possible outcomes in such unstable situations.

No person or entity is to blame for our Global Economic Crisis. It began in the US though Americans are not to blame. The individual is only responding to system stress experienced as social peer pressure. Simply contemplate how this Capitalist treatise had to be written in the form it has taken: by 200 men and women, each one with decades of accumulated knowledge of how the Global Economic System works on the monetary, financial and real level.

Academic economists lack the know-how to see and understand the system in its entirety. Their theoretical models have no predictive value. They weren't able to explain Japanese decline and their forecasts were contradicted by observable reality: this renders deliberation and choice obsolete.

Rate setters don't attach any value to money printing since there is no ultimate end that relates to money printing. They haven't chosen to print money. They were never in a position to decide otherwise.

The free market has disintegrated. You're only feeding off of its carcass.

It's either stock or flow? All the demand is being stocked away in company buy-backs of shares, Asian central banks sterilizing demand by keeping their currencies lower (to export deflation and internal devaluation elsewhere since 1997), and demand stored in luxury goods like condos that are a fraction of what they cost to construct, or Gucci bags.

We've seen this script before. It was the era before 1929, when it was the US exporting deflation with an undervalued exchange rate from a gold standard that resembles the Eurozone now. Some debtors couldn't take it anymore and Creditanstalt folded, creating a cascading event. The US resembled Japan, a creditor country with a bubble which is trickier to fix since creditors are within the country and can distort politics to prevent corrections that involve them taking a loss.

The wealthy can distort politics to make sure debtors always pay. This was true until the US government gained a lot of credibility after WWII by funding many construction projects that helped transfer private debt to the public book. The US government's debt exploded during the war, but it also shifted the power game away from creditors to a big debtor with a lot of political capital. Low and behold, the US jacked up tax rates on the wealthy and had a period of elevated inflation in the late 40s and into the 1950s — all of which slowly sucked out government bond-creditors, but also ushered in a unique middle class era in the West. The US also reformed extraction centric institutions in Europe and Japan to make sure an extractive-creditor class did not hobble growth...which was easy to do because the war wiped them out (same as in Korea).

Right now, demand is locked away in Asian countries (why are poor countries lending when there are more investment opportunities at home? - m-a-n-i-p-u-l-a-t-i-o-n). Demand is locked away by elites who are now multinational-global citizens who live away from public ire. In the US, they own the media to promote false Gods of capitalism while they run a crony game decrying socialism (until they need $700 billion magically appear overnight on a law bill that is only one sheet of paper long, but cannot do the same for healthcare).

They talk about debt — but every debtor has a creditor. If there are a lot of debts globally, there are a lot of savings. But that doesn't sound right, if things were spread out more equitably, people wouldn't need to borrow from anyone but their own selves. But the fact that there are so many debtors must mean there is a small but big concentration of creditors (which means they are powerful). Creditors evidently have a lot of money. If they had paid their workers better, who have a higher propensity to spend, there might in fact be investable ventures as there will be demand to make such investments profitable in a feedback loop (which would bring up yields).

What is unique now is that we are again seeing exploding government debt, imbalances (some manipulated, some circumstantial like Germany in the Eurozone), but we are not seeing rising government credibility to go after creditors. We see creditors owning governments. They're like lemmings, afraid for their wealth that they collectively bring down yields and boost up property values in global cities to find new "stores" of value.

Either stock or flow...

Investor

Interest rates go up asset prices go down. Once the balance of fear breaks—expect chaos. Why? Since 2007, global debt has grown by $57 trillion, raising the ratio of debt to GDP to 286%. There is no evidence that a credit event in one or more emerging markets can be contained.

Miles

What we can observe is a structural decline in productivity pretty much across all categories: labour, capital and innovation. Lower productivity means lower GDP growth and lower living standards. Even more interesting are some of the big items. There is a structural decline in investments in long–term industrial assets while 30 year nominal bond yields are at 2.6%. Investors seem to believe that returns from real economy investments will be even lower as uncertainty is high. Labour productivity growth is declining for a variety of reasons despite low labour participation. Innovation and entrepreneurship, always hard to measure, seem to be in decline.

None of the above can be influenced by central bankers or monetary policy. To revive entrepreneurship and long-term investment we need a pretty old-style cocktail of supply side programs including investment into infrastructure, education and research, reforms of labour markets and taxation and, last but not least, an end to the madness of arbitrary government intervention.

*An entrepreneurial economy needs low rents.

Cpl. Jones

We needed new leadership in 2005 at the Fed when it let the banks fake reform of the derivatives market for three years before collapsing. We needed new leadership in 2008 when government didn't let banks go bust, preventing the reform of banking that only investor rage could have achieved. Right now, we need a time machine.

Duvin Rouge – French Viewpoint

The central contradiction of capitalism: capital accumulation itself causes profit rates to decline (explained most accurately by Marx but acknowledge by classical economists like Ricardo). The long-term rate of interest cannot be greater than the rate of profit as interest comes out of profit (technically surplus value for Marxists). So as underlying profits have fallen (not the recorded ones for many that have been inflated by investment income from inflated asset prices), so the interest rate has fallen. Again, not a lack of demand and liquidity trap. The glut of savings isn't a glut of money capital; rather money has become divorced from productive capital. Adding more digits to finance capital's bank accounts does not create value, nor make new investments suddenly more profitable. We do indeed have a depression that isn't being allowed to take its course, and the more they try to prevent capital devaluation the bigger the crisis to come.

Sam

Dear Prof Wolf et al,
You Keynesians' cleverly used the leftist veneer to cover for blatant elitist support by central banks of 0.01% of the population which probably controls 75% of the assets. Central Banks have only increased their balance sheet to keep the interest rates low to protect the asset values of

0.1% of the population. The working poor never factored into their decision making and would have been better off with a free market.

If there wasn't excess cash, asset values would have had to go down, on paper deflation would have taken hold for a few years; money would have retained value and finally got back into the productive cycle. But the 0.01% don't have many physical needs except to keeping the fixed asset values high; the 1% population will continue to espouse the benefits of these loose monetary policy to protect their corner hoping it will give them the opportunity to reach the 0.01% cut.

Alas, the 99% will suffer, hopefully none of them are FT readers, but who cares, when even the powerful opinion makers have turned up to bat for the 0.01%. Interest rates must go up, deflation must be allowed and central bank balance sheets must reduce for the true benefit of the 99%.

Drake

It is pointless to talk about monetary issues without knowing how the money is created and for whom.

The problem with low rates and QE is that the wrong people get the money and decide what to do with it. They invest in what is the safest in their view and it is real estate and commodities. We did see inflation in those and still do in the real estate. But as it happened with the commodities bubble last year the same will happen with the real estate eventually. The speculation does not create new value and without creating new value there is no progress and growth.

Consider how the high real estate prices and cheap money affect the economy. The young have to save for a down payment. They do not spend and that slows the money velocity. The central banks increase the volume, but it ends up in the banker's hands; and they invest in the real estate or similar assets. The prices go up. All services from hair dressers to day care to groceries have to build the rent into their prices. This is another squeeze on savers and damper on economic activity. The money is not invested in productivity tools and machinery, or technological innovation. Using more money to do the same causes diminishing returns. It is really basic economics. The monetarism can give good results if it has a head start. Once the rates are near zero they use other tools that they call QE (we call printing money).

There is nowhere else to go from there. The central bankers do not have good choices any more, only bad ones. It is the question what will happen next. Damned if you do, damned if you don't. This is uncharted territory and whoever says that she knows what is the best course of action lies. Nobody knows. We need a genius, someone who will come up with the new "ism" that we cannot imagine right now. But she is too busy paying off her student loan, I'm afraid.

Johnny Julius Johnson

I think you fundamentally misconstrue society. Society is essentially a system of distributing privilege. In order to explain this to you, I'll take a page out of the bible and begin with Genesis: In the beginning, everyone was privileged and equally so. But, alas, it's a maxim that if everyone is privileged no one is: If I'm forced to pay your rents and you mine it's a wash. So, society is a system for concentrating privilege on a select few at the expense of the rest. This creates the meaningful privilege we all crave and it creates a pecking order. Within this context, monetary policy is merely a tool and not an ends. However a thorough examination of monetary policy, as you say, should shed light on not merely how money is created but for whom.

Drake

For a moment I thought you'd quote Mathew's Law:

"For whoever has will be given more, and they will have abundance. Whoever does not have, even what they have will be taken from them."

But my reasoning is that it is a very bad position to be rich and weak. Therefore those who are getting rich do not want to weaken the society that they are robbing to the point that the society becomes too weak to protect their riches. An example would be the Far East mandarins who could not protect their riches against the assault of industrialized nations. They were powerful enough to defend against their own people and did not conceive the external threat approaching. They did nothing to change their ways and fell as victims of their own ignorance. I know what Matthew's Law is about, but if you put wisdom in it, it also holds the truth.

"The Fed may find the US economy is not as strong as it believes" Martin Wolf, Financial Times, Dec 2015

The US economy is clearly not as strong as the Fed claims to believe. I say 'claims' because given the last 12 months of contradictory jawboning from voting and non-voting members alike, I'm not even sure THEY know what they believe.

Back to the data - there is plenty of data that indicates that the economy is not strong. Dr. Yellen is a labour economist, so unsurprisingly she appears to focus on jobs. The jobs number looks healthy enough, until you pull back the covers and look at what consists of a 'job' - 1 hour a week or more....until you look at who is taking these jobs – people 55 plus....until you look at where the bulk of the gains are – part-time low wage jobs...until you look at where the bulk of the losses are – high paid middle class jobs.

So it seems to me that either Dr. Yellen is a very poor labour economist, or she's convinced herself that this is the best that the US economy is capable of. I suspect it's the latter. Personally I totally disagree. A country as innovative and entrepreneurial as the US didn't just turn into a nation of part-timers. Something else is up, and Dr. Yellen doesn't know what it is.

Putting job numbers to one side – a strong economy would not be emitting the following signals, a full six years into a so-called 'recovery':

1. Between the pre-crisis peak in Q3 2007 and Q3 2015 labour productivity has grown at 1.1% per annum. The historic average is 2.3%

2. During the same period total labour hours worked has risen by less than one half of a percent

3. Business start-ups outpaced business failures by 100,000 per annum until 2008. In the past 6 years that trend has reversed – the net number of start-ups vs. failures is now minus 70,000 per annum.

4. Real net investment in US Business is 8% below that it was at the 2007

peak, and a full 17% below what it was in 2000.

Contrast these four figures with the following one:

5. The net worth of households and non-profit organisations in 2008 was $68,000. It is now...drumroll...$86,000.

What could possibly explain an economy that produces the first four of those signals in combination with the fifth one? How can an economy that is losing its productive flair, that is doing barely any more work than it was 8 years ago despite a higher population, that is closing down its businesses and failing to start new ones, that is not investing in its future...possibly have achieved a 25% increase in its household net worth?

The answer is QE. Asset price inflation. The Fed's main achievement over the past 6 years has been to inflate another bubble, just like they did after the dot-com bust. Every time they do this, it gets bigger. This one is enormous – when it bursts it will take down the bond market. This is an ersatz recovery, concocted by a group of ersatz economists.

Something is up and Dr. Yellen doesn't know what it is. The root of this malaise is not the productivity, or the willingness to work, or the entre-preneurial spirit of the American people.

The root of the problem is the central planning philosophy at the core of US political and economic life: Crony capitalism and socialism for the rich. Debt for Guns and Butter. Ponzi monetary policy and tooth fairy, 'something for nothing' economics.

Personally, I don't think it matters what the Fed believes about the economy, or what they do next week – we are way past that. But if and when the US shakes itself free from this travesty of central planning, there will be a real recovery. It will be very messy, but it will be real.

Cuibono

I think there are real merits to Andrew Mellon's liquidation arguments. The 1930's were a horrible decade but when the collapse came and the debt was wiped out, the bankers and finance artists were thoroughly dis-credited and new industries grew from the ashes. Specifically there was growth in the auto industry, the modern design movement with suburbs and everything from washing machines to phones and TVs in every house. These came from a drive to put the past behind us and build anew.

Incidentally, most of the innovations that were built upon in the Great Depression were developed or first launched in the mania phase of the bubble that burst in 1928/1929.

In the current system, we do everything to protect the past. We lower rates to protect debtors against the consequences of unaffordable debt levels. We refuse to allow banks to fail but instead force the weak onto the balance sheets of the strong and we refuse to allow auto manufacturers such as GM or Chrysler to go under. And to justify all of this we say "because we would get another depression". As if that alone is an argument to justify policies that are essentially anti market and anti capitalistic.

The hard fact is we can't have our cake and eat it. We can't on the one hand promote more innovation in, for example new auto technologies, but then on the other insist that the companies that exist today must survive forever. What will happen is what has always happened — you have a system politicized to such an extent that political access — and not profits from innovative new solutions become the core of the incentive structure.

*Reader, a central question is how can ingrained behaviour be changed? Please note that Pavlov proved that behaviour can be de-conditioned by pain/distress/fear.

MKC

It all boils down to ideology: Communism manipulated the markets in one way (central planning), the central banks manipulate it in a different and more devious fashion (by pulling money out of the pockets of the thrifty and hard working part of society and subsidizing borrowers, in particular zombie banks, spendthrift governments, financial speculators and simultaneously distorting the disciplining risk/reward function of the market).

Christopher

Economy and growth are mainly driven by the decisions of individuals to work hard and invest. Modern states, through taxes, now steal a big part of the rewards; mainly to buy the results of the next election and spoil people voting for the ruling party. Will I create a company or invest 10 million Euros because Draghi buys Greek bonds? No.

I also firmly believe debt levels scare a ton of people from investing. While main stream media pretends "all is safe". I'm sorry but 19 trillions of US debt is scary, not to mention crazy BOJ policies. How much money will ECB lose by buying junk debt? A ton, and they plan to make back their losses using taxes on my income. Smart people are careful, hide their money in tax free schemes (thank you Mr. Juncker and others), invest in real estate in booming cities as it's perceived as "less risky". Leave markets do what they do best: price discovery. Lower taxes and cut regulations and red tape. French work regulations is 5500 pages!!! Sadly, we are not going there...and, soon, the day will come—we'll be called to save the FED and ECB with trillions.

EinarBB

Printing may not be the problem. There is a far more probable alternate explanation which explains simultaneously that living standards are sliding and that growth is poor. I'm referring to the fact that millions of manufacturing jobs have moved to Asia since 1990. Economists act like there is no net loss for the countries that lose all these jobs. But over the same period we have witnessed rapidly growing indebtedness of the same Western countries and not the least, growth slowdown getting worse over time, and let us not forget constant net trade deficits with Asia. Clearly the growing debt problem, the growing problem with growth, which means a growing problem for the economies to create jobs and thus to maintain living standards—are all due to the massive movement of manufacturing jobs from Europe and N-America to Asia, that has been ongoing at an increasingly rapid rate since 1990.

The monetary policy isn't a cause—but a symptom of the overall problem, that manufacturing industries in Western countries have become uncompetitive and thus have been declining at a constant rate and at an ever growing rate since 1990. None of what's happening is a co-incidence.

GDCC

Don't stop there. Those that advocate QE (money printing) are always trying to divert attention away from fiscal deficits. If a BoP imbalance is the cause of the crisis, then what is the cause of BoP imbalance? Lack of competitiveness. OK, then what is the cause of lack of competitiveness? They elude the question but the answer is rather straightforward: misallocation of capital. Capital invested in cumulative fiscal deficits is simply not productive: a complete waste from a competitiveness standpoint.

Sanoran T

Printing Money (QE) = taxation via inflation. The unelected central bankers print cash and give to their Banks. The Banks make up for their losses, take their bonus and distribute the rest as loans. In a free-market-capitalist system, there should be no role for a Marxist Central Planning authority like the central banks, the free-market would punish bankers who lose. But Bankers have managed to have their moles like Draghi, Yellen/Bernanke to tax the masses and socialize their losses. In Europe, Germany keeps Draghi under control, but in the USA?

The Central Banks cannot create a single penny in wealth. All they can do is redistribute it. QE is essentially a wealth redistribution trick: inflation taxes the masses, and the recipients of the QE receive the collected tax. If the central banks were to print cash and distribute directly to Citizens, it would still cause taxation-via-inflation, but it would be more equitable. However, the Bankers wouldn't allow it: they didn't work so hard to have their moles in power for nothing. So, QE will definitely lower the standards of living (another way to say inflation will lower your purchasing power, or paying an extra tax will make you poorer, ... take your pick), but for the Bankers, it not only protects their jobs, but it also assures them fat bonuses. They love it.

GDCC

Indeed, QE succeeded in keeping the financial system alive after the crisis, a system which permits non-productive debt to balloon. Non-productive debt is debt which does not produce an income stream. This is today the case of most government and household debt. QE has therefore helped roll over debt which will not be repaid.

Is it that easy?

QE is the one true friend of the plutocrat, the speculator and the debtor —the true rentier. It ensures the wealthy can acquire assets with cheap debt, increase the price of such assets and then... wipe out the debt with inflation. And all paid for ensuring shrinking real wages for the poor and denying youngsters a roof over their heads. Genius... and I thought Mr Wolf had pretences to humanity.

History Matters

But the global affluent OWN debt as an asset, so it is in their interest to encourage debtors. If there is a default, all the better as the law allows them to seize the "secured" assets as collateral. Right now Bond holders rule, while democracy suffers.

Pepin

The situation we are in is not just one of persistent consumer price disinflation or deflation but also one of persistent asset price inflation. The combination of both is where the problem lies.

It is wonderful if you're a baby-boomer. Having bought assets on the cheap and having enjoyed the compounding effect at positive real interest rates during your lifetime, you can now convert those assets into gigantic mountains of cash given the incredible multiple of earnings they trade at (50 - 70 times for an apartment, 30 - 50 times for most decent common stocks, 50 - 100 times for AAA bonds), whereas that cash is almost guaranteed to keep its value. For young people the picture is the opposite. There's no possibility to grow savings through the route of compounding as real interest rates are stuck at zero. Acquiring assets is almost impossible. It takes a mountain of debt to buy a place to live. And consumer price disinflation means there's no real prospect for wage growth to help with that mountain of debt.

Michael McPhillips

When the goods and services on sale are too expensive to buy for the majority of consumers how can more QE make them less expensive and affordable? When homes are too expensive to buy how can more lending to prospective buyers make them less so when wages are not sufficient to service the debt? When taxes are too high for the problem economies to generate growth how can more bond buying by the ECB lower them if they have to be higher for government to service the increased debt?

German Viewpoint - German Mittelstand Company, CEO

Most of the money printing, probably 95% of it, is currently done by buying bonds of governments or bonds effectively guaranteed by governments providing purchasing power in an immediate sense to the debtor. The US central bank, the Fed, might do it to create banking reserves at the Fed for primary dealers selling government bonds or mortgage paper to the Fed. A foreign central bank, the Bank of China, might do it to gain access to dollar reserves to found its own banking system upon it and/or to keep its currency down to increase exports. Fannie Mae used the money of foreign central banks to refinance a local housing bubble, a futile but comparatively harmless endeavour.

The US government on the other hand **may**—on Planet Krugman—use that money wisely to competently finance infrastructure and education. That would mean: **NOT making a racket out of it**. Unfortunately, that is not what humans do in general or what lobbyists specialize in. So governments mostly create Departments with budgets to nurture rackets out of it: The War Racket, the Education racket, the Incarceration racket, the Agriculture Racket, the Health-Care Racket and — never to be forgotten — the Banking Racket.

And then, most importantly, the Deep State and "Intelligence" Racket. So corruption gets widely stretched. As these activities, buying politicians, draw profit margins of up to 100%, while normal industry has trouble competing with 0-15% margins per dollar invested.

These rackets suck money out of government budgets increasing the supply of government bonds to be refinanced by central banks buying those bonds.

It is a self-reinforcing cycle of debt and corruption sweeping around the globe, where it gets mixed up with geopolitics.

When and how does this end? We are bound to find out.

Bretton James   ***   **Apr, 2014**

Only the ignorant believe you.
If you have studied history, every time governments engaged in printing too much money, it always resulted in (hyper) inflation. The reasons for "low" inflation in the USA are:

1) Core inflation excludes food and energy prices.
2) Most of newly created dollars are used outside of the USA because countries need them to for trade and reserves.
3) Inflation does not show up in wages this time because the USA off shored most of its economy to China.

If you are looking for evidence of inflation, check out the prices of financial assets and the real estate market in the UK.

Bernhard Otto – German Viewpoint

Hyperinflation is a phenomenon which occurs only when there are exceptional circumstances. It all comes down to lost trust or non acceptance of a currency for political reasons. The US Dollar is good money as long as it is accepted and trusted with no restrictions all around the world. As long as this is the case, hyperinflation is not on the cards, only high inflation is possible. Hyperinflation is always a political phenomena. If China, India, Iran, Brazil, Russia and other very important market participants would decide from one day to the other — we do not accept US Dollars anymore — then the US Dollar is under political attack which may then lead to hyperinflation. Or to hyperinflation in these countries, it just depends which side is the winner in this confrontation.

The Reichsmark after WWI was attacked by US/UK/France etc. so that it totally lost its value. It was one of the major goals of the opponents of Germany to destroy the value of the Reichsmark. If the Reichsmark would have been stable in value the Germany economy would have quickly recovered, which was not something wanted by the winners of WWI.

Destroy the currency by not accepting it, then buy cheap the important assets of the opponent taking advantage of the situation. Destroying the currency means destroying the "working capital" of this nation. Inject foreign capital—which can be withdrawn anytime—and charge high interest rates with everything fixed exclusively to foreign currency, and wait for the right moment to buy the hard assets for a fraction of their value. This is one of the best proven recipes of economic slavery and post WWI period in Germany can be regarded as a model of such a policy.

This cannot happen to the US because the situation is not comparable to Germany after WWI. But one should not forget that the US has many powerful enemies (or better, economic competitors): Russia, China, Iran, Brazil and other important countries no longer want to accept the dominant role of the US. It's a fact, that the US Dollar is the most important weapon in the arsenal in Washington. Only because of the reserve currency status of the US Dollar (Petro Dollar) the US is capable to continue its imperialistic policy by maintaining military presence in more than 150 nations with a gigantic military budget. And this is the reason why the US Dollar is under attack. China and Russia (as the driving forces of the Shanghai Group) do want to bring the US down to their level. The only way to do this is to diminish the importance and dominance of the US Dollar. This is their great plan. Only the future will tell the outcome.

I personally believe the US is going to lose this fight for the following reasons:

1) The US is not militarily capable of defeating Russia/China since both countries have a high caliber nuclear arsenal. Not to mention their potential in biological, chemical, cyber space, orbital etc., warfare. A direct conflict between such superpowers does not have any winner — the whole of mankind is going to lose, the danger of mankind's extinction is clear to see on the horizon.

2) Economically the US is presently in a very weak position but what is more important is the prognosis for the coming years, (maybe a decade) and that is not good at all. On the other side China is showing an outstanding economic dynamic and the US is unable to hold them down, simply for the fact that Russia is a close ally of China. But also Iran is a close partner of China when it comes to fight the US Dollar. As a conclusion it can be said, that the Dollar is under political attack which might one day lead to hyperinflation of the US Dollar with all the devastating consequences.

Felix – Austia

Your account of the German hyperinflation is not accurate. WWI winners did not specifically attack the German currency — nor would it have been in their interest!! Naturally, the reparations imposed a choice of bad policy options for Germany, and some economists have tried (controversially) to defend the choice for inflation rather than unemployment. One thing is clear: the choice for inflation was made in Germany. But the fact is that in the early 1920s many countries in Europe (including WWI winners France, Italy and Belgium) were experiencing very high inflation due to deficit financing.

German inflation was not really such a dramatic outlier until the battle of the Ruhr in 1923. In fact, it seems that the conventional definition of hyperinflation (as 50% inflation per month) was not applicable until spring or summer 1923. Then, the German government made a conscious decision to replace the lost productivity with ever greater liquidity, leading inevitably to hyperinflation. By endorsing the view that the fall in the exchange rate triggered hyperinflation you side with the defence of the Reichsbank at the time. But it was the other way around.

Bitcoin

Keynesian blather, from the man who thinks Ben Bernanke saved the world. The truth is only time will tell who is right here. Given the untenable amount of debt around, and the tendency of politicians to inflate away their problems instead of an honest default, I'm sticking with hard assets. Owning stack of paper money at this point in history is for the fool. The first place to hyper-inflate, probably, will be the US. Watch for Russia, China and Iran doing deals in each other's currency or gold, and dumping the US dollar as reserve. All of those US dollars residing outside of the US will then flood back into the US, prices will balloon. Given that most other paper currencies are backed by the dollar, what happens to them?

Is it that easy?

Mr Wolf, A young buck on·£30k wanted to buy a house in Barnet last year. He saved every penny for the last 12 months with the aim of achieving a deposit for the studio flat priced at £140k. He popped into the estate agency this month and found the type of flat he was after is now £182k...a 30% price movement over this time...he felt sick to the stomach...He needs to save for 9 more years, just to make up for last year's price gain. What does he think about hyper-inflation? Now, given he has to save much more and for much longer to make up for just one year's gain, what does this do to the rest of his spending power in the economy for the next 9 years?

Tim Young

The problem for the young buck from Barnet is that, by not participating in the house-buying madness, and even more so by saving in the form of a bank deposit, he makes himself part of a minority who electoral calculation makes ripe for plucking, such as by taxing him to subsidise mortgage borrowers or by a bit of monetary dilution. This is what makes me so angry about the BoE—they were given operational independence precisely to render futile, and therefore prevent, this kind of cynical ma-nipulation of the economy by politicians, but the individuals in charge of the BoE independently chose to align themselves with the politicians, perhaps out of their own similar vanity, to ingratiate themselves with people who might nominate them for a bigger role, or simply because they do fine out of asset price inflation themselves. They have let this country down badly.

Southbank

If those in charge (the politicians, economists, and other leaders) were on the other side of the housing market and other asset markets, rather than being the beneficiaries of rising prices, then I believe we'd live be living in an unrecognisably different economic world. I can find no other way to explain the complete lack of acknowledgement of the full implications of monetary policy on asset prices.

MarkGB

MrWolf,
It is not only the ignorant who foresee the possibility of hyperinflation, whether they are living in fear of it is another matter. There are potential scenarios that lead to hyperinflation just as there are for deflation. There is currently a 'war' going on between these two forces. These possibilities

The crash of 2008 was the beginning of a market 'clear out' of debt,

are not acknowledged by you or in the hubristic tone you use to dispel such possibilities.

The crash of 2008 was the beginning of a market 'clear out' of debt, misallocated capital and speculative lunacy that had been encouraged and enabled by governments and central banks. The clear out was not allowed to happen because governments and central banks fear deflation, which they can't control and can't tax. They think they can control inflation through neo-Keynesian nonsense like 'optimal control' - there is no optimal control of large complex systems.

So deflation was avoided and huge swathes of private debt became public debt, whilst the investment bankers retained their jobs and their bonuses, Hank Paulson got to pretend he knows something about economics and Ben Bernanke became the new 'maestro'.

Here's one POSSIBILITY - the Nasdaq bubble bursts when people finally realise that stocks with market cap of billions but no earnings, are not worth the paper they are printed on. This leads to an algorithmic avalanche of stops, the contagion spreads to the S&P and the DOW when investors have to face up to the reality that that they are leveraged beyond 2008 levels already and earnings are disappointing because CEOs can't borrow to do any more share buybacks, even at ZIRP. Janet Yellen ramps up the printing press because she believes that structural problems like unemployment can be solved with monetary solutions and the marketplace comes to the conclusion that the Fed hasn't got a clue what it's doing and never has.

There is an initial stampede of US money into US Treasuries, but foreign investors, who realise that the US dollar is living on borrowed time, accelerate their move into gold and increase their trading arrangements with each other through currency swaps. The Chinese stop inflating their own economy by printing Yuan to buy dollars, and the 17 trillion dollars held overseas start to find their way home again. US imports are now becoming increasingly expensive and the government is no longer able to doctor the inflation figures…a loss of confidence takes hold…

I'm sure that you could find flaws in the above scenario Prof. Wolf. I don't know, and I don't think you do either.

Antti Jokinen

There is an insight missing here, obviously:

It could be that the banks have decided that lending is now too risky. This is the market mechanism, how it should work. Now we have central banks who (by committee) have decided that the banks are not doing their job, so the system must be broken. How can we say that the banks are not doing their job, which is NOT to lend when the risk is too high? Central Banks are overriding the market mechanism, having decided it's not working. We do have a problem, because we know from experience how risk ignorant the Central Banks can be.

*This entry highlights a major internal contradiction in the current design. If the banks won't create new money/debt due to high risk then outstanding debt plus interest cannot be repaid. This would only serve to increase risk evermore. My hunch is that student debt would be the first to succumb to this contradiction.

Tim Young

It should be clear that only the ignorant (or apologists for the economic establishment's shameless can-kicking by propping up asset prices, including the likes of Paul Krugman as well as Martin Wolf) do NOT live in fear of hyper (or at least very high) inflation.

The present stock of UK base money (mostly reserves) is, on my rough estimate, about four times the stock that would be consistent in normal, non-financial-crisis conditions with the present quantity of broad money. The reason that this has been sustainable is that the financial crisis has made it attractive for banks to hold reserves even bearing a low rate of interest as a practically risk-free asset. If and when the financial crisis subsides, the banks will find their holdings of reserves excessive, and, begin to spend these reserves on higher-returning loan assets.

Of course, this "spending" will not extinguish the reserves, because they get passed on to another bank, which in turn tries to spend its excess, until the banking system stock of bank lending and broad money increases to be consistent, given the non-crisis money multiplier, with the stock of reserves. Assuming that the usual proportional relationship between the stock of base money and prices holds, the result would be a roughly four-fold increase in the price level - high inflation by any standard, if not quite hyperinflation (though hyperinflation could be triggered if high inflation generated a collapse in currency demand).

The obvious way for the central bank to prevent this process is to reverse QE by selling the government debt it bought to expand the stock of reserves and lower long-term interest rates in the first place. The trouble with this of course is that, by probably raising long-term interest rates, it runs the risk of restraining or even reversing the economic recovery, as well as raising the governments headline indebtedness and cost of funding. An alternative is to increase the interest paid on reserves to make banks less inclined to spend them, but that would not be much better than selling the debt accumulated under QE, because it would effectively involve issuing state floating rate notes instead.

And so we are led to another attempted escape, which is to force the banks to hold the reserves by way of reserves requirements, which is no doubt what Martin means to discuss in his future column on increased state creation of money, and which proposal I will criticise when he makes it.

To sum up, the present state of knowledge of the outcome of QE is akin to that of a man who jumps out of an aeroplane at ten thousand feet as he passes two thousand feet — it has all been a bit of a breeze so far, but unless he has a parachute, he can still come to a messy end.

This question is posed after a large constellation of nations, including NATO members, became members of China's Asian Infrastructure Investment Bank (AIIB), in spite of resistance from Larry Summers, Ex Treasury Secretary of the U.S.

JP   ***   2015

Such delicious irony! That Larry Summers — the swaggering US Deputy Treasury Secretary during the Asian crisis of 1997 (and later Treasury Secretary) — should today be appealing for sanity and pragmatism from his country's political class.

Some of us are not so young that we have forgotten how Summers and his young henchman in the Treasury Department, a certain Timothy Geithner, and his two skull-crackers in the IMF — Stanley Fischer and the late Michael Mussa — destroyed the Japanese suggestion that they fund the Asian Development Bank with an additional $100 Bn to create an FX stabilization facility to forestall the worst effects of the crisis in places like Indonesia and Malaysia.

The argument used by them was that the Asian economies needed to pay for their excesses. That meant exchange rates needed to depreciate hugely, monetary policy needed to be brutally tight to check pass-through inflation and public budgets would have to move into surplus, i.e. through austerity, if local banks were being bailed out.

But foreign (mainly US) investors who had invested in the domestic fixed income markets must be made whole and allowed to exit at a favourable rate. Summers flew to Manila for the ADB meeting and kiboshed the Japanese proposal. The hatred that some Asian countries still feel for Summers and Fischer has not disappeared.

The truth, of course, was that Japan was getting too big for its boots and needed to be taught a lesson.

Dhako – Chinese Viewpoint

It seems that Washington elites have realized that US ability to call the shots across the global financial governance is at an end, particularly so long as the Tea-party-influenced Republican Party refused to play ball in reforming the IMF/World Bank.

Furthermore, it's also the case that many nations across the global south are beginning to realize finally that the Chinese can offer them a better deal in investment when it comes to the development of their infrastructure than perpetually to wait at the door of the western-governed international financial institutions such as the IMF and the World-Bank. Hence, the alacrity in which nations are queuing up to join the China's AIIB.

Moreover, I must say something about the role in which Larry and his friend (Bob Rubin — who was the US's treasury secretary) along with Alan Greenspan at the Federal Reserve Bank, have played in the Asia's financial crisis of 1997. And, what happened was that, these three gentlemen, used the IMF to enforce draconian austerity, privatization of public assets, as well as forcing the payback of every dollar the Wall Street banks had lent to these stricken nations. Which means, nations like Indonesia, Thailand, and others have essentially carried the can of that financial crisis, while those who, foolishly lent them too much debt (mainly Wall Street banks) have been protected by the IMF's support to these nations.

And, what is galling was that, after all these self-serving agendas in which poor countries with fragile economies have paid the price of Wall Street's greed of lending money and given too much debt to some developing countries, the Times newspaper, saw fit to call Rubin, Summers, and Greenspan, "the committee that saved the world"; instead of calling them, what they really were, namely the "Committee that saved Wall Street" at the expense of Asia's teeming poor, who saw their national assets been bought off for a pittance in-order to pay back Wall Street's oligarchs.

Consequently, when Japan, which was flush with savings wanted to create a similar IMF outfit for the Asian countries right after the 1997 financial crisis, the US government, in particular Clinton's administration (in which Summers, Rubin had an outsized role to play), had effectively "nixed" that proposal.

Hence, today, the Obama's administration, unlike Clinton's one of late 1990s, can't stop the Chinese version of the Bretton Woods institutions, in which the currently planned Chinese Asian Infrastructure Investment Bank (AIIB), is only the first one that will be off the drawing-board. All in all, it's refreshing to see that, even, Larry Summers, can see the writing on the wall, whereby unlike his days at the US's treasury in the late 1990s, the likes of Jack Lew and Janet Yellen, can't play a committee that will rescue Wall Street banks at the behest of some poor and fragile nations. Especially since those nations have an alternative to the "conditional support" they are likely to get from the likes of the IMF.

In other words, the world now has an alternative to any self-serving Washington-based alleged "rescuing committee". And, that should at least be welcome by anyone who desires their national assets to be safe from the usual avarice of the Wall Street-Treasury Dept.-Fed faction.

Mustapha

How is it possible that we had 15 years of Democrat and 8 years of Republican Presidency and have had the same "Foreign" and "Monetary" policies for the last 23 years if US politics was so divided? And wasn't it Larry Summers himself, who advised a US Senator "insiders don't criticize insiders"?

Tarquin

The US government's use of its banks as an instrument of foreign policy is for me the last straw. I sell vital non-military basic raw material to a country the US does not like. The goods are made in the Far East. US flag ships are prohibited from carrying the cargo, the lines that do carry it have to invoice freight in Euros. My customer has to send funds 'on the back of a camel' to another country to be converted to USD because if he sent them from his own country the US banks are prohibited from forwarding the funds. Finally both the cargo and the documents need to be transshipped to reach their destination. The Dollar is the world's reserve currency at the moment — but its use for this trade is subject to an overtly political embargo. Another currency and non-US based clearing house for the transfer of funds is needed so long as Uncle Sam abuses his role as the custodian of the USD.

Bekin

The best way to engage a rising power is not to hem it in, especially in its own backyard. If Britain and France had engaged with Germany at the beginning of the 20th century, things might have worked out better during the period 1914 to 1945.

The US needs to face the fact that its 'unipolar moment' is over and that the dollar must eventually cease to be the world's reserve currency. This is hard because, when this happens, there will be a limit on the extent to which the US can finance its deficit, just as there is a limit on the extent to which other countries can run a deficit. If the RMB and other currencies gradually erode the primacy of the dollar as the currency of world trade, the rest of the world will gradually run down their stocks of US Treasuries and diversify their reserve portfolios, as prudent investment strategy would suggest.

The US, like all great military powers, will eventually run out of credit. It is the first country that has been able to effectively 'tax' the whole world by making its currency a universal currency and basing it solely on credit. It's a nice position to be in. But, if the rest of the world 'wants its money back' and starts to sell down US Treasuries and refrains from buying new issues, then the US will be forced to spend less or increase taxes (or both) or, alternatively, default. Britain is no longer a military power, it's a trading nation and it's making a canny commercial bet on the rise of China. There is no reason why this should imply a change of geopolitical alignment.

Business is business.

Prof. Wolf thinks the Global Economy is stuck in Endless Credit Cycles, is it?

Dr. Hu – U.S. Viewpoint   *****   **Oct, 2014**

1) Is there demand deficiency? Not everywhere. Think nations which prosper from "poaching" demand from their trading partners and feel entitled to run current account surpluses—indefinitely. China, Germany, Japan, and South Korea come to mind. That proven strategy of export-led growth has worked well, but only by short-circuiting mechanisms that would increase the value of a nation's currency commensurate with its economic strength. Some manipulate, others link themselves to weaker economies and prosper from a currency "cheaper than it oughta be."

Lord Keynes, always read selectively by neo-liberals, warned against the destabilizing imbalances that would ensue if such "currency hoarders" went unchecked. The WTO/EZ era has proven him prescient. Surplus nations reap growth and jobs while deficit nations reap cheap goods, deflationary pressures, unemployment, and debt. The USA's current willingness to enable others' export-led growth and run trade deficits seemingly forever, in spite of the stagnant wages of its middle class, can't be the magic engine that pulls the global economy from stagnation.

2) Stagnant productivity? Again, not everywhere. Since China's opening, capital has flowed there in torrents, resulting in enormous productivity gains. The Middle Kingdom's decades of double digit growth were fuelled as much or more by abundant capital expenditures as by its dirt cheap labour and dearth of regulations. Meanwhile, capital investment in the US and most other advanced economies has stagnated. After all, why invest where labour is expensive, and environmental regulations (etc.) make the cost of production far higher than in China? Like everything else, we must look at productivity globally.

Let's skip to my most important and most ominous point: Political Instability. We "know" unemployment in southern Europe, many American cities, Central America, parts of Paris, etc. remains extremely high among young people, particularly young men. We also know that's a recipe for political chaos. Germans mostly ignored Hitler until the Great Depression, when loss of faith in capitalism polarized many societies into radical left and right antagonists. Nationalistic demagogues in the former Yugoslavia likewise gained followings when the economy collapsed all around them. History is replete with such examples. Hopelessness evolves into extremism, even more so when extremes in inequality are so obvious. Certainly we are seeing the rise of ideologies and groups that should wake us up to imminent danger. What are we doing instead?

Now we see China, falsely assumed to be transforming into a "consumer society," planning to accelerate its export sector. At the same time the Eurozone is weakening its currency to make its exports "more competitive." Japan has embarked on a similar course. Everyone, save the US it seems, is determined to export their way out of stagnation—seeking to find that elusive demand somewhere off-shore, especially in America. Currency wars masking trade wars: all breeding chaos.

So yes, current ills defy easy cures (think QE). But if we are to solve them we need to get to the root of the problems and quit with desperate strategies that can only make things worse.

MarkGB

Bravo Mr Wolf! An article about the crucial issue of 'debt' is a refreshing change from the huge tonnage of scribbling the paper produces on aggregate demand.

We have indeed made a "Faustian bargain with private sector-driven credit booms" Mr Wolf. But it's worse than that - debt is inevitable in a system where money is created as debt and needs ever expanding debt to prevent it from collapsing in on itself.

We have made a Faustian pact with a banking system that waves credit into existence, charges people interest on it, pockets the spoils in the good times, and gets its lackeys in the government to fleece the plebs when the Ponzi scheme collapses, as it inevitably does. The root cause of our troubles is a fiat based monetary system with fractional reserve banking. It is sleight of hand and legalised theft of the highest order. It will collapse, as it has done every time in history it has been tried.

As for the US coming closest to getting it right, I think the US recovery is a chimera. Take the jobs report for example – 248k jobs sound great, until you look under the bonnet to see what's there – far too many part-time, minimum wage jobs for older people. There are other disturbing statistics in the report that the talking heads on CNBC and Fox don't seem to like talking about:

For example: the civilian labour force for September, 2014 is recorded as 155.9 million. In October 2008, just as the crisis was taking off, the figure was a million fewer at 154.9 million. Great you say, that's back to where we were! No it's not, for the simple reason that during the same period the working age civilian population rose from 234.6 million to 248.4 million; nearly 14 million. A ratio of 14:1 is not great by any standards – so never mind, we won't talk about that!

The debt problem has been brewing for decades, since the breakdown of Bretton Woods in 1971; in the nineties it reached the bend of the 'J' curve, since 2008/9 it has been exponential and I think we are now approaching the finale. It's been a long running serial, with central bankers as the star players – let's call it Debt Trek:

Debt...the final frontier...these are the voyages of the central bank 'Kill Enterprise'. Its five-year mission: to explore strange new monetary tools, to seek out new zombies and new bubbles, to boldly go where no man, and now no woman have gone before.

Rxex

Indeed, the private corporate sector clamours for cheaper money thrown at consumers to keep its revenue growing at high and possibly unsustainable rates, which are in turn demanded by equity investors. The private household sector demands cheaper money thrown at them to keep up with a well-marketed better life achievable through newer and shinier stuff that it cannot afford with stagnant real wages. China needs to keep its engine going so it can accommodate the enormous rural exodus created by its own promise of a better life that only a perennial 8% growth rate can fulfil. This is what Americans want, what the Chinese want, and what everybody wants, and it is not sustainable. It's become a cliché to blame mythical clueless government drones for all our ills, but the enemy might just be us.

Is it that easy?

Different types of activity have different sensitivities to the price of money.
- Speculation and the provision of credit against existing assets are strongly sensitive leading to volatile change in the price of said assets.
- Productive investment less so.
Move long term rates down from 5% to 2.5%:
-asset prices double and credit grows exponentially against these prices, especially housing
- productive investment barely reacts if total funding cost (cost of capital) is 8% vs 10%. This is what policy makers do not understand (among much else) and why they are pushing on a string in productive investment but creating asset bubbles everywhere.

Mike

"Today the US and UK may be escaping from the crises that hit seven years ago."-Financial Times.
You don't really believe that, do you? Government debt is 90% of GDP in the UK, 102% in the US. And don't even start with Total Debt to GDP: According to St Louis Fed, the US has over $60 trillion total debt in 2014, which is well over 340% of GDP, whereas even more alarming UK total debt to GDP was 500% in 2012 according to PWC, but since then no company has the guts to publish a figure yet.

Nick Antill

From the '60s to the '80s governments believed that they could control long term unemployment levels through fiscal policy. Since the '80s they have believed that they could control unemployment through monetary policy. Neither worked but both increased government debt — the first directly and the latter indirectly.

Ohneeigenschaften

Why has growth become credit led in the first place? Because of the increase in income inequality, so that the necessary consumption share in balanced growth can only be achieved by the rich lending to the poor or export-surplus countries to debtor ones through elaborate forms of financial intermediation (e.g., securitization).

Is it that easy?

No, it is because central banks have sought to stimulate through the price of money.
- Cheap money- excess credit creation - bust - free money - excess credit creation - bust - money printing - excess credit creation -bust.
And all just to make existing assets more expensive and some people wealthier than others.

Cathal Haughian

Reader, they're both correct.
Demand and Supply predate Capitalism, they are core forces that influence Price. Bankrupt Elites or Nation States negate these forces to dictate price so their bankruptcy is not crystallised. The result is alienation from the marketplace.

Reader, please note that geo-strategic economic planners in Beijing think they've tamed the business cycle. Banks in the West are privately owned, for-profit cost centres; if they feel they've over extended credit, they panic in a herd type manner and rapidly withdraw credit provision. This causes a negative feedback loop whereby a scarcity of money triggers defaults and ever more financial stress and so on. This negative feedback loop causes a recession and wipes out weak companies and households.

In contrast, banks in China are instruments of the State so economic planners can guarantee only gradual changes in the supply of new money to all economic agents. This increases *confidence* and so far China hasn't had a recession in decades.

Furthermore, this system difference is why China may become a target of aggression by our Families. For our Families prefer a central banking system which they own privately. They prefer the *power* to create money, privately. Any that challenge this preference is destroyed. Gaddafi, even Hitler, was destroyed.

MarkGB   *******   **Nov, 2014**

"Japan should tax savings instead. Unproductive savings should be discouraged."-
Financial Times, Martin Wolf

Who knew that savings were the problem? Now we're all saved! We can trust governments to tell us what is productive and unproductive for each of us. Praise be to the central planners who brought us to the brink by jacking up credit booms...they are now going to save us from our own savings by...jacking up credit booms!

Mrs Watanabe might actually buy it, with her legendary *trust* in government, but as for me, no thanks Mr Wolf.

Capitalism works through the process of creating surplus over current needs, and using that surplus to meet future needs, real and imagined, through the mechanisms of savings and investment. Savings also lead to a more fulfilling life because they facilitate freedom and choice. Strangely enough people's needs, wants, talents and time preferences are all different. Otherwise we'd have never bothered with trade and we'd all still be picking berries every day.

So now you want governments to tax savings and savers...those selfish folks whose insistence on self reliance has brought us to this sad turn of events. Rigging rates so these pesky thrifts get less than a 1% return on capital is obviously not enough 'incentive' for them to let go of their selfishness and trust the central planners.

No, no, the little blighters are too stubborn for that - we must motivate them to spend with higher inflation (but let's call it price stability so they don't rumble the scam).

Still no good...let's tax them into submission...if they won't spend it, we'll take it off them and spend it ourselves...*trust* us, look what we did with your money so far!

Sometimes the current lunacy in the global economy is criticised as 'Keynesian'. Sometimes it is criticised as 'monetarist'.

Personally, I think a better description would be 'nuts'.

I think even a statist like Keynes would get indigestion looking at this travesty of central planning. Here's what he said in The Economic Consequences of the Peace:

"Lenin is said to have declared that the best way to destroy the capitalist system was to debauch the currency. By a continuing process of inflation, governments can confiscate, secretly and unobserved, an important part of the wealth of their citizens. By this method they not only confiscate, but they confiscate arbitrarily; and, while the process impoverishes many, it actually enriches some. The sight of this arbitrary rearrangement of riches strikes not only at security but [also] at confidence in the equity of the existing distribution of wealth.

Those to whom the system brings windfalls, beyond their deserts and even beyond their expectations or desires, become "profiteers," who are the object of the hatred of the bourgeoisie, whom the inflationism has impoverished, not less than of the proletariat. As the inflation proceeds and the real value of the currency fluctuates wildly from month to month, all permanent relations between debtors and creditors, which form the ultimate foundation of capitalism, become so utterly disordered as to be almost meaningless; and the process of wealth-getting degenerates into a gamble and a lottery"

That was 1919. Reading it gives me a funny feeling of déjà vu even though I wasn't there. 'Wealth-getting' as Keynes called it, is degenerating into a gamble and a lottery. The lottery is being rigged by governments and central banks, and the booty is going to their cronies. The gamble is what savers are taking by investing their money further down the risk curve in order to find some yield. Now you want to tax savers.

Give me a break Mr Wolf...a tax break...I can use the money more productively than you can.

Risk Adjusted Return

Savings enable ordinary people to avoid becoming state dependants, so naturally the state must use its power to crush them.

Serf

Stop doubling down on failure. Stop monetary central planning. People respond to incentives, so stop setting perverse incentives. Zero rates mean no incentive to lend, hence no lending. Money printing means robbing Peter to pay Paul, hence Paul will do nothing but lobby for more robbing, and Peter chooses to 'stagnate' to avoid getting robbed. Losses on bad loans should not be collectivised by diktat from the monetary politburo, but rather allocated to debtors and creditors in a restructuring. If a government cannot fund itself, then perhaps it is time to restructure rather than seek stagnation and collapse by 'redistributive' monetary policy.

Central Planners have a dehumanized approach to demand. Demand is not an animal. Manipulating it veers on totalitarianism. The natural order is that people demand — or, more precisely, desire — the product of their work. This natural — and beautiful — order can momentously be tampered with by well-meaning or not so well-meaning people. 'Needs' can be decreed by tyrants, cravings can be artificially aroused by advertising gurus and affordability can be engineered by economists through debt. But the end result is alienation.

Sardonic   ***   2010-2015

There is a lot; I'll try to be brief:
- our central bankers are all schooled in the neoclassical approach, yet their jobs essentially require them to confront blatant contradictions to their very schooling on a daily basis — nothing good can come out of such cognitive dissonance long term; our monetary policy needs a new team;

- our fiscal leaders do not understand our monetary system — or are willing to act like they don't to score political points; their "budget balancing" fights are a waste of valuable time;

- the [neo]classical approach is not credible for these reasons AT LEAST:

(a) it does not have or understand "money" (c.f. Adam Smith) and hence the entire apparatus of modern finance
(b) it models entire groups of economic actors as {N x single rational agent}, thus suffering from "fallacy of composition"
(c) it believes in "supply/demand equilibria" which contradicts both our observed reality (natural gas glut, oil glut, etc) as well as Minsky-style arguments about the existence of positive feedback loops (e.g. increases in prices of assets used as further margin/debt collateral can fuel further asset appreciation, and vice versa)

- "money" is "credit" and thus has both quantitative (monetary unit, currency) and social ("trust, a social contract) aspects. Because of this, any economic theory with a chance of real breakthrough is likely to have elements of game theory and irrational behaviour modelling;

- operational realities of existing systems are relevant and should not be "abstracted away" from a theory too quickly: who creates money and purchasing power, how the interest rates are set, liquidity constraints of various actors, etc;

- being a sovereign currency issuer confers tangible benefits;

- gold and other "scarcity-based" standards do not solve problems of inflation, price stability in general, or liquidity crises. In fact, "money as credit entries in some ledger" has been in use for far longer than any metal-based currency;

- history presents a thought-provoking number of examples of economic systems that all experienced periods of very high growth while not being 100% "free market" systems: post-WWII Japan, recent China, recent Russia;

- capitalism appears to have a cyclical nature whereby it goes through periods of financial institutions having an out-sized amount of power and influence (as opposed to being just financial intermediaries); we appear to be going through such a period right now;

- all economy is always political economy: any rules of economic theory in vogue during a given period of time will be undermined to serve geopolitical goals;

- last but not least: except for interest rate suppression, QE is useless; there does not seem to exist a respectable theory of QE "modus operandi".

Stuttgart 88

Established journals won't publish anything that isn't founded on the main axioms of traditional economics, free markets with no barriers to entry, perfect information, rational profit or utility maximising agents, zero transaction costs etc. A whole discipline is founded on assumptions that don't hold in real life, but hey, as long as the results show that unfettered free markets lead to optimal allocation of resources and perpetual growth that benefits everyone then that doesn't matter. Not to mention that no financial system exists in traditional economics, savings magically find their own way to investment by some all-powerful equilibrium interest rate.

The movie Inside Job showed how the academic economics profession was captured by the financial establishment in the US. It's quite staggering that Minsky's opinions on financial instability and money manager capitalism were marginalised despite talking perfect sense, although his evocation of what he called Big Government in his book Stabilising an Unstable Economy was probably seen as heretical. (Please, no knee-jerk responses about size of government, Minsky's view was very nuanced, including no welfare transfers without recipients actually working for them).

Middle-Aged American

It seems to me that Western economists are still in denial. During the past twenty years very often European and American economists would berate Japan for the economic malaise in which it found itself, calling for QE and other unconventional measures to fix the problem. However, after more than five years of unconventional measures in the US and Europe, it would seem that even Mr. Wolf, Bernanke, Ms. Yellan, Summers and many other such strong proponents of these measures, would admit that in the long run they look like they are not going to work.

The inconvenient truth about the current world economic system is that it relies on growth of consumption, and consumption relies on ever increasing population. No matter how hard you try to stimulate 50, 60, and 70 year olds to spend more, it usually will not work. This is for many reasons, but the three main ones I would point out is that they are typically older and wiser than the younger generations, therefore they will not wantonly waste as much money on needless expenditures.

Secondly, they are also getting to a physical stage in their life where many activities are no longer appealing, and they simply do not spend money on those anymore.

Finally, most of the big purchases have been made in their lives, so they do not need to purchase new houses etc. Now many economists will tell you here that we need to increase productivity and then this will boost consumption. However, again, if one was to research it, one would see that there is a natural drop off in productivity in an ageing population (average wages rise steadily until about age 55 and then begin to decline from there).

To me, it would seem that Japan simply got there first, and the wise will realize that the whole world is headed in that direction.

Cathal Haughian

Economists are projecting their mind toward things that don't exist. (Children and adults fantasise in a similar way but remain aware that the things they are imagining don't exist.) Philosophers call this the mind projection fallacy and it occurs when someone thinks that the way they see the world reflects the way the world really is, going as far as assuming the real existence of imagined objects. That is, someone's subjective judgments are "projected" to be inherent properties of an object, rather than being related to personal perception. For instance, economists seem to assume 'equilibrium' is a property of the market. Or that 'cost' is a property of choice.

(You can see Capitalism as a cost continuum whereby the price of all goods gravitates toward and then orbits zero. Those prices that never drop are likely to be in orbit. They can only fall further if a more positive net gain energy source is discovered. This is the simplest and most sustainable way to reduce inequality of living standards and improve the material condition of man: reduction in population size and cost. Let's use a rustic way to describe this process with this illuminating story. First, your ancestors cut bog and trees and lit a campfire. Then they used tar and stick. After that oil and wick were used; afterwards candles and finally an incandescent light bulb followed today by a light emitting diode. The mass of inputs fell over time. Energy efficiency improved.

The price of so many goods has moved so far along the *continuum* that cost may no longer influence choice for many transactions. I can only speak for myself, but appetite is the only property that determines how much candy I buy. Though note that disruption in the supply, or depletion, of a core input can raise prices.)

The invisible hand, free market, perfect information, etc. are all assumed. So many assumptions: such paucity of proof. They tend to search for 'data' that lends confirmation to their bias and preconceptions. I failed in my studies to discover a single exception; Pickety is only the most recent example. One consequence is that other economists are assumed to share the same perception, or that they are irrational or misinformed if they do not: which would explain a lot of school boy behaviour between economists. I've deliberately tried to avoid this fallacy by employing a large international team and debating style.

In a similar vein, you'll note that the Koran is also riddled with this fallacy. No wonder then, that economists are the theologians of our time.

This fallacy is how the ego limits the mind.

Domovoy   *******   **2014-2015**

Sic Transit Gloria Mundi. Thus passes the glory of the world.

A truly historical moment.

B = f(x)

China has demonstrated that an intelligent, industrious nation can reverse quickly a downwards or stagnant trend. How? By bringing its societal behaviours under the control of long-term rather than short-term goals. Conversely, the USA and the EU, falling prey to the dictates of the mob via the ballot-box, have brought their respective behaviours under the control of short-term rather than long-term goals. The consequences have been self-defeating and may well prove disastrous.

Zhubajie

In human endeavours, there are many types of innovation. The most applicable to the 7 billion souls living on earth, are innovations that make technology AVAILABLE. Availability means affordable prices. In that regard, China is the most important innovator on Earth in the last 30 years. Well priced Made in China was literally, empirically, the most efficacious (and some say the only one working) poverty reduction program in the world, serving even most of the American poor. If not for the well priced Made in China, living standards for the less fortunate would have been 1/2 or a 1/3rd what they are today.

Thank God for Chinese innovations. And the results are impressive. In about 60 years, China has completed industrialization that took almost everyone else 200 years. Today China has the world's largest industries in steel, cement, and aluminium, ship building, autos, 90% of rare earths produced, No. 2 (No. 1?) supercomputer in the world, the fastest and biggest high speed train network, and no net foreign debts ($700 Billion in foreign currency debts, AND $3.8 Trillion in foreign currency holdings), what's not to like?

Just take one industry out of many. Solar panels had been around for many decades, but had never been competitive with grid power. Entered

China, and in a short few years, solar panel prices dropped by over 50%, and today parity is here. Multicrystalline Si panels have dropped to something like $0.40/W, lower than even the CIGA panels from First Solar. If that is not innovation, you try producing solar panels at that price.

In general, with the relentless innovation, costs are down in entire swaths of industries (engineering, cement, steel, etc.), Chinese engineering companies can bid 30% lower than the "more innovative" American counterparts, and still make money. Foresight, intelligent deployment of resources, innovative reordering of systems and markets have much greater impact than patents. Perhaps the job of the politician is to make feel good speeches. But ignoring reality and insisting that black is white, is not helpful to the real conversation needed.

Cathal Haughian – Chinese Viewpoint

The mind forms differently in different places. The incredible accumulation of wealth by Chinese households is due to the interplay of civilisational attributes such as honour/face, discipline, family worship, deference, cordial feeling and generosity. With respect to the Chinese government and the All-China Federation of Trade Unions, they have no contradiction of purpose when trying to prevent social unrest while claiming to stand behind the workers: a vast majority of Chinese workers prefer to work rather than fight, and the more stable the country and society, the faster the salaries can rise. Stability is not enough for rising wages, but it is one prerequisite.

They worship their ancestors; an unconscious process prepares their soul to join them. They do this by burning replica money, houses and so on, which they believe their ancestors can use in the *after-life*. They do not worship money per se but it is significant as it acts as a vehicle between this life and the next. They use money to sustain a psychic relationship with their family members that have passed away. Thus, it has holy and ritualistic properties. And so they have a very personal relationship with their dead ancestors. Their soul must account for the family lineage so childlessness is hateful. The elderly eke out an existence which is their habit, working where and when they can, spending almost nothing on themselves; avoiding medical care and cost. They want to enter the *after-life* with *face*, and that's determined by how well the family line is doing.

The one child policy allows a rich inheritance for the young especially because the elderly are strongly motivated to claim positional goods for them, such as a good education that will help them claim a high position in society. Both parents tend to use their prime working years earning income. So, the child often bonds strongest to the grandparent as they may be the primary care giver. Because your nearest and dearest companions in life are a part of your self-image, there's danger of a 'breakdown' in the continuity of the self when someone close to you passes away. So when the grandparent passes away the child internalises the *after-life* which supports the continuity of the self.

Western economists have supported 'free trade' and globalization on the expectation that a 'convergence' will occur between China and America. E.G., that the cost of labour will *'converge'* and money income will circulate by way of mutual and naturally occurring trade. Alas, the Chinese are an intelligent race that, since they almost worship the stuff, loves to think about money.

They save money to capture interest, so that they can claim wealth outright in the future. Property is preferably bought outright and related males may pool monies for such. Though note that male siblings, from rural families, may share monies before spouses and private property owned prior to marriage is **not** split in the event of divorce. Marriage may be seen as a temporary merger and acquisition of power and resources. The micro decisions concerning ownership of property are heavily influenced by the power relations between the respective families. They understand that debt based consumption is a recipe for a static station in society, for they would have to pay rent/interest to the money owner. And most importantly they value stability; credit carries risk which causes anxiety about the future.

Westerners' are encouraged to interpret money as a means of exchange. And for Chinese people money has that property as well. But, money for them has one **more** property.

Money is also a ***means to power***. At the macro and micro level, where and on what money is spent preferably promises power. At the micro level, they will be motivated by narcissism and position within their pecking order. There are no powerful poor people in China. Power is what motivates generosity and accumulated wealth; not greed. At the macro level, their nation state will deliberately spend monies where it strengthens China's position and preferably weakens competitors as well. This form of asymmetric behaviour operates at all levels of society.

I have worked for the Chinese State for 3 years. Their hierarchy of power is a complex matrix of power relations that is difficult to traverse well. Some Chinese people opt to 'stay low' or adopt gormless fearful obedience to survive. When I worked in Korea I made the error of learning well the Korean language. After which, their perception altered to see me as a potential disturbance to social harmony for I had become capable of independent action. They could no longer control or fool me. I have flourished in China, partly due to having never spoken Chinese.

I listen and adopt an equivalence of behavioural norms. If I spoke Chinese their behaviour would become defensive, or mistrustful, for I would be able to report inappropriate behaviour or speech, to authorities or foreign media. Also, they would be less helpful, so I use a bilingual assistant during the day and secretary in the evening. Workplace conversation is often asymmetrically defensive so real meaning, desire or intent can be the exact opposite of what has been said. They always cover their own back. Real meaning is conveyed via tone, pitch, micro expressions and (group) body language or simply by the silent recognition that the other knows how the game is played.

When lying is a way of speaking then what's the point of talking? Pointless, if understanding is your goal. Almost all of their accumulated knowledge and wisdom is stored in the governing culture. The Communist government inherited knowledge pertaining to governance via adoption of the administrative culture of Sino Imperial dynasties. You can only access their knowledge of such by working amongst them in government.

If I spoke their language they would see it as an attempt to enter their hierarchy of power. The structure of their language corresponds to how they think. Words in English that are substantives function more as verbs in Chinese, corresponding to and reinforcing an experience of *being* and the world as dynamic process.

A *dynamic competition* delivered by ancient and often cruel historical experiences, population density, habitat and ecological stress. Thus, empathy may be completely absent in manifold situational settings. They may be untouched by a distressed child in a public place. It was only last year that a child died due to multiple strikes on a public road while adults passed by without offering aid. In contrast and as compensation, a Chinese teacher has a great store of empathy and loyalty for her students. Because her student body as a whole, is competing for *face* against other classes. So, they empathise when it's within the proper context which is determined by their culture. By not speaking Chinese they simply observe me while I observe them.

There are many 'rules' in China but they are unlike rules in the West. You can and may need to break rules here. Though, you can only break a rule if your action is within the culture. E.G., if a teacher helps her students cheat that is not evidence that's she's a bad teacher. It is only an expression of an excess of empathy, loyalty and competitiveness. Their mind sees this as a naturally occurring possibility, so even in primary school; a teacher is never allowed to invigilate the exams of her own students—no *trust*.

They are comforted by cyclical behaviour that is socially harmonious and cohesive. They desire an inner harmonious flow of life force and balance, and so require other selves to be in sync. They calibrate their social systems to attain such a result for cyclical behaviour is predictable, ordered and stable. This occurs seamlessly as they share a common conception of well-being. Attempts by foreign powers to destabilise *faith* or cohesion are systematically checked. E.G., the Chinese state appoints its own 'bishops' and makes moves to gain control over the recognition of the next Dali Lama so as to ensure Rome or India cannot build a parallel and destabilising hierarchy of power.

Authority figures in Christian and Muslim communities cover the reproductive area of children with clothing because it is assumed that sexual activity/thoughts may be sinful. Even in hot weather, children are forced to wear underwear. The child makes an unconscious assumption that genitalia have a wrongful property. This cultural practice encourages fixation on sex and formation of psycho-sexual problems, e.g. frigidity.

In contrast, child rearing in China is informed by observing Mother Nature. Genitalia of children is uncovered. Once the wife is confirmed to be pregnant sexual activity is discontinued. Thus, sex is interpreted as functional. The Chinese mind is naturalistic and ordered by practical problems (e.g. shelter, jobs, good health) addressed by practical philosophy. Naturally occurring desires are satisfied first, e.g. procreation is satisfied before career is taken seriously.

War is the great danger. *Proportional force* is an alien notion to them. It is largely absent, e.g. a recent power struggle at the top has resulted in more than 100,000 public officials indicted for corruption. Westerners' learn this concept from their combative sports and call it 'fair play'. War is hateful for war is chaotic, unpredictable, with uncertain results.

Miles

Of the risk factors in my book I can find only one overlap and even there only partially: geopolitical risk. But there is a high probability that one or a combination of the 4 following global trends will result in a crisis.

-Multipolarity is the driver of geopolitical risk in that we have more global and regional powers competing for influence and asserting whatever their definition is of national interest. Economically, we can see it in higher defence budgets worldwide but also in trade fragmentation, including following the much increased military conflicts or due to a proliferation of sanctions (e.g. Russia, Iran, China, Turkey), new trade blocs (e.g. TPP vs China, Eurasian customs union vs EU, China focused Silk Route), new supranational organizations (e.g. China focused AIIB) and failures of incumbent global supranational organizations to perform (e.g. WTO, UN, World Bank).

-Secular stagnation is a real threat. Economists have varying interpretations but the real world drivers are undisputed: demographics, low productivity, inequality, and low real investment. We can see it in ongoing low real growth, real interest rates and low real wage growth.

-Reversal of globalization caused by the upward adjustment of living standards and move up in the production value chain by the main Emerging Market actors, such as China. We can see it in the collapsing vessel and container freight rates but also in a reversal of the balance of payments where major Emerging Markets experience capital outflows as well as a drop in exports.

-Increasing global debt both in absolute terms and versus GDP. Deleveraging was always a myth when governments run record fiscal deficits even in an economic upswing, corporations borrow for share repurchases, M&A and dividends and individuals have to replace low real income growth with debt. So it happens that all 3 debt categories are at record highs way beyond 2008 levels. The point is that these are secular trends which – especially when combined – pose little upside and any black swan or known unknown can trigger a major crisis. I would categorize the known unknowns for capital markets in just 3 subcategories.

-First, any major geopolitical conflict can derail the global economy by, for example, affecting the oil price (Iran vs SA), demand or trade routes (e.g. any China related conflict).

-Second, governments and especially central banks and regulators will be prone to commit policy mistakes after 30 years of lowering interest rates, facilitating liquidity and leverage. From here, both, continuing on the same path or reversing the policies will be fraught with danger. But policy mistakes can also include the failure of China to change from the export and investment driven to a consumption driven economy and revert to last resort policies such as devaluation of the Yuan.

-Third, the incredible increase in corporate profits in absolute terms vs GDP can revert to mean any time because its drivers can: all above 4 secular trends reduce revenue growth while real wage growth cannot be much lower for longer without causing social unrest. In my view, the focus shifts from analysing drivers and risks for growth to timing the exit from markets. If this view becomes more widespread, it becomes circular in a way George Soros calls reflexivity.

Dr. Hu – U.S. Viewpoint

It's impossible for me to accept this half hearted analysis when northern China's citizens have been choking for weeks on the annual onslaught of winter-enhanced toxic coal smoke. Nothing new here, of course, except perhaps coverage by western media — those heart-rending photos of young children struggling for breath, awaiting their turns for what their distraught mothers hope will be life-saving IV drips. And, more importantly, new levels of outrage by citizens tired of watching their precious 'only child' succumb to the pollution, or develop agonizing respiratory illnesses, or seeing family members and neighbours dying in clusters in "cancer villages" plagued by toxic drinking water.

Yes, affluent ex-pats and wealthy Chinese can just "stay indoors," protected by cutting edge air purifiers and bottled water. They can venture out into the eternal gloom adorned with high-tech "gas masks." Their children can play in the filtered air of specially-constructed chambers at their private schools, but even they won't see the sun or track the moon and stars in the occluded night sky.

But look outside and you'll see an army of labour without such options —construction workers, street vendors, and those streams of desperate mothers carrying limp-armed children to emergency rooms—in those few cities fortunate enough to have decent medical facilities. "Race ahead to modern prosperity" said the slogan. "Build the harmonious society." But what is this new beast 'prosperity,' that lurches through China's industrial cities, killing its children and sickening its people? Where's the harmony with nature? Millions lifted out of poverty?

Certainly.

But the cost of which is the worst public health crisis in modern history. Can Beijing really keep a lid on the outrage by hiding the death toll, refusing to collect statistics that would show the world the terrible price of China's rise, and contracting for "impression management" by western PR firms?

The Middle Kingdom's ecological catastrophe has given the term 'China price' new meaning. A nation can take a short cut to riches if it's willing to sacrifice a generation or two of its children on the altar of prosperity, be willing to live with its blue skies be-smudged with coal smoke, its people's lungs burning with sulphur dioxide, their drinking water laced with industrial effluent, raw sewage, and agricultural chemicals, its lakes and rivers too polluted for fish or recreation, and its food supply tainted with mercury, arsenic, and other heavy metal fallout from coal burning. China's becoming an environment bereft of natural beauty and its once rich heritage of wildlife, a habitat suited only for foolish humans and the rare insects and vermin able to adapt to such levels of pollution.

As the American environmentalist Aldo Leopold observed back in the

1930s, "land abuse has evicted civilizations—and it will do so again." Our engineering feats may bedazzle us, he added, but when it comes to keeping land fit to live upon, "we still live in nomads' tents in the desert."

Indeed, that "eviction" has been under-way in China for some time now as land abuse creates the fierce "yellow dragon" sandstorms which are pushing desertification across vast expanses of northern and western China, burying thousands of villages in their path, and making nomads of their former residents. So, to me the China glass looks far less than half full, with its life-sustaining liquids draining rapidly. King Midas learned too late that life—and health—are far more precious than gold.

May the Chinese people take heed of his tragedy.

***

Let's begin this concluding chapter by offering readers a Chinese perspective of the Global Economic Order. Firstly, one should understand that the Chinese seek to understand the present by analysing historical forces.

They were the ones that saved the Global economy after 2008 with a super massive fiscal stimulus. It's what Lord Keynes had once suggested. Chinese city life has been transformed. Impressive sector wide productivity gains have improved standards of living for everyone and buying power was distributed. Few have suffered due to the global depression here. What infrastructure did the USA or Europe build? None.

The abandonment of the working class in the West is thoroughly shameful and a shocking dereliction of duty. Why didn't the West pour mega tonnes of concrete? This can be seen as an intensification of the assault on the working class that began in earnest with the Reagan and Thatcher administrations. There was a quiet coup during the Great Financial Crisis. The New York Fed played Russian Roulette with some Wall Street banks until Congress capitulated. A power faction working out of the Treasury Department, Federal Reserve Bank and Wall Street has taken control of the USA, which explains why no Wall Street executives were imprisoned.

But the problem with assaulting your working class is simple. They no longer add all the value they used to do. The financial sector simply extracts value. A Nation State needs a vibrant, industrious and highly motivated working class so that the country can run at a profit. The UK and US are broke because their working class can't compete with German and Chinese workers. Western workers are demoralised and depressed.

Consequently, the West, with the exception of Germany, has been running at a loss for decades. This is the root cause of their economic depression and real decline in living standards. Instead of building infrastructure this neo-liberal power faction's policy was a helicopter drop of trillions of dollars over Chelsea, Kensington and Manhattan, which inflated the price of existing assets worldwide. The World now stands on the precipice of a deflationary collapse in asset prices because

China's real stimulus has ended and China's dynamic in catching up has petered out. When the collapse happens Chinese people will take comfort in the rich inheritance of excellent infrastructure they built. Their private sector is large and dynamic. Their workers have gained knowledge and skills. They'll recover.

Germany is waging all out economic war with the ultimate goal of restoring full sovereignty: the removal of US bases from her soil. The English seem to believe their own lies and cannot accept that a country home to foreign military bases is effectively occupied and a vassal state. This is a simple Machiavellian dictum. Germany has taken control of the EU by means of the Euro and desires a dollar crisis. Such an outcome could result in catastrophe since German nationality is exclusive, as seen in their blood citizenship laws, and thus they cannot cope with Empire. European empires originating from Rome were stable for their religion was inclusive.

A more recent example is how the US used Religion to incorporate xenophobic South Korea into her empire. The Koreans emulate the appearance and form of America's hegemony without any analysis of the philosophy underlying Western civilisation; since religion functions by way of suggestion to the subconscious mind.

The Russian-Chinese axis anticipate war with NATO as a result of the coup in Kiev. The goal of this partnership between Kiev and the West was to destabilise Russia, get rid of Putin and replace him with a stooge, thereby plundering Russia for more profit and encircling China. An encircled China would be forced to genuflect or militarise her society.

China has responded by switching energy suppliers from the Middle East to Russia. Russia and China are trading energy for manufactured goods and advanced weapons systems, including the S-400 air defence system that is capable of destroying NATO stealth bombers, stealth fighter planes and naval vessels. And that system has been delivered. I realise that it's hard for readers to stomach these facts but they cannot be denied. No nation delivers such a weapon to their neighbour unless their leaders have plans to fight a common foe.

Mankind is currently reliving the nightmare that haunted the 1930's while the World staggers toward war. Wars don't suddenly break out; they are the result of small incremental increases in tension largely due to miscommunication. For example, late last year a Financial Times correspondent called President Putin the son of an unmarried woman. The Nazis killed Putin's grandmother and his mother buried his brother after the Battle of Stalingrad. As is, refugees are now being used to wage asymmetric warfare.

The current crisis stems from the current framework of capitalism which has three major operational problems:

1) A falling rate of profit as demonstrated by the need to offshore most of the US industrial base to China.
2) A profit realisation problem as demonstrated by the need to increase debt levels evermore.
3) A labour redundancy problem as demonstrated by the 48 million Americans on food aid.

The tried and tested solution is the waging of World War. War burns up and destroys excess capacity, labour redundancy is solved by mass death and the rate of return on investment can rise due to extreme exploitation of the working class, since war reduces the majority of humanity to a state of despair and diminished expectations. The China-Russia axis will not fold as time is on their side for their political system is static.

The origin of opposition and tension between world powers is the credit based reserve currency that allows the US to effectively tax the rest of the world. Whilst all economy is political economy, all international exchange is Geo-strategic. Capitalism now marches behind her older brother — Imperialism — in lockstep, these siblings can only deliver World War. No matter how this game is played, their tribute to our Empire has ended.

The central lesson of the Vietnam War was that armed forces are neither viable nor effective without the consent of the local population. This lesson was stressed by Robert Asprey in his monumental analysis of asymmetrical warfare but this thesis was studiously ignored by those who profit from and enjoy dominating others.

The doctrine of utilitarianism, which enjoys the blessing of the Neo-liberal State, should be feared. Humans enjoy and take pleasure from dominating others. They can be pack animals with a biological need for a hierarchy of power. Unemployment, an absence of opportunity, debt and declining power causes stress, anxiety and tension in the muscular structure and frustration of humans.

The human group either deals with the resulting aggression internally or directs violence externally. Many of the ailments that afflict the current form of Capitalism can, and have been resolved in the past, by the waging of war against peaceful populations. The Second World War serves as a classic example.

The invaders lay waste to the productive power of the competing nation. For example, Libya's ultra-cheap conventional oil production was destroyed to benefit expensive North Sea and Shale oil producers. Libya's share of the energy market was robbed. Not to mention its Gold.

War is rape and robbery. If the gold or other assets cannot be stolen from the injured nation then the working class of the belligerent nation are robbed, to pay for the psychological pleasure that the rulers and their lackeys enjoy. Little mention in the media of Libyans that now labour under anarchy and hideous pain. Simply put, death and destruction can be interpreted as positive events. You may disagree, and that is acceptable; but your opinion is biased by your class and remains irrelevant. You don't decide if war is waged.

Though in a strange way should the sycophants that gin up the public be judged so harshly? War is much more than rape and robbery—it's also a profitable way to ease unemployment, for the Dominant Class. Things are tense but a way forward has been found: The attitude of an elite faction may have changed somewhat because Absolutism cannot be attained — thermonuclear weapons and tribalism rule out Globalism as an intellectual solution. And their attitude matters, why?

Central Bank physical gold rarely moves, only claims of ownership. You should ask German "citizens" about the return of their "sovereign" gold from the USA. It moves very slowly, and is not the "same gold" as originally held.

The Bank of International Settlements holds claim over all Central Bank gold and that agreement is not so much written "in paper" as it is a plan for Mankind's continuing survival. Why challenge an agreement that is in the best interest of humanity? When all paper contracts are broken, the kind of contract that prevails is "written in gold". Easy for the "Old World" to grasp, much harder for "New Money" to understand.

This is the end of the FIAT time-line. For the FIAT only distributes buying power by hanging the working classes with debt. The FIAT always ends when we, the Dominant Class, are impacted by the collapse of the working classes, and the impact that collapse has on our Profit.

Traders do not and cannot think like true generational wealth — of the type that survives and continues past the fires of change. This is wealth that survives political and social upheaval and World War. This is the wealth behind the layers of perception that shape our geopolitical world. They are the senior bond holders of the banks that own the Central Banks, therefore, in essence, they own all "political" gold. They are The Market Makers.

They are The Families. They plan to accommodate the rise of the East, thus avoiding World War, by settling the dispute over what constitutes legal tender — which is easy since elite everywhere are loyal to Gold and Gold alone. Have you not noticed that the Gold Market is behaving a little differently this year? The Families are now united behind Gold. And then we have the little people, who own bits and pieces of it. Wealth will be redistributed in the only way that it can be, with the repricing of gold.

Here's the plan:

The East is forcing the issue by integrating their real and financial systems — recall that the USSR began to weaken after the USA and China integrated their resources and economical systems — by 2016 this dangerous stand-off united The Families behind a common campaign.

The global currency — the SDR — will be backed by gold — reducing tensions with the East.

The FIAT price of gold will be freed and go ballistic — a hyperinflation mentality takes hold of the general population in some places as working capital moves to countries with large gold holdings — this will also help to wipe away a big chunk of the debt ponzi.

So some of the debt ponzi will survive — averting a total system meltdown.

The surviving part of the debt claims will concentrate with banks politically connected to The Families — particularly banks in nation states with substantial gold holdings.

Now the Gold price represents stored labour time, the energy needed to refine bullion — and a Fiat value above that which represents debt claims on the underlying Gold.

The underlying reality is that those with accumulated capital — particularly in the form of gold, art and land — will flourish and survive.

The true capitalistic power structure remains the same — The Dynasties of Wealth — remain the leaders of the universal Religion, aka Capitalism.

And a new cycle shall commence — like Yin and Yang.

But hard problems caused by internal contradictions in the original framework, which called for and was papered over by properties of the FIAT — shall rise like a Phoenix from the ashes of its funeral pyre — to ignite a new class war. Unemployment will sky rocket in the US — cities which house the unemployed will become extremely unstable. In the words of one insider at The Bank of International Settlements — the Central Bankers' bank:

"If you didn't like the last system, you sure as Hell won't like the next."

But we do not know the deep games being played by other actors and whether such shall become reality. We have at least the following players in the West, which overlap and are connected by Freemasonry and other associations:

The City of London
The people who control MI5 and MI6
The people behind Netanyahu / Mossad
The people who currently control the CIA
The Military Industrial Complex

The NSA and other Intelligence Agencies
The Wall Street faction
The people behind and protecting Trump
Rockefeller and other Families
Big Oil

The knowledge of real power structures is part of power. But we know the universal template is Religion. At the scale of civilisation, particularly one in crisis, we can only try to have a "speculative working model" or "power hypothesis" and observe how things develop. If our model is closer to reality it might deliver some good predictions.

And always we must wonder about evil.

How evil, exactly, are the men and women behind the attack on Libya? How evil, exactly, are the men and women behind the creation and arming of ISIS? What's the nature of the evil that attacked Iraq repeatedly? Tribes have always fought over resources but our Empire is immensely wealthy, a compromise would have been easy. What's the nature of the evil behind opium production in Afghanistan — our colony — and the development of one million heroin addicts in the USA? Have we now added opiates to "the labour problem" solution? Are the prison, university and military systems used to warehouse future labour no longer large enough? Or do they not render enough Profit?

Is such evil the well known Power-mad type? Or an abnormal growth in the species? — Caused by Capitalism. Perhaps not. Perhaps philosophy failed and Man remains the image of evil — Lucifer.

The End

of

Before The Collapse

Volume Two

of

The Philosophy of Capitalism